Darkness and Daylight

Mary J. Holmes

Contents

CHAPTER I. COLLINGWOOD.	7
CHAPTER II. EDITH HASTINGS GOES TO COLLINGWOOD.	12
CHAPTER III. GRACE ATHERTON.	18
CHAPTER IV. RICHARD AND EDITH.	24
CHAPTER V. VISITORS AT COLLINGWOOD AND VISITORS AT BRIER HILL.	30
CHAPTER VI. ARTHUR AND EDITH.	41
CHAPTER VII. RICHARD AND ARTHUR.	47
CHAPTER VIII. RICHARD AND EDITH.	52
CHAPTER IX. WOMANHOOD.	60
CHAPTER X. EDITH AT HOME.	70
CHAPTER XI. MATTERS AT GRASSY SPRING.	78
CHAPTER XII. LESSONS.	91
CHAPTER XIII. FRIDAY.	97
CHAPTER XIV. THE MYSTERY AT GRASSY SPRING.	102
CHAPTER XV. NINA.	110
CHAPTER XVI. ARTHUR'S STORY.	117
CHAPTER XVII. NINA AND MIGGIE.	128
CHAPTER XVIII. DR. GRISWOLD.	137
CHAPTER XIX. EX-OFFICIO.	148
CHAPTER XX. THE DECISION.	154
CHAPTER XXI. THE DEERING WOODS.	160
CHAPTER XXII. THE DARKNESS DEEPENS.	168
CHAPTER XXIII. PARTING.	175
CHAPTER XXIV. THE NINETEENTH BIRTH-DAY.	185
CHAPTER XXV. DESTINY.	199
CHAPTER XXVI. EDITH AND THE WORLD.	209
CHAPTER XXVII. THE LAND OF FLOWERS.	222
CHAPTER XXVIII. SUNNYBANK.	231
CHAPTER XXIX. THE SISTERS.	238
CHAPTER XXX. ARTHUR AND NINA.	253
CHAPTER XXXI. LAST DAYS.	259
CHAPTER XXXII. PARTING WITH THE DEAD, AND PARTING WITH THE LIVING.	267
CHAPTER XXXIII. HOME.	275
CHAPTER XXXIV. NINA'S LETTER.	281
CHAPTER XXXV. THE FIERY TEST.	287
CHAPTER XXXVI. THE SACRIFICE.	293
CHAPTER XXXVII. THE BRIDAL.	299
CHAPTER XXXVIII. SIX YEARS LATER.	305

DARKNESS AND DAYLIGHT

BY

Mary J. Holmes

CHAPTER I.
COLLINGWOOD.

Collingwood was to have a tenant at last. For twelve long years its massive walls of dark grey stone had frowned in gloomy silence upon the passers-by, the terror of the superstitious ones, who had peopled its halls with ghosts and goblins, saying even that the snowy-haired old man, its owner, had more than once been seen there, moving restlessly from room to room and muttering of the darkness which came upon him when he lost his fair young wife and her beautiful baby Charlie. The old man was not dead, but for years he had been a stranger to his former home.

In foreign lands he had wandered--up and down, up and down--from the snow-clad hills of Russia to where the blue skies of Italy bent softly over him and the sunny plains of France smiled on him a welcome. But the darkness he bewailed was there as elsewhere, and to his son he said, at last, "We will go to America, but not to Collingwood--not where Lucy used to live, and where the boy was born."

So they came back again and made for themselves a home on the shore of the silvery lake so famed in song, where they hoped to rest from their weary journeyings. But it was not so decreed. Slowly as poison works within the blood, a fearful blight was stealing upon the noble, uncomplaining Richard, who had sacrificed his early manhood to his father's fancies, and when at last the blow had fallen and crushed him in its might, he became as helpless as a little child, looking to others for the aid he had heretofore been accustomed to render. Then it was that the weak old man emerged for a time from beneath the cloud which had enveloped him so long, and winding his arms around his stricken boy, said, submissively, "What will poor Dick have me do?"

"Go to Collingwood, where I know every walk and winding path, and where the world will not seem so dreary, for I shall be at home."

The father had not expected this, and his palsied hands shook nervously; but the terrible misfortune of his son had touched a chord of pity, and brought to his darkened mind a vague remembrance of the years in which the unselfish Richard had thought only of his comfort, and so he answered sadly, "We will go to Collingwood."

One week more, and it was known in Shannondale, that crazy Captain Harrington and his son, the handsome Squire Richard, were coming again to the old homestead, which was first to be fitted up in a most princely style. All through the summer months the extensive improvements and repairs went on, awakening the liveliest interest in the villagers, who busied themselves with watching and reporting the progress of events at Collingwood. Fires were kindled on the marble hearths, and the flames went roaring up the broad-mouthed chimneys, frightening from their nests of many years the croaking swallows, and scaring away the bats, which had so long held holiday in the deserted rooms. Partitions were removed, folding doors were made, windows were cut down, and large panes of glass were substituted for those of more ancient date. The grounds and garden too were reclaimed from the waste of briers and weeds which had so wantonly rioted there; and the waters of the fish- pond, relieved of their dark green slime and decaying leaves, gleamed once more in the summer sunshine like a sheet of burnished silver, while a fairy boat lay moored upon its bosom as in the olden time. Softly the hillside brooklet fell, like a miniature cascade, into the little pond, and the low music it made blended harmoniously with the fall of the fountain not far away.

It was indeed a beautiful place; and when the furnishing process began, crowds of eager people daily thronged the spacious rooms, commenting upon the carpets, the curtains, the chandeliers, the furniture of rosewood and marble, and marvelling much why Richard Harrington should care for surroundings so costly and elegant. Could it be that he intended surprising them with a bride? It was possible--nay, more, it was highly probable that weary of his foolish sire's continual mutterings of "Lucy and the darkness," he bad found some fair young girl to share the care with him, and this was her gilded cage.

Shannondale was like all country towns, and the idea once suggested, the story rapidly gained ground, until at last it reached the ear of Grace Atherton, the pretty young widow, whose windows looked directly across the stretches of meadow and woodland to where Collingwood lifted its single tower and its walls of dark grey stone. As became the owner of Brier Hill and the widow of a judge, Grace held herself somewhat above the rest of the villagers, associating with but few, and finding her society mostly in the city not many miles away,

When her cross, gouty, phthisicy, fidgety old husband lay sick for three whole months, she nursed him so patiently that people wondered if it could be she loved the SURLY DOG, and one woman, bolder than the others, asked her if she did.

"Love him? No," she answered, "but I shall do my duty."

So when he died she made him a grand funeral, but did not pretend that she was sorry. She was not, and the night on which she crossed the threshold of Brier Hill a widow of twenty-one saw her a happier woman than when she first crossed it as a bride. Such was Grace Atherton, a proud, independent, but well principled woman, attending strictly to her own affairs, and expecting others to do the same. In the gossip concerning Collingwood, she had taken no verbal part, but there was no one more deeply interested than herself, spite of her studied indifference.

"You never knew the family," a lady caller said to her one morning, when at a rather late hour she sat languidly sipping her rich chocolate, and daintily picking at the snowy rolls and nicely buttered toast, "you never knew them or you would cease to wonder why the village people take so much interest in their movements, and are so glad to have them back."

"I have heard their story," returned Mrs. Atherton, "and I have no doubt the son is a very fine specimen of an old bachelor; thirty- five, isn't he, or thereabouts?"

"Thirty-five!" and Kitty Maynard raised her hands in dismay. "My dear Mrs. Atherton, he's hardly thirty yet, and those who have seen him since his return from Europe, pronounce him a splendid looking man, with an air of remarkably high breeding. I wonder if there IS any truth in the report that he is to bring with him a bride."

"A bride, Kitty!" and the massive silver fork dropped from Grace Atherton's hand.

SHE was interested now, and nervously pulling the gathers of her white morning gown, she listened while the loquacious Kitty told her what she knew of the imaginary wife of Richard Harrington. The hands ceased their working at the gathers, and assuming an air of indifference, Grace rang her silver bell, which was immediately answered by a singular looking girl, whom she addressed as Edith, bidding her bring some orange marmalade from an adjoining closet. Her orders were obeyed, and then the child lingered by the door, listening eagerly to the conversation which Grace had resumed concerning Collingwood and its future mistress.

Edith Hastings was a strange child, with a strange habit of expressing her thoughts aloud, and as she heard the beauties of Collingwood described in Kitty Maynard's most glowing terms, she suddenly exclaimed, "Oh, JOLLY don't I wish I could live there, only I'd be afraid of that boy who haunts the upper rooms."

"Edith!" said Mrs. Atherton, sternly, "why are you waiting here? Go at once to Rachel and bid her give you something to do."

Thus rebuked the black-eyed, black-haired, black-faced little girl waited away, not cringingly, for Edith Hastings possessed a spirit as proud as that of her high born mistress, and she went slowly to the kitchen, where, under Rachel's directions, she was soon in the mysteries of dish-washing, while the ladies in the parlor continued their conversation.

"I don't know what I shall do with that child," said Grace, as Edith's footsteps died away. I sometimes wish I had left her where I found her."

"Why, I thought her a very bright little creature," said Kitty, and her companion replied,

"She's too bright, and that's the trouble. She imitates me in everything, walks like me, talks like me, and yesterday I found her in the drawing-room going through with a pantomime of receiving calls the way I do. I wish you could have seen her stately bow when presented to an imaginary stranger."

"Did she do credit to you?" Kitty asked, and Grace replied,

"I can't say that she did not, but I don't like this disposition of hers--to put on the airs of people above her. Now if she were not a poor--"

"Look, look!" interrupted Kitty, "that must be the five hundred dollar piano sent up from Boston," and she directed her companion's attention to the long wagon which was passing the house on the way to Collingwood.

This brought the conversation back from the aspiring Edith to Richard Harrington, and as old Rachel soon came in to remove her mistress' breakfast, Kitty took her leave, saying as she bade her friend good morning,

"I trust it will not be long before you know him."

"Know him!" repeated Grace, when at last she was alone. "Just as if I had not known him to my sorrow. Oh, Richard, Richard! maybe you'd forgive me if you knew what I have suffered," and the proud, beautiful eyes filled with tears as Grace Atherton plucked the broad green leaves from the grape vine over her head, and tearing them in pieces scattered the fragments upon the floor of the piazza. "Was there to be a bride at Collingwood?" This was the question which racked her brain, keeping her in a constant state of feverish excitement until the very morning came when the family were expected.

Mrs. Matson, the former housekeeper, had resumed her old position, and though she came often to Brier Hill to consult the taste of Mrs. Atherton as to the arrangement of curtains and furniture, Grace was too haughtily polite to question her, and every car whistle found her at the window watching for the carriage and a sight of its inmates. One after another the western trains arrived, and the soft September twilight deepened into darker night, showing to the expectant Grace the numerous lights shining from the windows of Collingwood. Edith Hastings, too, imbued with something of her mistress' spirit, was on the alert, and when the last train in which they could possibly come, thundered through the town, her quick ear was the first to catch the sound of wheels grinding slowly up the hill.

"They are coming, Mrs. Atherton!" she cried; and nimble as a squirrel she climbed the great gate post, where with her elf locks floating about her sparkling face, she sat, while the carriage passed slowly by, then saying to herself, "Pshaw, it wasn't worth the trouble--I never saw a thing," she slid down from her high position, and stealing in the back way so as to avoid the scolding Mrs. Atherton was sure to give her, she crept up to her own chamber, where she stood long by the open window, watching the lights at Collingwood, and wondering if it WOULD make a person perfectly happy to be its mistress and the bride of Richard Harrington.

CHAPTER II.
EDITH HASTINGS GOES TO COLLINGWOOD.

The question Edith had asked herself, standing by her chamber window, was answered by Grace Atherton sitting near her own. "Yes, the bride of Richard Harrington MUST be perfectly happy, if bride indeed there were." She was beginning to feel some doubt upon this point, for strain her eyes as she might, she had not been able to detect the least signs of femininity in the passing carriage, and hope whispered that the brightest dream she had ever dreamed might yet be realized.

"I'll let him know to-morrow, that I'm here," she said, as she shook out her wavy auburn hair, and thought, with a glow of pride, how beautiful it was. "I'll send Edith with my compliments and a bouquet of flowers to the bride. She'll deliver them better than any one else, if I can once make her understand what I wish her to do."

Accordingly, the next morning, as Edith sat upon the steps of the kitchen door, talking to herself, Grace appeared before her with a tastefully arranged bouquet, which she bade her take with her compliments to Mrs. Richard Harrington, if there was such a body, and to Mr. Richard Harrington if there were not.

"Do you understand?" she asked, and Edith far more interested in her visit to Collingwood than in what she was to do when she reached there, replied,

"Of course I do; I'm to give your compliments;" and she jammed her hand into the pocket of her gingham apron, as if to make sure the compliments were there. "I'm to give them to MR. Richard, if there is one, and the flowers to Mrs. Richard, if there ain't!"

Grace groaned aloud, while old Rachel, the colored cook, who on all occasions was Edith's champion, removed her hands from the dough she was kneading and coming towards them, chimed in, "She ain't fairly got it through her har, Miss Grace. She's such a substracted way with her that you mostly has to tell her twicet," and in her own peculiar style Rachel succeeded in making the "substracted" child comprehend the nature of her errand.

"Now don't go to blunderin'," was Rachel's parting injunction, as Edith left the yard and turned in the direction of Collingwood.

It was a mellow September morning, and after leaving the main road and entering the gate of Collingwood, the young girl lingered by the way, admiring the beauty of the grounds, and gazing with feelings of admiration upon the massive building, surrounded by majestic maples, and basking so quietly in the warm sunlight. At the marble fountain she paused for a long, long time, talking to the golden fishes which darted so swiftly past each other, and wishing she could take them in her hand "just to see them squirm."

"I mean to catch ONE any way," she said, and glancing nervously at the windows to make sure no Mrs. Richard was watching her, she bared her round, plump arm, and thrust it into the water, just as a footstep sounded near.

Quickly withdrawing her hand and gathering up her bouquet, she turned about and saw approaching her one of Collingwood's ghosts. She knew him in a moment, for she had heard him described too often to mistake that white-haired, bent old man for other than Capt. Harrington. He did not chide her as she supposed he would, neither did he seem in the least surprised to see her there. On the contrary, his withered, wrinkled face brightened with a look of eager expectancy, as he said to her, "Little girl, can you tell me where Charlie is?"

"Charlie?" she repeated, retreating a step or two as he approached nearer and seemed about to lay his hand upon her hair, for her bonnet was hanging down her back, and her wild gipsy locks fell in rich profusion about her face. "I don't know any boy by that name, I'm nobody but Edith Hastings, Mrs. Atherton's waiting maid, and she don't let me play with boys. Only Tim Doolittle and I went huckleberrying once, but I hate him, he has such great warts on his hands," and having thus given her opinion of Tim Doolittle, Edith snatched up her bonnet and placed it upon her head, for the old man was evidently determined to touch her crow-black hair.

Her answer, however, changed the current of his thoughts, and while a look of intense pain flitted across his face, he whispered mournfully, "The same old story they all tell. I might have known it, but this one looked so fresh, so truthful, that I thought maybe she'd seen him. Mrs. Atherton's waiting maid," and he turned toward Edith--"Charlie's dead, and we all walk in darkness now, Richard and all."

This allusion to Richard reminded Edith of her errand, and thinking to herself, "I'll ask the crazy old thing if there's a lady here," she ran after him as he walked slowly away and catching him by the arm, said, "Tell me, please, is there any Mrs. Richard Harrington?"

"Not that I know of. They've kept it from me if there is, but there's Richard, he can tell you," and he pointed toward a man in a distant part of the grounds.

Curtseying to her companion, Edith ran off in the direction of the figure moving so slowly down the gravelled walk.

"I wonder what makes him set his feet down so carefully," she thought, as she came nearer to him. "Maybe there are pegs in his shoes, just as there were in mine last winter," and the barefoot little girl glanced at her naked toes, feeling glad they were for the present out of torture.

By this time she was within a few rods of the strange acting man, who, hearing her rapid steps, stopped, and turning round with a wistful, questioning look, said,

"Who's there? Who is it?"

The tone of his voice was rather sharp, and Edith paused suddenly, while he made an uncertain movement toward her, still keeping his ear turned in the attitude of intense listening.

"I wonder what he thinks of me?" was Edith's mental comment as the keen black eyes appeared to scan her closely.

Alas, he was not thinking of her at all, and soon resuming his walk, he whispered to himself, "They must have gone some other way."

Slowly, cautiously he moved on, never dreaming of the little sprite behind him, who, imitating his gait and manner, put down her chubby bare feet just when his went down, looking occasionally over her shoulder to see if her clothes swung from side to side just like Mrs. Atherton's, and treading so softly that he did not hear her until he reached the summer-house, when the cracking of a twig betrayed the presence of some one, and again that sad, troubled voice demanded, "Who is here?" while the arms were stretched out as if to grasp the intruder, whoever it might be.

Edith was growing excited. It reminded her of blind man's buff; and she bent her head to elude the hand which came so near entangling itself in her hair. Again a profound silence ensued, and thinking it might have been a fancy of his brain that some one was there with him, poor blind Richard Harrington sat down within the arbor, where the pleasant September sunshine, stealing through the thick vine leaves, fell in dancing circles upon his broad white brow, above which his jet black hair lay in rings. He was a tall, dark, handsome man, with a singular cast of countenance, and Edith felt that she had never seen anything so grand, so noble, and yet so helpless as the man sitting there before her. She knew now that he was blind, and she was almost glad that it was so, for had it been otherwise she would never have dared to scan him as she was doing now. She would not for the world have met the flash of those keen black eyes, had they not been sightless, and she quailed even now, when they were bent upon her, although she knew their glance was meaningless. It seemed to her so terrible to be blind, and she wondered why he should care to have his house and grounds so handsome when he could not see them. Still she was pleased that they were so, for there was a singular fitness, she thought, between this splendid man and his surroundings.

"I wish he had a little girl like me to lead him and be good to him," was her next mental comment, and the wild idea crossed her brain that possibly Mrs. Atherton would let her come up to Collingwood and be his waiting maid. This brought to mind a second time the object of her being there now, and she began to devise the best plan for delivering the bouquet. "I don't believe he cares for the compliments," she said to herself, "any way, I'll keep them till another time," but the flowers; how should she give those to him? She was beginning to be very much afraid of the figure sitting there so silently, and at last mustering all her courage, she gave a preliminary cough, which started him to his feet, and as his tall form towered above her she felt her fears come back, and scarcely knowing what she was doing she thrust the bouquet into his hand, saying as she did so, "POOR blind man, I am so sorry and I've brought you some nice flowers."

The next moment she was gone, and Richard heard the patter of her feet far up the gravelled walk ere he had recovered from his surprise. Who was she, and why had she remembered him? The voice was very, very sweet, thrilling him with a strange melody, which carried him back to a summer sunset years ago, when on the banks of the blue Rhine he had listened to a beautiful, dark-eyed Swede singing her infant daughter to sleep. Then the river itself appeared before him, cold and grey with the November frosts, and on its agitated surface he saw a little dimpled hand disappearing from view, while the shriek of the dark-eyed Swede told that her child was gone. A plunge--a fearful struggle--and he held the limp, white object in his arms; he bore it to the shore; he heard them say that he had saved its life, and then he turned aside to change his dripping garments and warm his icy limbs. This was the first picture brought to his mind by Edith Hastings' voice. The second was a sadder one, and he groaned aloud as he remembered how from the time of the terrible cold taken then, and the severe illness which followed, his eyesight had begun to fail--slowly, very slowly, it is true--and for years he could not believe that Heaven had in store for him so sad a fate. But it had come at last--daylight had faded out and the night was dark around him. Once, in his hour of bitterest agony, he had cursed that Swedish baby, wishing it had perished in the waters of the Rhine, ere he saved it at so fearful a sacrifice. But he had repented of the wicked thought; he was glad he saved the pretty Petrea's child, even though be should never see her face again. He knew not where she was, that girlish wife, speaking her broken English for the sake of her American husband, who was not always as kind to her as he should have been. He had heard no tidings of her since that fatal autumn. He had scarcely thought of her for months, but she came back to him now, and it was Edith's voice which brought her.

"Poor blind man," he whispered aloud. "How like that was to Petrea, when she said of my father, 'Poor, soft old man;'" and then he wondered again who his visitor had been, and why she had left him so abruptly.

It was a child, he knew, and he prized her gift the more for that, for Richard Harrington was a dear lover of children and he kissed the fair bouquet as he would not have kissed it had he known from whom it came. Rising at last from his seat, he groped his way back to the house, and ordering one of the costly vases in his room to be filled with water, he placed the flowers therein, and thought how carefully he would preserve them for the sake of his unknown friend.

Meantime Edith kept on her way, pausing once and looking back just in time to see Mr. Harrington kiss the flowers she had brought.

"I'm glad they please him," she said; "but how awful it is to be blind;" and by way of trying the experiment, she shut her eyes, and stretching out her arms, walked just as Richard, succeeding so well that she was beginning to consider it rather agreeable than otherwise, when she unfortunately ran into a tall rose-bush, scratching her forehead, tangling her hair, and stubbing her toes against its gnarled roots. "'Taint so jolly to be blind after all," she said, "I do believe I've broken my toe," and extricating herself as best she could from the sharp thorns, she ran on as fast as her feet could carry her, wondering what Mrs. Atherton would say when she heard Richard was blind, and feeling a kind of natural delight in knowing she should be the first to communicate the bad news.

CHAPTER III.
GRACE ATHERTON.

"Edith," said Mrs. Atherton, who had seen her coming, and hastened out to meet her, "you were gone a long time, I think."

"Yes'm," answered Edith, spitting out the bonnet strings she had been chewing, and tossing back the thick black locks which nearly concealed her eyes from view. "Yes'm; it took me a good while to talk to old Darkness."

"Talk to whom?" asked Grace; and Edith returned,

"I don't know what you call him if 'taint old Darkness; he kept muttering about the dark, and asked "where Charlie was."

"Ole Cap'n Harrington," said Rachel. "They say how't he's allus goin' on 'bout Charlie an' the dark."

This explanation was satisfactory to Grace, who proceeded next to question Edith concerning Mrs. Richard Harrington, asking if she saw her, etc.

"There ain't any such," returned Edith, "but I saw Mr. Richard. Jolly, isn't he grand? He's as tall as the ridge-pole, and---"

"But what did he say to the flowers?" interrupted Grace, far more intent upon knowing how her gift had been received, than hearing described the personal appearance of one she had seen so often.

Edith felt intuitively that a narrative of the particulars attending the delivery of the bouquet would insure her a scolding, so she merely answered, "He didn't say a word, only kissed them hard, but he can't see them, Mrs. Atherton. He can't see me, nor you, nor anybody. He's blind as a bat--"

"Blind! Richard blind! Oh, Edith;" and the bright color which had stained Grace's cheeks when she knew that Richard had kissed her flowers, faded out, leaving them of a pallid hue. Sinking into the nearest chair, she kept repeating "blind--

blind--poor, poor Richard. It cannot be. Bring me some water, Rachel, and help me to my room. This intensely hot morning makes me faint."

Rachel could not be thus easily deceived. She remembered an old house in England, looking out upon the sea, and the flirtation carried on all summer there between her mistress, then a beautiful young girl of seventeen, and the tall, handsome man, whom they called Richard Harrington. She remembered, too, the white-haired, gouty man, who, later in the autumn, came to that old house, and whose half million Grace had married, saying, by way of apology, that if Richard chose to waste his life in humoring the whims of his foolish father, she surely would NOT waste hers with him. SHE would see the world!

Alas, poor Grace. She had seen the world and paid dearly for the sight, for, go where she might, she saw always one face, one form; heard always one voice murmuring in her ear, "Could you endure to share my burden?"

No, she could not, she said, and so she had taken upon herself a burden ten-fold heavier to bear--a burden which crushed her spirits, robbed her cheek of its youthful bloom, after which she sent no regret when at last it disappeared, leaving her free to think again of Richard Harrington. It was a terrible blow to her that he was blind, and talk as she might about the faintness of the morning, old Rachel knew the real cause of her distress, and when alone with her, said, by way of comfort,

"Law, now, Miss Grace, 'taint worth a while to take on so. Like 'nough he'll be cured--mebby it's nothin' but them fetch-ed water- falls--CAT-A-RATS, that's it--and he can have 'em cut out. I wouldn't go to actin' like I was love-sick for a man I 'scarded oncet."

Grace was far too proud to suffer even her faithful Rachel thus to address her, and turning her flashing eyes upon the old woman, she said haughtily,

"How dare you talk to me in this way--don't you know I won't allow it? Besides, what reason have you for asserting what you have?"

"What reason has I? Plenty reason--dis chile ain't a fool if she is a nigger, raised in Georgy, and a born slave till she was turned of thirty. Your poor marm who done sot me free, would never spoke to me that way. What reason has I? I'se got good mem'ry--I 'members them letters I used to tote forrid and back, over thar in England; and how you used to watch by the winder till you seen him comin', and then, gal-like, ran off to make him think you wasn't particular 'bout seein' him. But, it passes me, what made you have ole money bags. I never could see inter that, when I knowd how you hated his shiny bald head, and slunk away if he offered to tache you with his old, soft, flappy hands. You are glad he's in Heaven, yon know you be; and though I never said nothin', *I* knowd you was glad that Squire Herrin'ton was come back to Collingwood, just as I knowd what made you choke like a chicken with the pip when Edith tole you he was blind. Can't cheat dis chile," and adjusting her white turban with an air of injured dignity, Rachel left her mistress, and returned to the kitchen.

"What ails Mrs. Atherton?" asked Edith, fancying it must be something serious which could keep the old negress so long from her bread.

On ordinary occasions the tolerably discreet African would have made some evasive reply, but with her feathers all ruffled, she belched out, "The upshot of the matter is, she's in love?"

"In love? Who does Mrs. Atherton love?"

"Him--the blind man," returned Rachel, adding fiercely, "but if you ever let her know I told you, I'll skin you alive--do you hear? Like enough she'll be for sendin' you up thar with more posies, an' if she does, do you hold your tongue and take 'em along."

Edith had no desire to betray Rachel's confidence, and slipping one shoulder out of her low dress she darted off after a butterfly, wondering to herself if it made everybody faint and sick at their stomach to be in love! It seemed very natural that one as rich and beautiful as Grace should love Richard Harrington, and the fact that she did, insensibly raised in her estimation the poor, white-faced woman, who, in the solitude of her chamber was weeping bitterer tears than she had shed before in years.

Could it he so? She hoped there was some mistake--and when an hour later she heard Kitty Maynard's cheerful voice in the lower hall her heart gave a bound as she thought, "She'll know--she's heard of it by this time."

"Please may I come in?" said Kitty, at her door. "Rachel told me you had a headache, but I know you won't mind me," and ere the words were half out of her mouth, Kitty's bonnet was off and she was perched upon the foot of the bed. HAVE you heard the news?" she began. "It's so wonderful, and so sad, too. Squire Harrington is not married; he's worse off than that--he's hopelessly blind."

"Indeed!" and Grace Atherton's manner was very indifferent.

"Yes," Kitty continued, "His French valet, Victor, who travelled with him in Europe, told brother Will all about it. Seven or eight years ago they were spending the summer upon the banks of the Rhine, and in a cottage near them was an American with a Swedish wife and baby. The man, it seems, was a dissipated fellow, much older than his wife, whom he neglected shamefully, leaving her alone for weeks at a time. The baby's name was Eloise, and she was a great pet with Richard who was fond of children. At last, one day in autumn, the little Eloise, who had just learned to run alone, wandered off by herself to a bluff, or rock, or something, from which she fell into the river. The mother, Petrea, was close by, and her terrific shrieks brought Richard to the spot in time to save the child. He had not been well for several days, and the frightful cold he took induced a fever, which seemed to settle in his eyes, for ever since his sight has been failing until now it has left him entirely. But hark! isn't some one in the next room?" and she stepped into the adjoining apartment just as the nimble Edith disappeared from view.

She had been sent up by Rachel with a message to Mrs. Atherton, and was just in time to hear the commencement of Kitty's story. Any thing relating to the blind man was interesting to her, and so she listened, her large black eyes growing larger and blacker as the tale proceeded. It did NOT seem wholly new to her, that story of the drowning child--that cottage on the Rhine, and for a moment she heard a strain of low, rich music sung as a lullaby to some restless, wakeful child. Then the music, the cottage and the blue Rhine faded away. She could not recall them, but bound as by a spell she listened still, until the word Petrea dropped from Kitty's lips. Then she started suddenly. Surely, she'd heard that NAME before. Whose was it? When was it? Where was it? She could not tell, and she repeated it in a whisper so loud that it attracted Kitty's attention.

"I shall catch it if she finds me listening," thought Edith, as she heard Kitty's remark, and in her haste to escape she forgot all about Petrea--all about the lullaby, and remembered nothing save the noble deed of the heroic Richard. "What a noble man he must be," she said, "to save that baby's life, and how she would pity him if she knew it made him blind. I wonder where she is. She must be most as big as I am now;" and if it were possible Edith's eyes grew brighter than their wont as she thought how had SHE been that Swedish child, she would go straight up to Collingwood and be the blind man's slave. She would read to him. She would see for him, and when he walked, she would lead him so carefully, removing all the ugly pegs from his boots, and watching to see that he did not stub his toes, as she was always doing in her headlong haste. "What a great good man he is," she kept repeating, while at the same time she felt an undefinable interest in the Swedish child, whom at that very moment, Grace Atherton was cursing in her heart as the cause of Richard's misfortune.

Kitty was gone at last, and glad to be alone she wept passionately over this desolation of her hopes, wishing often that the baby had perished in the river ere it had wrought a work so sad. How she hated that Swedish mother and her child--how she hated all children then, even the black haired Edith, out in the autumn sunshine, singing to herself a long-forgotten strain, which had come back to her that morning, laden with perfume from the vine- clad hills of Bingen, and with music from the Rhine. Softly the full, rich melody came stealing through the open window, and Grace Atherton as she listened to the mournful cadence felt her heart growing less hard and bitter toward fate, toward the world, and toward the innocent Swedish babe. Then as she remembered that Richard kissed the flowers, a flush mounted to her brow. He did love her yet; through all the dreary years of their separation he had clung to her, and would it not atone for her former selfishness, if now that the world was dark to him, she should give herself to the task of cheering the deep darkness? It would be happiness, she thought, to be pointed out as the devoted wife of the blind man, far greater happiness to bask in the sunlight of the blind man's love, for Grace Atherton did love him, and in the might of her love she resolved upon doing that from which she would have shrunk had he not been as helpless and afflicted as he was. Edith should be the medium between them. Edith should take him flowers every day, until he signified a wish for her to come herself, when she would go, and sitting by his side, would tell him, perhaps, how sad her life had been since that choice of hers made on the shore of the deep sea. Then, if he asked her again to share his lonely lot, she would gladly lay her head upon his bosom, and whisper back the word she should have said to him seven years ago.

It was a pleasant picture of the future which Grace Atherton drew as she lay watching the white clouds come and go over the distant tree tops of Collingwood, and listening to the song of Edith, still playing in the sunshine, and when at dinner time she failed to appear at the ringing of the bell, and Edith was sent in quest of her, she found her sleeping quietly, dreaming of the Swedish babe and Richard Harrington.

CHAPTER IV.
RICHARD AND EDITH.

On Richard's darkened pathway, there WAS now a glimmer of daylight, shed by Edith Hastings' visit, and with a vague hope that she might come again, he on the morrow groped his way to the summer house, and taking the seat where he sat the previous day, he waited and listened for the footstep on the grass which should tell him she was near. Nor did he wait long ere Edith came tripping down the walk, bringing the bouquet which Grace had prepared with so much care.

"Hist!" dropped involuntarily from her lips, when she descried him, sitting just where she had, without knowing why, expected she should find him, and her footfall so light that none save the blind could have detected it.

To Richard there was something half amusing, half ridiculous in the conduct of the capricious child, and for the sake of knowing what she would do, he professed to be ignorant of her presence, and leaning back against the lattice, pretended to be asleep, while Edith came so near that he could hear her low breathing as she stood still to watch him. Nothing could please her more than his present attitude, for with his large bright eyes shut she dared to look at him as much and as long she chose. He was to her now a kind of divinity, which she worshipped for the sake of the Swedish baby rescued from a watery grave, and she longed to wind her arms around his neck and tell him how she loved him for that act; but she dared not, and she contented herself with whispering softly, "If I wasn't so spunky and ugly, I'd pray every night that God would make you see again. Poor blind man."

It would be impossible to describe the deep pathos of Edith's voice as she uttered the last three words. Love, admiration, compassion and pity, all were blended in the tone, and it is not strange that it touched an answering chord in the heart of the "poor blind man." Slowly the broad chest heaved, and tears, the first he had shed since the fearful morning when they led him into the sunlight he felt but could not see, moistened his lashes, and dropped upon his face.

"He's dreaming a bad dream," Edith said, and with her little chubby hand she brushed his tears away, cautiously, lest she should rouse him from his slumbers.

Softly she put back from the white forehead his glossy hair, taking her own round comb to subdue an obdurate look, while he was sure that the fingers made more than one pilgrimage to the lips as the little barber found moisture necessary to her task.

"There, Mr. Blindman, you look real nice," she said, with an immense amount of satisfaction, as she stepped back, the better to inspect the whole effect. "I'll bet you'll wonder who's been here when you wake up, but I shan't tell you now. Maybe, though, I'll come again to-morrow," and placing the bouquet in his hands, she ran away.

Pausing for a moment, and looking back, she saw Richard again raise to his lips her bouquet, and with a palpitating heart, as she thought, "what if he weren't asleep after all!" she ran on until Brier Hill was reached.

"Not any message this time either?" said Grace, when told that he had kissed her flowers, and that was all.

Still this was proof that he was pleased, and the infatuated woman persisted in preparing bouquets, which Edith daily carried to Collingwood, going always at the same time, and finding him always in the same spot waiting for her. As yet no word had passed between them, for Edith, who liked the novelty of the affair, was so light-footed that she generally managed to slip the bouquet into his hand, and run away ere he had time to detain her. One morning, however, near the middle of October, when, owing to a bruised heel, she had not been to see him for more than a week, he sat in his accustomed place, half-expecting her, and still thinking how improbable it was that she would come. He had become strangely attached to the little unknown, as he termed her; he thought of her all the day long, and when, in the chilly evening, he sat before the glowing grate, listening to the monotonous whisperings of his father, he wished so much that she was there beside him. His life would not be so dreary then, for in the society of that active, playful child, he should forget, in part, how miserable he was. She was blue-eyed, and golden-haired, he thought, with soft, abundant curls veiling her sweet young face; and he pictured to himself just how she would look, flitting through the halls, and dancing upon the green sward near the door,

"But it cannot be," he murmured on that October morning, when he sat alone in his wretchedness. "Nothing I've wished for most has ever come to pass. Sorrow has been my birthright from a boy. A curse is resting upon our household, and all are doomed who come within its shadow. First my own mother died just when I needed her the most, then that girlish woman whom I also called my mother; then, our darling Charlie. My father's reason followed next, while *I* am hopelessly blind. Oh, sometimes I wish that I could die."

"Hold your breath with all your might, and see if you can't," said the voice of Edith Hastings, who had approached him cautiously, and heard his sad soliloquy.

Richard started, and stretching out his long arm, caught the sleeve of the little girl, who, finding herself a captive, ceased to struggle, and seated herself beside him as he requested her to do.

"Be you holding your breath?" she asked, as for a moment he did not speak, adding as he made no answer, "Tell me when you're dead, won't you?"

Richard laughed aloud, a hearty, merry laugh, which startled himself, it was so like an echo of the past, ere his hopes were crushed by cruel misfortune.

"I do not care to die now that I have you," he said; "and if you'd stay with me always, I should never be unhappy."

"Oh, wouldn't that be jolly," cried Edith, using her favorite expression, "I'd read to you, and sing to you, only Rachel says my songs are weird-like, and queer, and maybe you might not like them; but I'd fix your hair, and lead you in the smooth places where you wouldn't jam your heels;" and she glanced ruefully at one of hers, bound up in a cotton rag. "I wish I could come, but Mrs. Atherton won't let me, I know. She threatens most every day to send me back to the Asylum, 'cause I act so. I'm her little waiting-maid, Edith Hastings."

"Waiting maid!" and the tone of Richard's voice was indicative of keen disappointment.

The Harringtons were very proud, and Richard would once have scoffed at the idea of being particularly interested in one so far below him as a waiting-maid. He had never thought of this as a possibility, and the child beside him was NOT of quite so much consequence as she had been before. Still he would know something of her history, and he asked her where she lived, and why she had brought him so many flowers.

"I live with Mrs. Atherton," she replied. "She sent the flowers, and if you'll never tell as long as you live and breathe, I'll tell you what Rachel says. Rachel's an old colored woman, who used to be a nigger down South, but she's free now, and says Mrs. Atherton loves you. I guess she does, for she fainted most away that day I went home and told her you were blind."

"Mrs. Atherton!" and Richard's face grew suddenly dark. "Who is Mrs. Atherton, child?"

"Oh-h-h!" laughed Edith deprecatingly; "don't you know her? She's Grace Atherton--the biggest lady in town; sleeps in linen sheets and pillow cases every night, and washes in a bath-tub every morning."

"Grace Atherton!" and Edith quailed beneath the fiery glance bent upon her by those black sightless eyes. "Did Grace Atherton send these flowers to me?" and the bright-hued blossoms dropped instantly from his hand.

"Yes, sir, she did. What makes you tear so? Are you in a tantrum?" said Edith, as he sprang to his feet and began unsteadily to pace the summer-house.

Richard Harrington possessed a peculiar temperament, Grace Atherton had wounded his pride, spurned his love, and he THOUGHT he hated her, deeming it a most unwomanly act in her to make these overtures for a reconciliation. This was why he TORE so, as Edith had expressed it, but soon growing more calm, he determined to conceal from the quick-witted child the cause of his agitation, and resuming his seat beside her, he asked her many questions concerning Grace Atherton and herself, and as he talked he felt his olden interests in his companion gradually coming back. What if she were now a waiting-maid, her family might have been good, and he asked her many things of her early life. But Edith could tell him nothing. The Orphan Asylum was the first home of which she had any vivid remembrance, though it did seem to her she once had lived where the purple grapes were growing rich and ripe upon the broad vine stalk, and where all the day long there was music such as she'd never heard since, but which came back to her sometimes in dreams, staying long enough for her to catch the air. Her mother, the matron told her, had died in New York, and she was brought to the Asylum by a woman who would keep her from starvation. This was Edith's story, told without reserve or the slightest suspicion that the proud man beside her would think the less of her because she had been poor and hungry. Neither did he, after the first shock had worn away; and he soon found himself wishing again that she would come up there and live with him. She was a strange, odd child, he knew, and he wondered how she looked. He did not believe she was golden-haired and blue-eyed now. Still he would not ask her lest he should receive a second disappointment, for he was a passionate admirer of female beauty, and he could not repress a feeling of aversion for an ugly face.

"Is Mrs. Atherton handsome?" he suddenly asked, remembering the fresh, girlish beauty of Grace Elmendorff, and wishing to know if it had faded.

"Oh, jolly," said Edith, "I guess she is. Such splendid blue hair and auburn eyes."

"She must be magnificent," returned Richard, scarcely repressing a smile. "Give her my compliments and ask her if she's willing NOW to share my self-imposed labor. Mind, don't you forget a word, and go now. I'll expect you again to-morrow with her answer."

He made a gesture for Edith to leave, and though she wanted so much to tell him how she loved him for saving that Swedish baby, she forbore until another time, and ran hastily away, repeating his message as she ran lest she should forget it.

"Sent his compliments, and says ask you if you're willing to share, his--his--his--share his--now--something--anyway, he wants you to come up there and live, and I do so hope you'll go. Won't it be jolly?" she exclaimed, as half out of breath she burst into the room where Grace sat reading a letter received by the morning's mail.

"Wants me to what?" Grace asked, fancying she had not heard aright, and as Edith repeated the message, there stole into her heart a warm, happy feeling, such as she had not experienced since the orange wreath crowned her maiden brow.

Edith had not told her exactly what he said, she knew, but it was sufficient that he cared to see her, and she resolved to gratify him, but with something of her olden coquetry she would wait awhile and make him think she was not coming. So she said no more to Edith upon the subject, but told her that she was expecting her cousin Arthur St. Claire, a student from Geneva College, that he would be there in a day or two, and while he remained at Brier Hill she wished Edith to try and behave herself.

"This Mr. St. Claire," said she, "belongs to one of the most aristocratic Southern families. He is not accustomed to anything low, either in speech or manner."

"Can't I even say JOLLY?" asked Edith, with such a seriously comical manner that Grace had great difficulty to keep from smiling.

"Jolly" was Edith's pet word, the one she used indiscriminately and on all occasions, sometimes as an interjection, but oftener as an adjective. If a thing suited her it was sure to be jolly--she always insisting that 'twas a good proper word, for MARIE used it and SHE knew. Who Marie was she could not tell, save that 'twas somebody who once took care of her and called her jolly. It was in vain that Grace expostulated, telling her it was a slang phrase, used only by the vulgar. Edith was inexorable, and would not even promise to abstain from it during the visit of Arthur St. Claire.

CHAPTER V.
VISITORS AT COLLINGWOOD AND VISITORS AT BRIER HILL.

The morning came at last on which Arthur was expected, but as he did not appear, Grace gave him up until the morrow, and toward the middle of the afternoon ordered out her carriage, and drove slowly in the direction of Collingwood. Alighting before the broad piazza, and ascending the marble steps, she was asked by Richard's confidential servant into the parlor, where she sat waiting anxiously while he went, in quest of his master.

"A lady, sir, wishes to see you in the parlor," and Victor Dupres bowed low before Richard, awaiting his commands.

"A lady, Victor? Did she give her name?"

"Yes, sir; Atherton--Mrs. Grace Atherton, an old friend, she said," Victor replied, marveling at the expression of his master's face, which indicated anything but pleasure.

He had expected her--had rather anticipated her coming; but now that she was there, he shrank from the interview. It could only result in sorrow, for Grace was not to him now what she once had been. He could value her, perhaps, as a friend, but Edith's tale had told him that he to her was more than a friend. Possibly this knowledge was not as distasteful to him as he fancied it to be; at all events, when he remembered it, he said to Victor:

"Is the lady handsome?" feeling a glow of satisfaction in the praises heaped upon the really beautiful Grace. Ere long the hard expression left his face, and straightening up his manly form, he bade Victor take him to her.

As they crossed the threshold of the door, he struck his foot against it, and instantly there rang in his ear the words which little Edith had said to him so pityingly, "Poor blind man!" while he felt again upon his brow the touch of those childish fingers; and this was why the dark, hard look came back. Edith Hastings rose up between him and the regal creature waiting so anxiously his coming, and who, when he came and stood before her, in his helplessness, wept like a child.

"Richard! oh, Richard! that it should be thus we meet again!" was all that she could say, as, seizing the groping hand, she covered it with her tears.

Victor had disappeared, and she could thus give free vent to her emotions, feeling it almost a relief that the eyes whose glance she once had loved to meet could not witness her grief.

"Grace," he said at last, the tone of his voice was so cold that she involuntarily dropped his hands and looked him steadily in the face. "Grace, do not aggravate my misfortune by expressing too much sympathy. I am not as miserable as you may think, indeed, I am not as unhappy even now as yourself."

"It's true, Richard, true," she replied, "and because I am unhappy I have come to ask your forgiveness if ever word or action, or taunt of mine caused you a moment's pain. I have suffered much since we parted, and my suffering has atoned for all my sin."

She ceased speaking and softened by memories of the past, when he loved Grace Elmendorf, Richard reached for her hand, and holding it between his own, said to her gently, "Grace, I forgave you years ago. I know you have suffered much, and I am sorry for it, but we will understand each other now. You are the widow of the man you chose, I am hopelessly blind--our possessions adjoin each other, our homes are in sight. I want you for a neighbor, a friend, a sister, if you like. I shall never marry. That time is past. It perished with the long ago, and it will, perhaps, relieve the monotony of my life if I have a female acquaintance to visit occasionally. I thank you much for your flowers, although for a time I did not know you sent them, for the little girl would place them in my hands without a word and dart away before I could stop her. Still I knew it was a child, and I preserved them carefully for her sake until she was last here, when I learned who was the real donor. I am fond of flowers and thank you for sending them. I appreciate your kindness. I like you much better than I did an hour since, for the sound of your voice and the touch of your hands seem to me like old familiar friends. I am glad you came to see me, Grace. I wish you to come often, for I am very lonely here. We will at least be friends, but nothing more. Do you consent to my terms?"

She had no alternative but to consent, and bowing her head, she answered back, "Yes, Richard; that is all I can expect, all I wish. I had no other intention in sending you bouquets."

He knew that she did not tell him truly, but he pitied her mortification, and tried to divert her mind by talking upon indifferent subjects, but Grace was too much chagrined and disappointed to pay much heed to what he said, and after a time arose to go.

"Come again soon," he said, accompanying her to the door, "and send up that novelty Edith, will you?"

"Edith," muttered Grace, as she swept haughtily down the box-lined walk, and stepped into her carriage. "I'll send her back to the Asylum, as I live. Why didn't she tell me just how it was, and so prevent me from making myself ridiculous?"

Grace was far too much disturbed to go home at once. She should do or say something unlady-like if she did, and she bade Tom drive her round the village, thus unconsciously giving the offending Edith a longer time in which to entertain and amuse the guest at Brier Hill, for Arthur St. Claire had come.

Edith was the first to spy him sauntering slowly up the walk, and she watched him curiously as he came, mimicing his gait, and wondering if he didn't feel big.

"Nobody's afraid of you," she soliloquised, "if you do belong to the firstest family in Virginia." Then, hearing Rachel, who answered his ring, bid him walk into the parlor and amuse himself till Mrs. Atherton came, she thought, "Wouldn't it be jolly to go down and entertain him myself. Let me see, what does Mrs. Atherton say to the Shannondale gentlemen when they call? Oh, I know, she asks them if they've read the last new novel; how they liked it, and so on. I can do all that, and maybe he'll think I'm a famous scholar. I mean to wear the shawl she looks so pretty in," and going to her mistress' drawer, the child took out and threw around her shoulders a crimson scarf, which Grace often wore, and then descended to the parlor, where Arthur St. Claire stood, leaning against the marble mantel, and listlessly examining various ornaments upon it.

At the first sight of him Edith felt her courage forsaking her, there seemed so wide a gulf between herself and the haughty-looking stranger, and she was about to leave the room when he called after her, bidding her stay, and asking who she was.

"I'm Edith Hastings," she answered, dropping into a chair, and awkwardly kicking her heels against the rounds in her embarrassment at having those large, quizzical brown eyes fixed so inquiringly upon her.

He was a tall, handsome young man, not yet nineteen years of age, and in his appearance there certainly was something savoring of the air supposed to mark the F. F. V's. His manners were polished in the extreme, possessing, perhaps, a little too much hauteur, and impressing the beholder with the idea that he could, if he chose, be very cold and overbearing. His forehead, high and intellectually formed, was shaded by curls of soft brown hair, while about his mouth there lurked a mischievous smile, somewhat at variance with the proud curve of his upper lip, where an incipient mustache was starting into life. Such was Arthur St. Claire, as he stood coolly inspecting Edith Hastings, who mentally styling him the "hatefullest upstart" she ever saw, gave him back a glance as cool and curious as his own.

"You are an odd little thing," he said at last.

"No I ain't neither," returned Edith, the tears starting in her flashing black eyes.

"Spunky," was the young man's next remark, as he advanced a step or two toward her. "But don't let's quarrel, little lady. You've come down to entertain me, I dare say; and now tell me who you are."

His manner at once disarmed the impulsive Edith of all prejudice, and she replied:

"I told you I was Edith Hastings, Mrs. Atherton's waiting maid."

"Waiting maid!" and Arthur St. Claire took a step or two backwards as he said: "Why are you in here? This is not your place."

Edith sprang to her feet. She could not misunderstand the feeling with which he regarded her, and with an air of insulted dignity worthy of Grace herself, she exclaimed,

"Oh, how I hate you, Arthur St. Claire! At first I thought you might be good, like Squire Harrington; but you ain't. I can't bear you. Ugh!"

"Squire Harrington? Does he live near here?" and the face which at the sight of her anger had dimpled all over with smiles, turned white as Arthur St. Claire asked this question, to which Edith replied:

"Yes; he's blind, and he lives up at Collingwood. You can see its tower now," and she pointed across the fields.

But Arthur did not heed her, and continued to ply her with questions concerning Mr. Harrington, asking if he had formerly lived near Geneva, in western New York, if he had a crazy father, and if he ever came to Brier Hill.

Edith's negative answer to this last query seemed to satisfy him, and when, mistaking his eagerness for a desire to see her divinity, Edith patronizingly informed him that he might go with her some time to Collingwood, he answered her evasively, asking if Richard recognized voices, as most blind people did.

Edith could not tell, but she presumed he did, for he was the smartest man that ever lived; and in her enthusiastic praises she waxed so eloquent, using, withal, so good language, that Arthur forgot she was a waiting maid, and insensibly began to entertain a feeling of respect for the sprightly child, whose dark face sparkled and flashed with her excitement. She WAS a curious specimen, he acknowledged, and he began adroitly to sound the depths of her intellect. Edith took the cue at once, and not wishing to be in the background, asked him, as she had at first intended doing, if he'd read the last new novel.

Without in the least comprehending WHAT novel she meant, Arthur promptly replied that he had.

"How did you like it?" she continued, adjusting her crimson scarf as she had seen Mrs. Atherton do under similar circumstances.

"Very much indeed," returned the young man with imperturbable gravity, but when with a toss of her head she asked; "Didn't you think there was too much 'PHYSICS in it?" he went off into peals of laughter so loud and long that they brought old Rachel to the door to see if "he was done gone crazy or what."

Taking advantage of her presence, the crest-fallen Edith crept disconsolately up the stairs, feeling that she had made a most ridiculous mistake, and wondering what the word COULD be that sounded so much like 'PHYSICS, and yet wasn't that at all. She know she had made herself ridiculous, and was indulging in a fit of crying when Mrs. Atherton returned, delighted to meet her young cousin, in whom she felt a pardonable pride.

"You must have been very lonely," she said, beginning to apologize for her absence.

"Never was less so in my life," he replied. "Why, I've been splendidly entertained by a little black princess, who called herself your waiting maid, and discoursed most eloquently of METAPHYSICS and all that."

"Edith, of course," said Grace. "It's just, like her. Imitated me in every thing, I dare say."

"Rather excelled you, I think, in putting on the fine lady," returned the teasing Arthur, who saw at once that Edith Hastings was his fair cousin's sensitive point.

"What else did she say?" asked Grace, but Arthur generously refrained from repeating the particulars of his interview with the little girl who, as the days went by, interested him so much that he forgot his Virginia pride, and greatly to Mrs. Atherton's surprise, indulged with her in more than one playful romp, teasingly calling her his little "Metaphysics," and asking if she hated him still.

She did not. Next to Richard and Marie, she liked him better than any one she had ever seen, and she was enjoying his society so much when a most unlucky occurrence suddenly brought her happiness to an end, and afforded Grace an excuse for doing what she had latterly frequently desired to do, viz. that of sending the little girl back to the Asylum from which she had taken her.

Owing to the indisposition of the chambermaid, Edith was one day sent with water to Mr. St. Claire's room. Arthur was absent, but on the table his writing desk lay open, and Edith's inquisitive eyes were not long in spying a handsome golden locket, left there evidently by mistake. Two or three times she had detected him looking at this picture, and with an eager curiosity to see it also, she took the locket in her hand, and going to the window, touched the spring.

It was a wondrously beautiful face which met her view--the face of a young girl, whose golden curls rippling softly over her white shoulders, and whose eyes of lustrous blue, reminded Edith of the angels about which Rachel sang so devoutly every Sunday. To Edith there was about that face a nameless but mighty fascination, a something which made her warm blood chill and tingle in her veins, while there crept over her a second time dim visions of something far back in the past--of purple fruit on vine-clad hills--of music soft and low--of days and nights on some tossing, moving object-- and then of a huge white building, embowered in tall green trees, whose milk-white blossoms she gathered in her hand; while distinct from all the rest was this face, on which she gazed so earnestly. It is true that all these thoughts were not clear to her mind; it was rather a confused mixture of ideas, one of which faded ere another came, so that there seemed no real connection between them; and had she embodied them in words, they would have been recognized as the idle fancies of a strange, old-fashioned child. But the picture--there WAS something in it which held Edith motionless, while her tongue seemed struggling to articulate a NAME, but failed in the attempt; and when, at last, her lips did move, they uttered the word MARIE, as if she too, were associated with that sweet young face.

"Oh, but she's jolly," Edith said, "I don't wonder Mr. Arthur loves her," and she felt her own heart throb with a strange affection for the beautiful original of that daguerreotype.

In the hall without there was the sound of a footstep. It was coming to that room. It was Grace herself, Edith thought; and knowing she would be censured for touching what did not belong to her, she thrust the locket into her bosom, intending to return it as soon as possible, and springing out upon the piazza, scampered away, leaving the water pail to betray her recent presence.

It was NOT Grace, as she had supposed, but Arthur St. Claire himself come to put away the locket, which he suddenly remembered to have left upon the table. Great was his consternation when he found it gone, and that no amount of searching could bring it to light. He did not notice the empty pail the luckless Edith had left, although he stumbled over it twice in his feverish anxiety to find his treasure. But what he failed to observe was discovered by Grace, whom he summoned to his aid, and who exclaimed:

"Edith Hastings has been here! She must be the thief!"

"Edith, Grace, Edith--it cannot be," and Arthur's face indicated plainly the pain it would occasion him to find that it was so.

"I hope you may be right, Arthur, but I have not so much confidence in her as you seem to have. There she is now," continued Grace, spying her across the yard and calling to her to come.

Blushing, stammering, and cowering like a guilty thing, Edith entered the room, for she heard Arthur's voice and knew that he was there to witness her humiliation.

"Edith," said Mrs. Atherton, sternly, "what have you been doing?"

No answer from Edith save an increase of color upon her face, and with her suspicions confirmed, Grace went on,

"What have you in your pocket?"

"'Taint in my pocket; it's in my bosom," answered Edith, drawing it forth and holding it to view.

"How dare you steal it," asked Grace, and instantly there came into Edith's eyes the same fiery, savage gleam from which Mrs. Atherton always shrank, and beneath which she now involuntarily quailed.

It had never occurred to Edith that she could be accused of theft, and she stamped at first like a little fury, then throwing herself upon the sofa, sobbed out, "Oh, dear--oh, dear, I wish God would let me die. I don't want to live any longer in such a mean, nasty world. I want to go to Heaven, where everything is jolly."

"You are a fit subject for Heaven," said Mrs. Atherton, scornfully, and instantly the passionate sobbing ceased; the tears were dried in the eyes which blazed with insulted dignity as Edith arose, and looking her mistress steadily in the face, replied,

"I suppose you think I meant to steal and keep the pretty picture, but the one who was in here with me knows I didn't."

"Who was that?" interrupted Grace, her color changing visibly at the child's reverent reply.

"God was with me, and I wish he hadn't let me touch it, but he did. It lay on the writing desk and I took it to the window to see it. Oh, isn't she jolly?" and as she recalled the beautiful features, the hard expression left her own, and she went on, "I couldn't take my eyes from her; they would stay there, and I was almost going to speak her name, when I heard you coming, and ran away. I meant to bring it back, Mr. Arthur," and she turned appealingly to him. "I certainly did, and you believe me, don't you? I never told a lie in my life."

Ere Arthur could reply, Grace chimed in.

"Believe you? Of course not. You stole the picture and intended to keep it. I cannot have you longer in my family, for nothing is safe. I shall send you back at once."

There was a look in the large eyes which turned so hopelessly from Arthur to Grace, and from Grace back to Arthur, like that the hunted deer wears when hotly pursued in the chase. The white lips moved but uttered no sound and the fingers closed convulsively around the golden locket which Arthur advanced to take away.

"Let me see her once more," she said.

He could not refuse her request, and touching the spring he held it up before her.

"Pretty lady," she whispered, "sweet lady, whose name I most know, speak, and tell Mr. Arthur that I didn't do it. I surely didn't."

This constant appeal to Arthur, and total disregard of herself, did not increase Mrs. Atherton's amiability, and taking Edith by the shoulder she attempted to lead her from the room.

At the door Edith stopped, and said imploringly to Arthur,

"DO you think I stole it?"

He shook his head, a movement unobserved by Grace, but fraught with so much happiness for the little girl. She did not heed Grace's reproaches now, nor care if she was banished to her own room for the remainder of the day. Arthur believed her innocent; Uncle Tom believed her innocent, and Rachel believed her innocent, which last fact was proved by the generous piece of custard pie hoisted to her window in a small tin pail, said pail being poised upon the prongs of a long pitch-fork. The act of thoughtful kindness touched a tender chord in Edith's heart, and the pie choked her badly, but she managed to eat it all save the crust, which she tossed into the grass, laughing to see how near it came to hitting Mrs. Atherton, who looked around to discover whence it could possibly have come.

That night, just before dark, Grace entered Edith's room, and told her that as Mr. St. Claire, who left them on the morrow, had business in New York, and was going directly there, she had decided to send her with him to the Asylum. "He will take a letter from me," she continued, "telling them why you are sent back, and I greatly fear it will be long ere you find as good a home as this has been to you."

Edith sat like one stunned by a heavy blow. She had not really believed that a calamity she so much dreaded, would overtake her, and the fact that it had, paralyzed her faculties. Thinking her in a fit of stubbornness Mrs. Atherton said no more, but busied herself in packing her scanty wardrobe, feeling occasionally a twinge of remorse as she bent over the little red, foreign-looking chest, or glanced at the slight figure sitting so motionless by the window.

"Whose is this?" she asked, holding up a box containing a long, thick braid of hair.

"Mother's hair! mothers hair! for Marie told me so. You shan't touch THAT!" and like a tigress Edith sprang upon her, and catching the blue-black tress, kissed it passionately, exclaiming, "'Tis mother's--'tis. I remember now, and I could not think before, but Marie told me so the last time I saw her, years and years ago. Oh, mother, if I ever had a mother, where are you to- night, when I want you so much?"

She threw herself upon her humble bed, not thinking of Grace, nor yet of the Asylum, but revelling in her newborn joy. Suddenly, like a flash of lightning, an incident of the past had come back to her bewildered mind, and she knew now whose was the beautiful braid she had treasured so carefully. Long ago--oh, how long it seemed to her--there had come to the Asylum a short, dumpy woman, with a merry face, who brought her this hair in a box, telling her it was her mother's, and also that she was going to a far country, but should return again sometime--and this woman was Marie, who haunted her dreams so often, whispering to her of magnolias and cape-jessamines. All this Edith remembered distinctly, and while thinking of it she fell asleep, nor woke to consciousness even when Rachel's kind old hands undressed her carefully and tucked her up in bed, saying over her a prayer, and asking that Miss Grace's heart might relent and keep the little girl. It had not relented when morning came, and still, when at breakfast, Arthur received a letter, which made it necessary for him to go to New York by way of Albany, she did suggest that it might be too much trouble to have the care of Edith.

"Not at all," he said; and half an hour later Edith was called into the parlor, and told to get herself in readiness for the journey.

"Oh, I can't, I can't," cried Edith, clinging to Mrs. Atherton's skirt, and begging of her not to send her back.

"Where will you go?" asked Grace. "I don't want you here."

"I don't know," sobbed Edith, uttering the next instant a scream of joy, as she saw, in the distance, the carriage from Collingwood, and knew that Richard was in it. "To him! to him!" she exclaimed, throwing up her arms. "Let me go to Mr. Harrington! He wants me, I know."

"Are you faint?" asked Grace, as she saw the sudden paling of Arthur's lips.

"Slightly," he answered, taking her offered salts, and keeping his eyes fixed upon the carriage until it passed slowly by, "I'm better now," he said, returning the salts, and asking why Edith could not go to Collingwood.

Grace would rather she should go anywhere else, but she did not say so to Arthur. She merely replied that Edith was conceited enough to think Mr. Harrington pleased with her just because he had sometimes talked to her when she carried him flowers.

"But of course he don't care for her," she said. "What could a blind man do with a child like her? Besides, after what has occurred, I could not conscientiously give her a good name."

Arthur involuntarily gave an incredulous whistle, which spoke volumes of comfort to the little girl weeping so passionately by the window, and watching with longing eyes the Collingwood carriage now passing from her view.

"We must go or be left," said Arthur, approaching her gently, and whispering to her not to cry.

"Good bye, Edith," said Mrs. Atherton, putting out her jewelled band; but Edith would not touch it, and in a tone of voice which sank deep into the proud woman's heart, she answered:

"You'll be sorry for this some time."

Old Rachel was in great distress, for Edith was her pet; and winding her black arms about her neck, she wept over her a simple, heartfelt blessing, and then, as the carriage drove from the gate, ran back to her neglected churning, venting her feelings upon the dasher, which she set down so vigorously that the rich cream flew in every direction, bespattering the wall, the window, the floor, the stove, and settling in large white flakes upon her tawny skin and tall blue turban.

Passing through the kitchen, Grace saw it all, but offered no remonstrance, for she knew what had prompted movements so energetic on the part of odd old Rachel. She, too, was troubled, and all that, day she was conscious of a feeling of remorse which kept whispering to her of a great wrong done the little girl whose farewell words were ringing in her ear: "You'll be sorry for this some time."

CHAPTER VI.
ARTHUR AND EDITH.

If anything could have reconciled Edith to her fate, it would have been the fact that she was travelling with Arthur St. Claire, who, after entering the cars, cared for her as tenderly as if she had been a lady of his own rank, instead of a little disgraced waiting maid, whom he was taking back, to the Asylum. It was preposterous, he thought, for Grace to call one as young as Edith a waiting maid, but it was like her, he knew. It had a lofty sound, and would impress some people with a sense of her greatness; so he could excuse it much more readily than the injustice done to the child by charging her with a crime of which he knew she was innocent. This it was, perhaps, which made him so kind to her, seeking to divert her mind from her grief by asking her many questions concerning herself and her family. But Edith did not care to talk. All the way to Albany she continued crying; and when, at last, they stood within the noisy depot, Arthur saw that the tears were still rolling down her cheeks like rain.

"Poor little girl. How I pity her!" he thought, as she placed her hand confidingly in his, and when he saw how hopelessly she looked into his face, as she asked, with quivering lip, if "it wasn't ever so far to New York yet?" the resolution he had been trying all the day to make was fully decided upon, and when alone with Edith in the room appropriated to her at, the Delavan House, he asked her why she supposed Richard Harrington would be willing to take her to Collingwood.

Very briefly Edith related to him the particulars of her interviews with the blind man, saying, when she had finished,

"Don't you believe he likes me?"

"I dare say he does," returned Arthur, at the same time asking if she would be afraid to stay alone one night in that great hotel, knowing he was gone?"

"Oh, Mr. Arthur, you won't leave me here?" and in her terror Edith's arms wound themselves around the young man's neck as if she would thus keep him there by force.

Unclasping her hand's, and holding them in his own, Arthur said,

"Listen to me, Edith. I will take the Boston train which leaves here very soon, and return to Shannondale, reaching there some time to-night. I will go to Collingwood, will tell Mr. Harrington what has happened, and ask him to take you, bringing him back here with me, if he will---"

"And if he won't?" interrupted Edith, joy beaming in every feature. "If he won't have me, Mr. Arthur, will you? Say, will you have me if he won't?"

"Yes, yes, I'll have you," returned Arthur, laughing to himself, as he thought of the construction which might be put upon this mode of speech.

But a child nine and a half years old could not, he knew, have any designs upon either himself or Richard Harrington, even had she been their equal, which he fancied she was not. She was a poor, neglected orphan, and as such he would care for her, though the caring compelled him to do what scarcely anything else could have done, to wit, to seek an interview with the man who held his cherished secret.

"Are you willing to stay here alone now?" he said again. "I'll order your meals sent to your room, and to-morrow night I shall return."

"If I only knew you meant for sure," said Edith, trembling at the thought of being deserted in a strange city.

Suddenly she started, and looking him earnestly in the face, said to him,

"Do you love that pretty lady in the glass--the one Mrs. Atherton thinks I stole?"

Arthur turned white but answered her at once.

"Yes, I love her very, very much."

"Is she your sister, Mr. Arthur?" and the searching black eyes seemed compelling him to tell the truth.

"No, not my sister, but a dear friend."

"Where is she, Mr. Arthur? In New York?"

"No, not in New York."

"In Albany then?"

"No, not in Albany. She's in Europe with her father," and a shade of sadness crept over Arthur's face, "She was hardly a young lady when this picture was taken, and he drew the locket from its hiding place. She was only thirteen. She's not quite sixteen now."

Edith by this time had the picture in her hand, and holding it to the light exclaimed, "Oh, but she's so jolly, Mr. Arthur. May I kiss her, please?"

"Certainly," he answered, and Edith's warm red lips pressed the senseless glass, which seemed to smile upon her.

"Pretty--pretty--pretty N-n-n-Nina!" she whispered, and in an instant Arthur clutched her so tightly that she cried out with pain.

"Who told you her name was Nina?" he asked in tones so stern and startling that Edith's senses all forsook her, and trembling with fright she stammered,

"I don't know, sir--unless you did. Of course you did, how else should I know. I never saw the lady."

Yes, how else should she know, and though he would almost have sworn that name had never passed his lips save in solitude, he concluded be most have dropped it inadvertently in Edith's hearing, and still holding her by the arm, he said, "Edith, if I supposed yon would repeat the word Nina, either at Collingwood or elsewhere, I certainly should be tempted to leave you here alone."

"I won't, I won't, oh, Mr. Arthur, I surely won't!" and Edith clung to him in terror. "I'll never say it--not even to Mr. Harrington. Ill forget it, I can, I know."

"Not to Mr. Harrington of all others," thought Arthur, but he would not put himself more in Edith's power than he already was, and feeling that he must trust her to a certain extent, he continued, "If you stay at Collingwood, I may sometime bring this Nina to see you, but until I do you must never breathe her name to any living being, or say a word of the picture."

"But Mr. Harrington," interrupted the far-seeing Edith, "He'll have to know why Mrs. Atherton sent me away.

"I'll attend to that," returned Arthur. "I shall tell him it was a daguerreotype of a lady friend. There's nothing wrong in that, is there?" he asked, as he noticed the perplexed look of the honest-hearted Edith.

"No," she answered hesitatingly. "It is a lady friend, but--but-- seems as if there was something wrong somewhere. Oh, Mr. Arthur-- "and she grasped his hand as firmly as he had held her shoulder. "You ain't going to hurt pretty Nina, are you?

You never will do her any harm?"

"Heaven forbid," answered Arthur, involuntarily turning away from the truthful eyes of the dark-haired maiden pleading with him not to harm the Nina--who, over the sea, never dreamed of the scene enacted in that room between the elegant Arthur St. Claire and the humble Edith Hastings. "Heaven forbid that I should harm her---"

He said it twice, and then asked the child to swear solemnly never to repeat that name where any one could hear.

"I won't swear," she said, "but I'll promise as true as I live and breathe, and draw the breath of life, and that's as good as a swear."

Arthur felt that it was, and with the compact thus sealed between them, he arose to go, reaching out his hand for the picture.

"No," said Edith, "I want her for company. I shan't be lonesome looking in her eyes, and I know you will come back if I keep her."

Arthur understood her meaning, and answered laughingly, "Well, keep her then, as a token that I will surely return," and pressing a kiss upon the beautiful picture he left the room, while Edith listened with a beating heart, until the sound of his footsteps had died away. Then a sense of dreariness stole over her; the tears gathered in her eyes, and she sought by a one-sided conversation with her picture to drive the loneliness away.

"Pretty Nina! Sweet Nina! Jolly Nina!" she kept repeating, "I guess I used to see you in Heaven, before I came down to the nasty old Asylum. And mother was there, too, with a great long veil of hair, which came below her waist. Where was it?" she asked herself as Nina, her mother and Marie were all mingled confusedly together in her mind; and while seeking to solve the mystery, the darkness deepened in the room, the gas lamps were lighted in the street, and with a fresh shudder of loneliness Edith crept into the bed, and nestling down among her pillows, fell asleep with Nina, pressed lovingly to her bosom.

At a comparatively early hour next morning, the door of her room, which had been left unfastened, was opened, and a chambermaid walked in, starting with surprise at sight of Edith, sitting up in bed, her thick black hair falling over her shoulders, and her large eyes fixed inquiringly upon her.

"An, sure," she began, "is it a child like you staying here alone the blessed night? Where's yer folks?"

"I hain't no folks," answered Edith, holding fast to the locket, and chewing industriously the bit of gum which Rachel, who knew her taste, had slipped into her pocket at parting.

"Hain't no folks! How come you here then?" and the girl Lois advanced nearer to the bedside.

"A man brought me," returned Edith. "He's gone off now, but will come again to-night."

"Your father, most likely," continued the loquacious Lois.

"My father!" and Edith laughed scornfully, "Mr. Arthur ain't big enough to be anybody's father--or yes, maybe he's big enough, for he's awful tall. But he's got the teentiest whiskers growing you ever saw," and Edith's nose went up contemptuously at Arthur's darling mustache. "I don't believe he's twenty," she continued, "and little girl's pa's must be older than that I guess, and have bigger whiskers."

"How old are you?" asked Lois, vastly amused at the quaint speeches of the child, who replied, with great dignity,

"Going on TEN, and in three years more I'll be THIRTEEN!"

"Who are you, any way?" asked Lois, her manner indicating so much real interest that Edith repeated her entire history up to the present time, excepting, indeed, the part pertaining to the locket held so vigilantly in her hand.

She had taken a picture belonging to Mr. Arthur, she said, and as Lois did not ask what picture, she was spared any embarrassment upon that point.

"You're a mighty queer child," said Lois, when the narrative was ended; "but I'll see that you have good care till he comes back;" and it was owing, in a measure, to her influence, that the breakfast and dinner carried up to Edith was of a superior quality, and comprised in quantity far more than she could eat.

Still the day dragged heavily, for Lois could not give her much attention; and even Nina failed to entertain her, as the western sunlight came in at her window, warning her that it was almost night.

"Will Arthur come? or if he does, will Mr. Harrington be with him?" she asked herself repeatedly, until at last, worn out with watching and waiting, she laid her head upon the side of the bed, and fell asleep, resting so quietly that she did not hear the rapid step in the hall, the knock upon the door, the turning of the knob, or the cheery voice which said to her:

"Edith, are you asleep?"

Arthur had come.

CHAPTER VII.
RICHARD AND ARTHUR.

It was not a common occurrence for a visitor to present himself at Collingwood at so early an hour as that in which Arthur St. Claire rung for admittance, and Victor, who heard the bell, hastened in some surprise to answer it,

"Tell Mr. Harrington a stranger wishes to see him," said Arthur, following the polite valet into the library, where a fire was slowly struggling into life.

"Yes, sir. What name?" and Victor waited for a moment, while Arthur hesitated, and finally stammered out:

"Mr. St. Claire, from Virginia."

Immediately Victor withdrew, and seeking his master, delivered the message, adding that the gentleman seemed embarrassed, and he wouldn't wonder if he'd come to borrow money."

"St Claire--St. Claire," Richard repeated to himself. "Where have I heard that name before? Somewhere, sure."

"He called himself a stranger," returned Victor, adding that a youth by that name was visiting at Brier Hill, and it was probably of him that Mr. Harrington was thinking,

"It may be, though I've no remembrance of having heard that fact," returned Richard; "but, lead on," and he took the arm of Victor, who lead him to the library floor and then, as was his custom, turned away.

More than once during the rapid journey, Arthur had half resolved to turn back and not run the fearful risk of being recognized by Richard Harrington, but the remembrance of Edith's mute distress should he return alone, emboldened him to go on and trust to Providence, or, if Providence failed, trust to Richard's generosity not to betray his secret. He heard the uncertain footsteps in the hall, and forgetting that the eyes he so much dreaded could not see, he pulled his coat collar up around his face so as to conceal as much of it as possible.

"Mr. St. Claire? Is there such a person here?" and Richard Harrington had crossed the threshold of the door, and with his sightless eyes rolling around the room, stood waiting for an answer.

How well Arthur remembered that rich, full, musical voice. It seemed to him but yesterday since, he heard it before, and he shrank more and more from the reply which must be made to that question, and quickly, too, for the countenance of the blind man was beginning to wear a look of perplexity at the continued silence.

Summoning all his courage he stepped forward and taking the hand groping in the air, said rapidly, "Excuse me, Mr. Harrington, I hardly know what to say, I've come upon so queer an errand. You know Edith Hastings, the little girl who lived with Mrs. Atherton?"

He thought by introducing Edith at once to divert the blind man from himself; but Richard's quick ear had caught a tone not wholly unfamiliar as he replied,

"Yes, I know Edith Hastings, and it seems to me I ought to know you, too. I've heard your name and voice before. Wasn't it in Geneva?" and the eagle eves fastened themselves upon the wall just back of where Arthur stood.

Arthur fairly gasped for breath, and for an instant he was as blind as Richard himself; then, catching at the word Geneva, he answered, "Did you ever live in Geneva, sir?"

"Not in the village, but near there on the lake shore," answered Richard, and Arthur continued,

"You probably attended the examinations then at the Academy, and heard me speak. I was a pupil there nearly two years before entering the college."

Arthur fancied himself remarkably clever for having suggested an idea which seemed so perfectly to satisfy his companion and which was not a falsehood either. He had been a student in the Academy for nearly two years, had spoken at all the exhibitions, receiving the prize at one; he had seen Richard Harrington among the spectators, and had no doubt that Richard might have observed him, though not very closely, else he had never put himself in his power by the one single act which was embittering his young life.

"It is likely you are right," said Richard, "I was often at the examinations, and since my misfortune I find myself recognizing voices as I never could have done when I had sight as well as hearing upon which to depend. But you spoke of Edith Hastings. I trust no harm has befallen the child. I am much interested in her and--wonder she has not been here long ere this. What would you tell me of her?"

Briefly Arthur related the particulars of his visit at Brier Hill, a visit which had ended so disastrously to Edith, and even before he reached the important point, Richard answered promptly, "She shall come here, I need her, I want her--want her for my sister, my child. I shall never have another;" then pressing his hands suddenly up on his forehead, whose blue veins seemed to swell with the intensity of his emotions, he continued. "But, no, Mr. St. Claire. It cannot be, she is too young, too merry-hearted, too full of life and love to be brought into the shadow of our household. She would die upon my hands. Her voice would grow sadder and more mournful with the coming of every season, until at last when I had learned to love her as my life, I should some morning listen for what, would never greet my ear again. It's a great temptation, but it must not be. A crazy old man and his blind son are not fit guardians for a child like Edith Hastings. She must not walk in our darkness."

"But might not her presence bring daylight to that darkness?" asked Arthur, gazing with mingled feelings of wonder and admiration upon the singularly handsome noble-looking man, who was indeed walking in thick darkness.

"She might," said Richard. "Yes, she might bring the full rich daylight to us, but on her the shadow would fail with a fearful blackness if she linked her destiny with mine. Young man, do you like Edith Hastings, if so, take her yourself and if money----"

Arthur here interrupted him with, "I have money of my own, sir; but I have no home at present. I am a student in college. I can do nothing with her there, but--" and his voice sunk almost to a whisper. "Years hence, I hope to have a home, and then, if you are tired of Edith I will take her. Meantime keep her at Collingwood for me. Is it a bargain?"

"You are young, I think," said Richard, smiling at Arthur's proposition, and smiling again, when in tones apologetical, as if to be only so old were something of which he ought to be ashamed, Arthur returned,

"I am nineteen this month."

"And I was thirty, last spring," said Richard. "An old man, you think, no doubt. But to return to Edith Hastings. My heart wants her so much, while my better judgment rebels against it. Will she be greatly disappointed if I refuse?"

"Oh, yes, yes," said Arthur, grasping the hand laying on Richard's knee. "I CAN'T go back to her without you. But, Mr. Harrington, before I urge it farther, let me ask as her friend, will she come here as a SERVANT, or an equal."

There was an upward flashing of the keen black eyes, a flush upon the high, white forehead, and Richard impatiently stamped upon the floor as he answered proudly,

"She comes as an equal, or not at all. She shall be as highly educated and as thoroughly accomplished as if the blood of the Harrington's flowed in her veins."

"Then take her," and Arthur seemed more anxious than before. "She will do justice to your training. She will be wondrously beautiful. She will grace the halls of Collingwood with the air of England's queen. You will not be ashamed of her, and who knows but some day--"

Arthur began to stammer, and at last managed to finish with, "There is NOT such a vast difference in your ages. Twenty-one years is nothing when weighed against the debt of gratitude she will owe you--"

"There, I've made a fool of myself," he thought, as he saw the forehead tie itself up in knots, and the corners of the mouth twitch with merriment.

"By that last speech you've proved how YOUNG and romantic you are," answered Richard. "Winter and spring go not well together. Edith Hastings will never be my wife. But she shall come to Collingwood. I will return with you and bring her back myself."

Ringing the bell for Victor, he bade him see that breakfast was served at once, saying that he was going with his friend to Albany.

"Without ME?" asked Victor in much surprise, and Richard replied,

"Yes, without you," adding in an aside to Arthur, "Victor is so much accustomed to waiting upon me that he thinks himself necessary to every movement, but I'd rather travel alone with Edith, she'll do as well as Victor, and I have a fancy to keep my movements a secret, at least until the child is fairly in the house. It will be a surprise to Mrs. Atherton; I'll have John drive us to the next station, and meet me there to-morrow,"

So saying, he excused himself for a few moments and groped his way up stairs to make some necessary changes in his dress. For several minutes Arthur was alone, and free to congratulate himself upon his escape from detection.

"In my dread of recognition I undoubtedly aggravated its chances," he thought. "Of course this Mr. Harrington did not observe me closely. It was night, and he was almost blind, even then. My voice and manner are all that can betray me, and as he is apparently satisfied on that point, I have nothing further to apprehend from him."

Arthur liked to feel well--disagreeable reflections did not suit his temperament, and having thus dismissed from his mind the only thing annoying him at the present, he began to examine the books arrayed so carefully upon the shelves, whistling to himself as he did so, and pronouncing Arthur St. Claire a pretty good fellow after all, if he had a secret of which most people would not approve. He had just reached this conclusion when Richard reappeared, and breakfast was soon after announced by the valet, Victor. That being over, there was not a moment to be lost if they would reach the cars in time for the next train, and bidding his father a kind adieu, Richard went with Arthur to the carriage, and was driven to the depot of the adjoining town. More than one passenger turned their heads to look at the strangers as they came in, the elder led by the younger, who yet managed so skillfully that but few guessed how great a calamity had befallen the man with the dark hair, and black, glittering eyes. Arthur took a great pride in ministering to the wants of his companion, and in all he did there was a delicacy and tenderness which touched a chord almost fraternal in the heart of the blind man, who, as the day wore on, found himself drawn more and more toward his new acquaintance.

"I believe even I might be happy if both you and Edith could live with me," he said, at last, when Albany was reached, and they were ascending the steps to the Delevan.

"Poor little Edith," rejoined Arthur, "I wonder if she has been very lonely? Shall we go to her at once?"

"Yes," answered Richard, and leaning on Arthur's arm, he proceeded to the door of Edith's room.

CHAPTER VIII.
RICHARD AND EDITH.

"Oh, Mr. Arthur, you did come back," and forgetting, in her great joy, that Arthur was a gentleman, and she a waiting-maid, Edith wound her arms around his neck, and kissed him twice ere he well knew what she was doing.

For an instant the haughty young man felt a flush of insulted dignity, but it quickly vanished when he saw the tall form of Richard bending over the little girl and heard him saying to her,

"Have you no welcoming kiss for me?"

"Yes, forty hundred, if you like," and in her delight Edith danced about the room like one insane.

Thrusting the locket slily into Arthur's hand, she whispered,

"I slept with her last night, and dreamed it was not the first time either. Will you ask her when you see her if she ever knew me?"

"Yes, yes," he answered, making a gesture for her to stop as Richard was about to speak.

"Edith, said Richard, winding his arm around her, "Edith, I have come to take you home--to take you to Collingwood to live with me. Do you wish to go?"

"Ain't there ghosts at Collingwood?" asked Edith, who, now that what she most desired was just within her reach, began like every human being to see goblins in the path. "Ain't there ghosts, at Collingwood?--a little boy with golden curls, and must I sleep in the chamber with him?"

"Poor child," said Richard, "You too, have heard that idle tale. Shall I tell you of the boy with golden hair?" and holding her so close to him that he could feel the beating of her heart and hear her soft, low breathing, he told her all there was to tell of his half-brother Charlie, who died just one day after his young mother, and was buried in the same coffin.

They could not return to Collingwood that night, and the evening was spent in the private parlor which Arthur engaged for himself and his blind friend. It was strange how fast they grew to liking each other, and it was a pleasant sight to look at them as they sat there in the warm firelight which the lateness of the season made necessary to their comfort--the one softened and toned down by affliction and the daily cross he was compelled to bear, the other in the first flush of youth when the world lay all bright before him and he had naught to do but enter the Elysian fields and pluck the fairest flowers.

It was late when they separated, but at a comparatively early hour the next morning they assembled again, this time to bid good-by, for their paths hereafter lay in different directions.

"You must write to me, little metaphysics," said Arthur, as with hat and shawl in hand he stood in the depot on the east side of the Hudson.

"Yes," rejoined Richard, "she is to be my private amanuensis, and shall let you know of our welfare, and now, I suppose, we must go."

It was a very pleasant ride to Edith, pleasanter than when she came with Arthur, but a slight headache made her drowsy, and leaning on Richard's arm she fell asleep, nor woke until West Shannondale was reached. The carriage was in waiting for them, and Victor sat inside. He had come ostensibly to meet his master, but really to see the kind of specimen he was bringing to the aristocratic halls of Collingwood.

Long and earnest had been the discussion there concerning the little lady; Mrs. Matson, the housekeeper, sneering rather contemptuously at one who heretofore had been a servant at Brier Hill. Victor, on the contrary, stood ready to espouse her cause, thinking within himself how he would teach her many points of etiquette of which he knew she must necessarily be ignorant; but firstly he would, to use his own expression, "see what kind of metal she was made of."

Accordingly his first act at the depot was to tread upon her toes, pretending he did not see her, but Edith knew he did it purposely, and while her black eyes blazed with anger, she exclaimed,

"You wretch, how dare you be so rude?"

Assisting Richard into the carriage, Victor was about to turn away, leaving Edith to take care of herself, when with all the air of a queen, she said to him,

"Help me in, sir. Don't you know your business!"

"Pardonnez, moi," returned Victor, speaking in his mother tongue, and bowing low to the indignant child, whom he helped to a seat by Richard.

An hour's drive brought them to the gate of Collingwood, and Edith was certainly pardonable if she did cast a glance of exultation in the direction of Brier Hill, as they wound up the gravelled road and through the handsome grounds of what henceforth was to be her home.

"I guess Mrs. Atherton will be sorry she acted so," she thought, and she was even revolving the expediency of putting on airs and not speaking to her former mistress, when the carriage stopped and Victor appeared at the window all attention, and asking if he should "assist Miss Hastings to alight."

In the door Mrs. Matson was waiting to receive them, rubbing her gold-bowed spectacles and stroking her heavy silk with an air which would have awed a child less self-assured than Edith. Nothing grand or elegant seemed strange or new to her. On the contrary she took to it naturally as if it were her native clement, and now as she stepped upon the marble floor of the lofty hall she involuntarily cut a pirouette, exclaiming, "Oh, but isn't this jolly! Seems as if I'd got back to Heaven. What a splendid room to sing in," and she began to warble a wild, impassioned air which made Richard pause and listen, wondering whence came the feeling which so affected him carrying him back to the hills of Germany.

Mrs. Matson looked shocked, Victor amused, while the sensible driver muttered to himself as he gathered up his reins, "That gal is just what Collingwood needs to keep it from being a dungeon."

Mrs. Matson had seen Edith at Brier Hill, but this did not prevent her from a close scrutiny as she conducted her to the large, handsome chamber, which Richard in his hasty directions of the previous morning had said was to be hers, and which, with its light, tasteful furniture, crimson curtains, and cheerful blazing fire seemed to the delighted child a second paradise. Clapping her hands she danced about the apartment, screaming, "It's the jolliest place I ever was in."

"What do you mean by that word JOLLY?" asked Mrs. Matson, with a great deal of dignity; but ere Edith could reply, Victor, who came up with the foreign chest, chimed in, "She means PRETTY, Madame Matson, and understands French, no doubt. Parley vous Francais?" and he turned to Edith, who, while recognizing something familiar in the sound, felt sure he was making fun of her and answered back, "Parley voo fool! I'll tell Mr. Harrington how you tease me."

Laughing aloud at her reply, Victor put the chest in its place, made some remark concerning its quaint appearance, and bowed himself from the room, saying to her as he shut the door,

"Bon soir, Mademoiselle."

"I've heard that kind of talk before," thought Edith, as she began to brush her hair, preparatory to going down to supper, which Mrs. Matson said was waiting.

At the table she met with the old man, who had seen her alight from the carriage, and had asked the mischievous Victor, "Who was the small biped Richard had brought home?"

"That," said Victor. "Why, that is Charlie turned into a girl." And preposterous as the idea seemed, the old man seized upon it at once, smoothing Edith's hair when he saw her, tapping her rosy cheeks, calling her Charlie, and muttering to himself of the wonderful process which had transformed his fair-haired boy into a black-haired girl.

Sometimes the utter impossibility of the thing seemed to penetrate even his darkened mind, and then he would whisper, "I'll make believe it's Charlie, any way," so Charlie he persisted in calling her, and Richard encouraged him in this whim, when he found how much satisfaction it afforded the old man to "make believe."

The day following Edith's arrival at Collingwood there was a long consultation between Richard and Victor concerning the little girl, about whose personal appearance the former would now know something definite.

"How does Edith Hastings look?" he asked, and after a moment of grave deliberation, Victor replied,

"She has a fat round face, with regular features, except that the nose turns up somewhat after the spitfire order, and her mouth is a trifle too wide. Her forehead is not very high--it would not become her style if it were. Her hair is splendid--thick, black and glossy as satin, and her eyes,--there are not words enough either in the French or English language with which to describe her eyes--they are so bright and deep that nobody can look into them long without wincing. I should say, sir, if put on oath, there was a good deal of the deuce in her eyes."

"When she is excited, you mean," interrupted Richard. "How are they in repose?"

"They are never there," returned Victor. "They roll and turn and flash and sparkle, and light upon one so uncomfortably, that he begins to think of all the badness he ever did, and to wonder if those coals of fire can't ferret out the whole thing."

"I like her eyes," said Richard, "but go on. Tell me of her complexion."

"Black, of course," continued Victor, "but smooth as glass, with just enough of red in it to make rouge unnecessary. On the whole I shouldn't wonder if in seven or eight years' time she'd be as handsome as the young lady of Collingwood ought to be."

"How should she be dressed?" asked Richard, who knew that Victor's taste upon such matters was infallible, his mother and sister both having been Paris mantua-makers.

"She should have scarlet and crimson and dark blue trimmed with black," said Victor, adding that he presumed Mrs. Atherton would willingly attend to those matters.

Richard was not so sure, but he thought it worth the while to try, and he that night dispatched Victor to Brier Hill with a request that she would, if convenient, call upon him at once.

"Don't tell her what I want," he said, "I wish to surprise her with a sight of Edith."

Victor promised obedience and set off for Brier Hill, where he found no one but Rachel, sitting before this kitchen fire, and watching the big red apples roasting upon the hearth.

"Miss Grace had started that morning for New York," she said, "and the Lord only knew when she'd come home."

"And as he probably won't tell, I may as well go back," returned Victor, and bidding Rachel send her mistress to Collingwood as soon as she should return, he bowed himself from the room.

As Rachel said, Grace had gone to New York, and the object of her going was to repair the wrong done to Edith Hastings, by taking her a second time from the Asylum, and bringing her back to Brier Hill. Day and night the child's parting words, "You'll be sorry sometime," rang in her ears, until she could endure it no longer, and she astonished the delighted Rachel by announcing her intention of going after the little girl. With her to will was to do, and while Victor was reporting her absence to his master, she, half-distracted, was repeating the words of the matron,

"Has not been here at all, and have not heard from her either! What can it mean?"

The matron could not tell, and for several days Grace lingered in the city, hoping Arthur would appear, but as he failed to do this, she at last wrote to him at Geneva, and then, in a sad, perplexed state of mind, returned to Shannondale, wondering at and even chiding old Rachel for evincing so little feeling at her disappointment.

But old Rachel by this time had her secret which she meant to keep, and when at last Grace asked if any one had called during her absence, she mentioned the names of every one save Victor, and then tried very hard to think "who that 'tother one was. She knowed there WAS somebody else, but for the life of her she couldn't"--Rachel did not quite dare to tell so gross a falsehood, and so at this point she concluded to THINK, and added suddenly,

"Oh, yes, I remember now. 'Twas that tall, long-haired, scented- up, big-feelin' man they call Squire Herrin'ton's VALLY."

"Victor Dupres been here!" and Grace's face lighted perceptibly.

"Yes, he said MOUSE-EER, or somethin' like that--meanin' the squire, in course--wanted you to come up thar as soon as you got home, and my 'pinion is that you go to oncet. 'Twont be dark this good while."

Nothing could be more in accordance with Grace's feelings than to follow Rachel's advice, and, half an hour later, Victor reported to his master that the carriage from Brier Hill had stopped before their door. It would be impossible to describe Mr. Atherton's astonishment when, on entering the parlor, the first object that met her view was her former waiting-maid, attired in the crimson merino which Mrs. Matson, Lulu, the chambermaid, and Victor had gotten up between them; and which, though not the best fit in the world, was, in color, exceedingly becoming to the dark-eyed child, who, perched upon the music-stool, was imitating her own operatic songs to the infinite delight of the old man, nodding his approval of the horrid discords.

"Edith Hastings!" she exclaimed, "What are you doing here?" Springing from the stool and advancing towards Grace, Edith replied,

"I live here. I'm Mr. Richard's little girl. I eat at the table with him, too, and don't have to wash the dishes either. I'm going to be a lady just like you, ain't I, Mr. Harrington?" and she turned to Richard, who had entered in time to hear the last of her remarks.

There was a world of love in the sightless eyes turned toward the little girl, and by that token, Grace Athertoa knew that Edith had spoken truly.

"Run away, Edith," he said, "I wish to talk with the lady alone."

Edith obeyed, and when she was gone Richard explained to Grace what seemed to her so mysterious, while she in return confessed the injustice done to the child, and told how she had sought to repair the wrong.

"I am glad you have taken her," she said. "She will be happier with you than with me, for she likes you best. I think, too, she will make good use of any advantages you may give her. She has a habit of observing closely, while her powers of imitation are unsurpassed. She is fond of elegance and luxury, and nothing can please bar more than to be an equal in a house like this. But what do you wish of me? What can I do to assist you?"

In a few words Richard stated his wishes that she should attend to Edith's wardrobe, saying he had but little faith in Mrs. Matson's taste. He could not have selected a better person to spend his money than Grace, who, while purchasing nothing out of place, bought always the most expensive articles in market, and when at last the process was ended, and the last dressmaker gone from Collingwood, Victor, with a quizzical expression upon his face, handed his master a bill for five hundred dollars, that being the exact amount expended upon Edith's wardrobe. But Richard uttered no word of complaint. During the few weeks she had lived with him she had crept away down into his heart just where Charlie used to be, and there was nothing in his power to give which he would withhold from her now. She should have the best of teachers, he said, particularly in music, of which she was passionately fond.

Accordingly, in less than a week there came to Collingwood a Boston governess, armed and equipped with all the accomplishments of the day; and beneath the supervision of Richard and Victor, Grace Atherton and Mrs. Chapen, Edith's education began.

CHAPTER IX.
WOMANHOOD.

Eight times have the Christmas fires been kindled on the hearths of Shannondale's happy homes; eight times the bell from St Luke's tower has proclaimed an old year dead, and a new one born; eight times the meek-eyed daisy struggling through the April snow, has blossomed, faded and died; eight times has summer in all her glowing beauty sat upon the New England hills, and the mellow autumnal light of the hazy October days falls on Collingwood for the eighth time since last we trod the winding paths and gravelled walks where now the yellow leaves are drifting down from the tall old maples and lofty elms, and where myriad flowers of gorgeous hue are lifting their proud heads unmindful of the November frosts hastening on apace. All around Collingwood seems the same, save that the shrubs and vines show a more luxurious growth, and the pond a wider sweep, but within there is an empty chair, a vacant place, for the old man has gone to join his lost ones where there is daylight forever, and the winter snows have four times fallen upon his grave. They missed him at first and mourned for him truly, but they have become accustomed to live without him, and the household life goes on much as it did before.

It is now the afternoon of a mild October day, and the doors and windows are opened wide to admit the warm south wind, which, dallying for a moment with the curtains of costly lace, floats on to the chamber above, where it toys with the waving plumes a young girl is arranging upon her riding hat, pausing occasionally to speak to the fair blonde who sits watching her movements, and whose face betokens a greater maturity than her own, for Grace Atherton's family Bible says she is thirty-two, while Edith is seventeen.

Beautiful Edith Hastings. Eight years of delicate nurture, tender care and perfect health have ripened her into a maiden of wondrous beauty, and far and near the people talk of the blind man's ward, the pride and glory of Collingwood. Neither pains nor money, nor yet severe discipline, have been spared by Richard Harrington to make her what she is, and while her imperious temper has bent to the one, her intellect and manners have expanded and improved beneath this influence of the other, and Richard has not only a plaything and pet in the little girl he took from obscurity, but also a companion and equal, capable of entering with him the mazy labyrinths of science, and astonishing him with the wealth of her richly stored mind. Still, in everything pertaining to her womanhood she is wholly feminine and simple-hearted as a child. Now, as of old, she bounds through the spacious grounds of Collingwood, trips over the grassy lawn, dances up the stairs, and fills the once gloomy old place with a world of melody and sunlight. Edith knows that she is beautiful! old Rachel has told her so a thousand times, while Victor, the admiring valet, tells her so every day, taking to himself no little credit for having taught her, as he thinks, something of Parisian manners. Many are the conversations she holds with him in his mother tongue, for she has learned to speak that language with a fluency and readiness which astonished her teachers and sometimes astonished herself. It did not seem difficult to her, but rather like an old friend, and Marie at first was written on every page of Ollendorff. But Marie has faded now almost entirely from her mind, as have those other mysterious memories which used to haunt her so. Nothing but the hair hidden in the chest binds her to the past, and at this she often looks, wondering where the head it once adorned is lying, whether in the noisy city or on some grassy hillside where the wild flowers she loves best are growing, and the birds whose songs she tries to imitate, pause sometimes to warble a requiem for the dead. Those tresses are beautiful, but not so beautiful as Edith's. Her blue-black hair is thicker, glossier, more abundant than in her childhood, and is worn in heavy braids or bands around her head, adding greatly to her regal style of beauty. Edith has a pardonable pride in her satin hair, and as she stands before the mirror she steals an occasional glance at her crowning glory, which is this afternoon arranged with far more care than usual; not for any particular reason, but because she had a fancy that it should be so.

They were going to visit Grassy Spring, a handsome country seat, whose grounds lay contiguous to those of Collingwood, and whose walls were in winter plainly discernible from the windows of the upper rooms. It had recently been purchased and fitted up somewhat after the style of Collingwood, and its owner was expected to take possession in a few days. Edith's heart always beat faster when she heard his name, for Arthur St. Claire was one of the links of the past which still lingered in the remembrance. She had never seen him since they parted in Albany, and after his leaving college she lost sight of him entirely. Latterly, however, she had heard from Grace, who knew but little more of him than herself, that he was coming into their very neighborhood; that at he had purchased Grassy Spring, and was to keep a kind of bachelor's hall inasmuch as he had no wife, nor yet a prospect of any. So much Edith knew and no more. She did not dare to speak of NINA, for remembering her solemn promise, she had never breathed that name to any living being. But the picture in the glass, as she ever termed it, was not forgotten, and the deep interest she felt in Grassy Spring was owing, in a great measure, to the fact that Nina was in her mind intimately associated with the place. Sooner or later she should meet her there, she was sure; should see those golden curls again, and look into those soft blue eyes, whose peculiar expression she remembered as if it were but yesterday since they first met her view.

"It is strange your cousin never married; he must, by this time, be nearly twenty-seven," she said to Grace, thinking the while of Nina, and carelessly adjusting the jaunty hat upon her head.

"I think so too," returned Grace. "When quite young he was very fond of the ladies, but I am told that he now utterly ignores female society. Indeed, in his last letter to me, he states distinctly that he wishes for no company except occasional calls in a friendly way."

"Been disappointed, probably," suggested Edith, still thinking of Nina, and wondering if Arthur did love her so very much as to put faith in no one because of her treachery.

"It may be," said Grace; "and if so, isn't it a little queer that he and Mr. Harrington should live so near each other; both so eccentric; both so handsome and rich; both been disappointed; and both so desirable as husbands?"

"Disappointed, Mrs. Atherton! Has Mr. Harrington been disappointed?" and the rich bloom on Edith's cheek deepened to a scarlet hue, which Grace did not fail to notice.

Her friendship for Edith Hastings had been a plant of sluggish growth, for she could not, at once, bring herself to treat as an equal one whom she formerly held as a servant, but time and circumstances had softened her haughty pride, while Edith's growing popularity, both in the village and at Collingwood, awakened in her a deep interest for the young girl, who, meeting her advances more than half the way, compelled her at last to surrender, and the two were now as warm friends as individuals well can be when there is between them so great a disparity of years and so vast a difference in disposition. In Grace's heart the olden love for Richard had not died out, and hitherto, it had been some consolation to believe that no other ear would ever listen to the words of love, to remember which continually would assuredly drive her mad. But matters now were changed. Day by day, week by week, month by month, and year by year, a rose had been unfolding itself at Collingswood, and with every opening petal had grown more and more precious to the blind man, until more than one crone foretold the end; and Grace Atherton, grown fonder of gossip than she was wont to be, listened to the tale, and watched, and wondered, and wept, and still caressed and loved the bright, beautiful girl, whom she dreaded as a powerful rival. This it was which prompted her to speak of Richard's disappointment; and when she saw the effect produced upon Edith, it emboldened her to go on, and tell how, years and years ago, when Richard Harrington first went to Europe, be had sued for the hand of a young girl whom he met there, and who, while loving him dearly, shrank from walking in his shadow, and gave herself to another.

"I must not tell you the name of this faithless girl," said Grace. "It is sufficient that her refusal made Richard gloomy, eccentric and misanthropical; in short, it nearly ruined him."

"My curse be on the woman's head who wrought this ruin, then," said Edith, her black eyes flashing with something of their former fire.

She had forgotten the scene in the kitchen of Brier Hill when Rachel whispered to her that Grace Atherton was in love, and she had now no suspicion that the calm, white-faced woman sitting there before her was the being she would curse. Neither was her emotion caused, as Grace imagined, by any dread lest the early love of Richard Harrington should stand between herself and him. The thought that SHE could be his wife had never crossed her brain, and her feelings were those of indignation toward a person who could thus cruelly deceive a man as noble and good as Richard, and of pity for him who had been so deceived.

"I will love him all the more and be the kinder to him for this vile creature's desertion," she thought, as she beat the floor nervously with the little prunella gaiter, and this was all the good Grace Atherton had achieved.

Edith had cursed her to her face, and with a sigh audible only to herself she arose and said laughingly, "It's time we were off, and you've certainly admired that figure in the glass long enough. What do you think of yourself, any way?"

"Why," returned Edith, in the same light, bantering tone, "I think I'm rather jolie, as I used to say. I wonder where I picked up that word. Victor says I must have had a French nurse, but I'm sure I was too poor for that. I wish I knew where I did come from and who I am. It's terrible, this uncertainty as to one's birth. I may be marrying my brother one of these days, who knows?"

"See rather that you do not marry your father," retorted Grace, following Edith as she tripped down the stairs and down the walk, whipping the tufts of box as she went, and answering to Grace who asked if she did not sometimes find her duties irksome at Collingwood. "Never, never. The links of my chains are all made of love and so they do not chafe. Then, too, when I remember what Richard has done for me and how few sources of happiness he has, I am willing to give my whole life to him, if need be. Why, Mrs. Atherton, you can't imagine how his dark features light up with joy, when on his return from riding or from transacting business he hears me in the hall, and knows that I am there to meet him," and Edith's bright face sparkled and glowed as she thought how often the blind man had blessed her with his sightless but speaking eyes, when she gave up some darling project which would take her from his side and stayed to cheer his solitude.

They had mounted their horses by this time, and at the speed which characterized Edith's riding, dashed down the road and struck into the woods, the shortest route to Grassy Spring. With the exception of Collingwood, Grassy Spring was the handsomest country seat for miles around, and thinking, as she continually did, of Nina, Edith rather gave it the preference as she passed slowly through the grounds and drew near to the building. Grace had seen the housekeeper, Mrs. Johnson, a talkative old lady, who, big with the importance of her office, showed them over the house, pointing out this elegant piece of furniture and that handsome room with quite as much satisfaction as if it had all belonged to herself.

In the third story, and only accessible by two flights of stairs leading from Arthur's suite of rooms, was a large square apartment, the door of which Mrs. Johnson unlocked with a mysterious shake of the head, saying to the ladies, "The Lord only knows what this place is for. Mr. St. Claire must have fixed it himself for I found it locked tighter than a drum, but I accidentally found on the but'ry shelf a rusty old key, that fits it to a T. I've been in here once and bein' you're his kin," nodding to Grace, "and t'other one is with you, it can't do an atom of harm for you to go. He's took more pains with this chamber than with all the rest, and when I asked what 'twas for, he said it was his "den," where he could hide if he wanted to."

"Don't go," whispered Edith, pulling at Grace's dress, "Mr. St. Claire might not like it."

But Grace felt no such scruples, and was already across the threshold, leaving Edith by the door.

"It's as bad to look in as to go in," thought Edith, and conquering her curiosity with a mighty effort, she walked resolutely down stairs, having seen nothing save that the carpet was of the richest velvet and that the windows had across them slender iron bars, rather ornamental than otherwise, and so arranged as to exclude neither light nor air.

Grace, on the contrary, examined the apartment thoroughly, thinking Mrs. Johnson right when she said that more pains had been taken with this room than with all the others. The furniture was of the most expensive and elegant kind. Handsome rosewood easy- chairs and sofas covered with rich satin damask, the color and pattern corresponding with the carpet and curtains. Ottomans, divans and footstools were scattered about--pictures and mirrors adorned the walls, while in one corner, covered with a misty veil of lace, hung the portrait of a female in the full, rich bloom of womanhood, her light chestnut curls falling about her uncovered neck, and her dreamy eyes of blue having in them an expression much like that which Edith had once observed in Nina's peculiar eyes. The dress was quite old-fashioned, indicating that the picture must have been taken long ago, and while Grace gazed upon it her wonder grew as to whose it was and whence it came.

"Look at the bed," said Mrs. Johnson, and touching Grace's elbow, she directed her attention to a side recess, hidden from view by drapery of exquisite lace, and containing a single bed, which might have been intended for an angel, so pure and white it looked with its snowy covering.

"What does it mean?" asked Grace, growing more and more bewildered, while Mrs. Johnson replied in her favorite mode of speech.

"The Lord only knows--looks as if he was going to make it a prison for some princess; but here's the queerest thing of all," and she thumped upon a massive door, which was locked and barred, and beyond which her prying eyes had never looked.

Over the door was a ventilator, and Grace, quite as curious as Mrs. Johnson, suggested that a chair or table be brought, upon which she, being taller than her companion, might stand and possibly obtain a view.

"What DO you see?" asked Mrs. Johnson, as Grace, on tip-toe, peered into what seemed to be a solitary cell, void of furniture of every kind, save a little cot, corresponding in size with the fairy bed in the recess, but in naught else resembling it, for its coverings were of the coarsest, strongest materials, and the pillows scanty and small.

Acting from a sudden impulse, Grace determined not to tell Mrs. Johnson what she saw, and stepping down from the table, which she quickly rolled back to its place, she said,

"It's nothing but a closet, where, I dare say, Mr. St. Claire will keep his clothes when he occupies his den. You must not let any one else in here, for Arthur might be offended."

Mrs. Johnson promised obedience, and turning the rusty key, followed her visitor down the two long flights of stairs, she, returning to her duties, while Grace went to the pleasant library, where, with her hat and whip upon the floor, Edith sat reading the book she had ventured to take from the well-filled shelves, and in which she had been so absorbed as not to hear the slight rustling in the adjoining room, where a young man was standing in the enclosure of the deep bay window, and gazing intently at her. He had heard from Mrs. Johnson's daughter that some ladies were going over the house, and not caring to meet them, he stepped into the recess of the window just as Edith entered the library. As the eye of the stranger fell upon her, he came near uttering an exclamation of surprise that anything so graceful, so queenly, and withal so wondrously beautiful, should be found in Shannondale, which, with the city ideas still clinging to him, seemed like an out-of-the-way place, where the girls were buxom, good-natured and hearty, just as he remembered Kitty Maynard to have been, and not at all like this creature of rare loveliness sitting there before him, her head inclined gracefully to the volume she was reading, and showing to good advantage her magnificent hair.

"Who can she be?" he thought, and a thrill of unwonted admiration ran through his veins as Edith raised for a moment her large eyes of midnight blackness, and from his hiding-place he saw how soft and mild they were in their expression, "Can Grace have spirited to her retreat some fair nymph for company? Hark! I hear her voice, and now for the solution of the mystery."

Standing back a little further, so as to escape observation, the young man waited till Grace Atherton came near.

"Here you are," she said, "poring over a book as usual. I should suppose you'd had enough of that to do in reading to Mr. Harrington--German Philosophy, too! Will wonders never cease? Arthur was right, I declare, when he dubbed you Metaphysics!"

"Edith Hastings!" The young man said it beneath his breath, while he involuntarily made a motion forward.

"Can it be possible, and yet now that I know it, I see the little black-eyed elf in every feature. Well may the blind man be proud of his protege. She might grace the saloons of Versailles, and rival the Empress herself!"

Thus far he had soliloquised, when something Grace was saying caught his ear and chained his attention at once.

"Oh, Edith," she began, "you don't know what you lost by being over squeamish. Such a perfect jewel-box of a room, with the tiniest single bed of solid mahogany! Isn't it queer that Arthur should have locked it up, and isn't it fortunate for us that Mrs. Johnson found that rusty old key which must have originally belonged to the door of the Den, as she says he calls it?"

Anxiously the young man awaited Edith's answer, his face aglow with indignation and his eyes flashing with anger.

"Fortunate for YOU, perhaps," returned Edith, tying on her riding- hat, "but I wouldn't have gone in for anything."

"Why not?" asked Grace, walking into the hall.

"Because," said Edith, "Mr. St. Claire evidently did not wish any one to go in, and I think Mrs. Johnson was wrong in opening the door."

"What a little Puritan it is!" returned Grace, playfully caressing the rosy cheeks of Edith, who had now joined her in the hall. "Arthur never will know, for I certainly shall not tell either him or any one, and I gave Mrs. Johnson some very wholesome advice upon that subject. There she is now in the back-yard. If you like, we'll go round and give her a double charge."

The young man saw them as they turned the corner of the building, and gliding from his post, he hurried up the stairs and entering the Den, locked the door, and throwing himself upon the sofa, groaned aloud, while the drops of perspiration oozed out upon his forehead, and stood thickly about his lips. Then his mood changed, and pacing the floor he uttered invectives against the meddlesome Mrs. Johnson, who, by this one act, had proved that she could not be trusted. Consequently SHE must not remain longer at Grassy Spring, and while in the yard below Mrs. Johnson was promising Grace "to be as still as the dead," Arthur St. Claire was planning her dismissal. This done, and his future course decided upon, the indignant young man felt better, and began again to think of Edith Hastings, whom he admired for her honorable conduct in refusing to enter a place where she had reason to think she was not wanted.

"Noble, high-principled girl," he said. "I'm glad I told Mr. Harrington what I did before seeing her. Otherwise he might have suspected that her beauty had something to do with my offer, and so be jealous lest I had designs upon his singing-bird, as he called her. But alas, neither beauty, nor grace, nor purity can now avail with me, miserable wretch that I am," and again that piteous moan, as of a soul punished before its time, was heard in the silent room.

But hark, what sound is that, which, stealing through the iron-latticed windows, drowns the echo of that moan, and makes the young man listen? It is Edith Hastings singing one of her wild songs, and the full rich melody of her wonderful voice falls upon his ear, Arthur St. Claire bows his head upon his hands and weeps, for the music carries him back to the long ago when he had no terrible secret haunting every hour, but was as light-hearted as the maiden whom, as she gallops away on her swift-footed Arabian, he looks after, with wistful eyes, watching her until the sweep of her long riding-skirt and the waving of her graceful plumes disappear beneath the shadow of the dim woods, where night is beginning to fall. Slowly, sadly, he turns from the window-- merrily, swiftly, the riders dash along, and just us the clock strikes six, their panting steeds pause at the entrance to Collingwood.

CHAPTER X.
EDITH AT HOME.

It was too late for Grace to call, and bidding her companion good-bye, she galloped down the hill, while Edith, in a meditative mood, suffered her favorite Bedouin to walk leisurely up the carriage road which led to the rear of the house.

"Victor Dupres!" she exclaimed, as a tall figure emerged from the open door and came forward to meet her. "Where did you come from?"

"From New York," he replied, bowing very low, "Will Mademoiselle alight?" and taking the little foot from out the shoe he lifted her carefully from the saddle.

"Is HE here?" she asked, and Victor replied,

"Certainement; and has brought home a fresh recruit of the blues, too, judging from the length and color of his face."

"Why did he go to New York?" interrupted Edith, who had puzzled her brain not a little with regard to the business which had taken Richard so suddenly from home.

"As true as I live I don't know," was Victor's reply. "For once he's kept dark even to me, scouring all the alleys, and lanes, and poor houses in the city, leaving me at the hotel, and taking with him some of those men with brass buttons on their coats. One day when he came back he acted as if he were crazy and I saw the great tears drop on the table over which he was leaning, then when I asked 'if he'd heard bad news,' he answered, 'No, joyful news. I'm perfectly happy now. I'm ready to go home,' and he did seem happy, until we drove up to the gate and you didn't come to meet him. 'Where's Edith?' he asked, and when Mrs. Matson said you were out, his forehead began to tie itself up in knots, just as it does when he is displeased. It's my opinion, Miss Edith, that you humor him altogether too much, You are tied to him as closely as a mother to her baby."

Edith sighed, not because she felt the bonds to which Victor had alluded, but because she reproached herself for not having been there to welcome the blind man home when she knew how much he thought of these little attentions.

"I'll make amends though, now," she said, and remembering the story of his disappointment, her heart swelled with a fresh feeling of pity for the helpless Richard, who, sitting before the blazing fire in the library, did not hear the light step coming so softly toward him.

All the way from the station, and indeed all the way from New York, he had pictured to himself Edith's sylph-like form running down the steps to meet him; had felt her warm hands in his, heard her sweet voice welcoming him home again, and the world around him was filled with daylight, but Edith was the sun which shone upon his darkness. She was dearer to him now, if possible, than when he left Collingwood, for, during his absence he had learned that which, if she knew it, would bind her to him by cords of gratitude too strong to be lightly broken. SHE owed everything to him, and he, alas, he groaned when he thought WHAT he owed to her, but he loved her all the same, and this it was which added to the keenness of his disappointment when among the many feet which hastened out to meet him, he listened for hers in vain. He knew it was very pleasant in his little library whither Victor led him; very pleasant to sit in his accustomed chair, and feel the fire- light shining on his face, but there was something missing, and the blue veins were swelling on his forehead, and the lines deepening about his mouth, when a pair of soft, white arms were wound about his neck, two soft white hands patted his bearded cheeks, and a voice, whose every tone made his heart throb and beat with ecstasy, murmured in his ear,

"Dear Mr. Richard, I am so glad you've come home, and so sorry I was not here to meet you. I did not expect you to-night. Forgive me, won't you? There, let me smooth the ugly wrinkles away, they make you look so cross and old," and the little fingers he vainly tried to clasp, wandered caressingly over the knit brows, while, for the first time since people began to call her Miss Hastings, Edith's lips touched his.

Nor was she sorry when she saw how beautiful the lovelight broke all over the dark, stern face, irradiating every feature, and giving to it an expression almost divine.

"Kiss me again, Birdie," he said. "It is not often you grant me such a treat," and he held her arms about his neck until she pressed her lips once more against his own.

Then he released her, and making her sit down beside him, rested his hand upon her shining hair, while he asked her how she had busied herself in his absence, if she had missed the old dark cloud, a bit, and if she was not sorry to have him back.

He know just what her answer would be, and when it was given, he took her face between his hands, and turning it up toward him, said, "I'd give all Collingwood, darling, just to look once into your eyes and see if---" then, apparently changing his mind, he added, "see if you are pleased with what I've brought you, look;" and taking from his pocket a square box he displayed to her view an entire set of beautiful pearls. "I wanted to buy diamonds, but Victor said pearls were more appropriate for a young girl like you. Are they becoming?" and he placed some of them amid the braids of her dark hair.

Like all girls of seventeen, Edith was in raptures, nor could he make her sit still beside him until, divested of her riding habit, she had tried the effect of the delicate ornaments, bracelets, ear-rings, necklace and all.

"I am so glad you like them," he said, and he did enjoy it very much, sitting there and listening to her as she danced about the room, uttering little girlish screams of delight, and asking Victor, when at last he came in--"if she wasn't irresistible?"

Victor FELT that she was, and in his polite French way he complimented her, until Richard bade him stop, telling him "she was already spoiled with flattery."

The pearls being laid aside and Victor gone, Edith resumed her accustomed seat upon a stool at Richard's feet, and folding both hands upon his knee, looked into his face, saying, "Well, monsieur, why did you go off to New York so suddenly? I think you might tell me now unless it's something I ought not to know."

He hesitated a moment as if uncertain whether to tell her or not; then said to her abruptly, "You've heard, I believe, of the little child whom I saved from drowning?"

"Yes," she answered. "Don't you know I told you once how I used to worship you because you were so brave. I remember, too, of praying every night in my childish way that you might some day find the little girl."

"Edith, I have found her," and the nervous hands pressed tenderly upon the beautiful head almost resting in his lap.

"Found her!" and Edith sprang to her feet, her large eyes growing larger, but having in them no shadow of suspicion. "Where did you find her? Where is she now? What is her name? Why didn't you bring her home?" and out of breath with her rapid questioning, Edith sat down again, while Richard laughingly replied, "Where shall I begin to answer all your queries? Shall I take them in order? I found out all about her in New York."

"That explains your scouring the alleys and lanes as Victor said you did," interrupted Edith, and Richard rejoined rather sharply, "What does HE know about it?"

"Nothing, nothing," returned Edith, anxious to shield Victor from his master's anger. "I asked him what you did in New York, and he told me that. Go on--what is her name?"

"Eloise Temple. Her mother was a Swede, and her father an American, much older than his wife."

"Eloise--Eloise--Eloise."

Edith repealed it three times.

"Where have I heard that name before? Oh, I know. I heard Kitty Maynard telling the story to Mrs. Atherton. Where is she, did you say, and how does she look?"

"She is with the family who adopted her as their own, for her mother is dead. Eloise is an orphan, Edith," and again the broad hand touched the shining hair, pityingly this time, while the voice which spoke of the mother was sad and low.

Suddenly a strange, fanciful idea flashed on Edith's mind, and looking into Richard's face she asked, "How old is Eloise?"

"Seventeen, perhaps. Possibly, though, she's older."

"And you, Mr. Harrington--how old are you, please? I'll never tell as long as I live, if you don't want me to."

She knew he was becoming rather sensitive with regard to his age, but she thought he would not mind HER knowing, never dreaming that SHE of all others was the one from whom he would, if possible, conceal the fact that he was thirty-eight. Still he told her unreservedly, asking her the while if she did not consider him almost her grandfather.

"Why, no," she answered; "you don't look old a bit. You haven't a single grey hair. *I* think you are splendid, and so I'm sure did the mother of Eloise; didn't she?" and the roguish black eyes looked up archly into the blind man's face.

Remembering what Grace had said of his love affair in Europe many years since, and adding to that the evident interest he felt in little Eloise Temple, the case was clear to her as daylight. The Swedish maiden was the girl who jilted Richard Harrington, and hence his love for Eloise, for she knew he did love her from his manner when speaking of her and the pains he had taken to find her. He had not answered her last question yet, for he did not understand its drift, and when at last he spoke he said,

"Mrs. Temple esteemed me highly, I believe; and I admired her very much. She had the sweetest voice I ever heard, not even excepting yours, which is something like it."

Edith nodded to the bright face on the mirror opposite, and the bright face nodded back as much was to say, "I knew 'twas so."

"Was she really handsome, this Mrs. Temple?" she asked, anxious to know how Richard Harrington's early love had looked.

Instinctively the hands of the blind man met together round Edith's graceful neck, as he told her how beautiful that Swedish mother was, with her glossy, raven hair, and her large, soft, lustrous eyes, and as he talked, there crept into Edith's heart a strange, inexplicable affection for that fair young Swede, who Richard said was not as happy with her father-husband as she should have been, and who, emigrating to another land, had died of a homesick, broken heart.

"I am sorry I cursed her to-day," thought Edith, her tears falling fast to the memory of the lonely, homesick woman, the mother of Eloise.

"Had she married Richard," she thought, "he would not now be sitting here in his blindness, for SHE would be with him, and Eloise, too, or some one very much like her. I wish she were here now," and after a moment she asked why he had not brought the maiden home with him. "I should love her as much as my sister," she said; "and you'd be happier with two of us, wouldn't you?"

"No," he answered; "one young girl is enough for any house. I couldn't endure two."

"Then *I* ought to go away," said Edith promptly, her bosom swelling with a dread lest she should eventually have to go. "Eloise has certainly the best right here. You loved her mother, yon know, and you'd rather have her than me, wouldn't you?"

She held both his hands now within her own. She bent her face upon them, and he felt her tears trickling through his fingers. Surely he was not to blame if, forgetting himself for the moment, he wound his arms about her and hugging her to his bosom, told her that of all the world SHE was the one he most wanted there at Collingwood, there just where she was now, her head upon his shoulder, her cheek against his own. Once she felt slightly startled, his words were so fraught with tender passion, but regarding him as her father, or at least her elder brother, she could not believe he intended addressing her save as his sister or his child, and releasing herself from his embrace, she slid back upon her stool and said, "I'm glad you're willing I should stay. It would kill me to go from Collingwood now. I've been so happy here, and found in you so kind a FATHER."

She WOULD say that last word, and she did, never observing that Richard frowned slightly as if it were to him an unwelcome sound.

Presently Edith went on, "I think, though, this Eloise ought to come, too, no matter how pleasant a home she has. It is her duty to care for you who lost your sight for her. Were I in her place, I should consider no sacrifice too great to atone for the past. I would do everything in the world you asked of me, and then not half repay you."

"Every thing, Edith? Did you say every thing?" and it would seem that the blind eyes had for once torn away their veil, so lovingly and wistfully they rested upon the bowed head of the young girl, who, without looking up, answered back,

"Yes, every thing. But I'm glad I am not this Eloise."

"Why, Edith, why?" and the voice which asked the question was mournful in its tone.

"Because," returned Edith, "I should not care to be under so great obligations to any one. The burden would be oppressive. I should be all the while wondering what more I could do, while you, too, would be afraid that the little kindnesses which now are prompted in a great measure by love would be rendered from a sense of gratitude and duty. Wouldn't it be so, Mr. Richard?"

"Yes, yes," he whispered. "You are right. I should be jealous that what my heart craved as love would be only gratitude. I am glad you suggested this, Edith; very, very, glad, and now let us talk no more of Eloise."

"Ah, but I must," cried Edith. "There are so many things I want to know, and you've really told me nothing. Had she brothers or sisters? Tell me that, please."

"There was a half sister, I believe, hut she is dead," said Richard. "They are all dead but this girl. She is alive and happy, and sometime I will tell you more of her, but not now. I am sorry I told you what I have."

"So am I if I can't hear the whole," returned Edith, beginning to pout.

"I DID intend to tell you all when I began," said Richard, "but I've changed my mind, and Edith, I have faith to believe you will not repeat to any one our conversation. Neither must you tease me about this girl. It is not altogether an agreeable subject."

Edith saw that he was in earnest, and knowing how useless it would be to question him further, turned her back upon him and gazing steadily into the fire, was wondering what made him so queer, when by way of diverting her mind, he said, "Did Victor tell you that Mr. St. Claire came with us all the way from New York?"

"Mr. St. Claire, no," and Edith brightened at once, forgetting all about Eloise Temple. "Why then didn't Mrs. Atherton and I see him? We went over the house this afternoon. It's a splendid place, most as handsome us Collingwood."

"How would you like to live there?" asked Richard, playfully. "One of the proposed conditions on which I consented to receive you, was that when Mr. St. Claire had a home of his own he was to take you off my hands; at least, that was what he said, standing here where you sit; and on my way from New York he reminded me of it, inquiring for little Metaphysics, and asking if I were ready to part with her."

"Do you wish me to go and let Eloise come?" Edith asked, pettishly, and Richard replied,

"No, Edith, I need you more than Arthur ever can, and you'll stay with me, too, stay always, won't you? Promise that you will."

"Of course I shall," she answered. "I'll stay until I'm married, as I suppose I shall he sometime; everybody is."

Richard tried to be satisfied with this reply, but it grated harshly, and it seemed to him that a shadow deeper, darker than any he had ever known, was creeping slowly over him, and that Arthur St. Claire's was the presence which brought the threatening cloud. He knew this half jealous feeling was unworthy of him, and with a mighty effort he shook it off and saying to Edith, calmly, "Mr. St. Claire asked many questions concerning you and your attainments, and when I spoke of your passion for drawing, lamenting that since Miss Chapin's departure, there was in town no competent instructor, he offered to be your teacher, provided you would come up there twice a week. He is a very sensible young man, for when I hesitated he guessed at once that I was revolving the propriety of your going alone to the house of a bachelor, where there were no females except the servants, and he said to me 'You can come with her, if you like.'"

"So it's more proper for a young lady to be with two gentlemen than with one, is it?" and Edith laughed merrily, at the same time asking if Richard had accepted the offer.

"I did, provided it met your approbation," was the reply, and as Victor just then appeared, the conversation for the present ceased.

But neither Eloise nor Arthur left the minds of either Richard or Edith, and while in her sleep that night the latter dreamed of the gentle Eloise, who called her sister, and from whom Arthur St. Claire strove to part her, the former tossed restlessly upon his pillow, moaning to him-self, "I am glad I did not tell her. She must answer me for love and not for gratitude."

CHAPTER XI.
MATTERS AT GRASSY SPRING.

The next morning as the family at Collingwood sat at their rather late breakfast a note was brought to Richard, who immediately handed it to Edith. Breaking the seal, and glancing at the name at the end, she exclaimed, "It's from Mr. St. Claire, and he says,-- let me see:
GRASSY SPRING, Oct. 18--

"Dear Sir:--A wholly unexpected event makes it necessary for me to be absent from home for the next few weeks. During this time my house will be shut up, and I shall be very glad if in her daily rides Miss Hastings will occasionally come round this way and see that everything is straight. I would like much to give the keys into her charge, knowing as I do that I can trust her. The books in my library are at her disposal, as is also the portfolio of drawings, which I will leave upon the writing table.

"When I return, and have become somewhat domesticated, I hope to have her for my pupil, as proposed yesterday. Please let me know at once if she is willing to take charge of my keys.

In haste,
ARTHUR ST. CLAIRE."

"What does he mean?" asked Edith, as she finished reading this note aloud. "What does he wish me to do?"

"Why," returned Richard, "He is to shut up his house, which, being brick, will naturally become damp, and I suppose he wishes you to air it occasionally, by opening the windows and letting in the sunlight.

"Wishes me, in short, to perform a servant's duty," said Edith, haughtily. "Very well, I'll do it. Perhaps it will pay my TUITION in part; who knows?" and in spite of Richard's remonstrances, she seized a pen and dashed off the following:

"Mr. St. Claire:

"Dear Sir,--Miss Hastings accepts the great honor of looking after your house, and will see that nothing gets mouldy during your absence."

In haste, RICHARD HARRINGTON, "Per Edith Hastings."

"P.S. Will you have her CLEAN it before you return?"

"Edith!" and Richard's voice was very stern. "Arthur St. Claire never intended to insult you and you shall NOT send that note. Tear it up at once."

Edith stood a moment irresolute, while her eyes flashed with indignation, but she had been too long accustomed to obey the man, who, groping his way to her side, stood commandingly before her to resist his authority now, and mechanically tearing the note in pieces, she tossed them into the fire.

"Victor," said Richard, wishing to spare Edith the mortification of writing a second answer, "tell the man from Grassy Spring that Mr. St. Claire can leave his keys at Collingwood."

Victor departed with the message, and Edith, somewhat recovered from her pet, said,

"Isn't it queer, though, that Mr. St. Claire should ask to leave his keys with me? One would suppose he'd trust his cousin to rummage his goods and chattels sooner than a stranger."

"He has his reasons, I dare say, for preferring you," returned Richard, adding that he himself would go with her some day to Grassy Spring, and assist her in airing the house.

Toward the middle of the afternoon, the keys of Collingwood were delivered to Edith, together with a sealed note, containing a single line,

"The iron broken key unlocks the DEN."

Had Arthur wished to puzzle Edith he could not have done so more effectually than he did by these few words.

"What do I care," she said, "which unlocks the Den. I certainly should not cross its threshold were the door left wide open. What does he mean?" and she was still wondering over the message when Grace Atherton was announced.

As she grew older Grace assumed a more familiar, youthful manner than had characterized her early womanhood, and now, tossing her riding hat and whip upon the bed, she sank into Edith's easy chair and began: "The funniest thing imaginable has happened at Grassy Spring. His Royal Highness, Lord St. Claire, has flown into a violent passion with Mrs. Johnson for having shown us into that room."

"Shown YOU, you mean. I didn't go in," interrupted Richard, and Grace continued, "Well, shown ME, then, though I think you might at least share in the disgrace. I never saw Arthur as indignant as he was last night when he called on me. 'Women were curious, prying creatures, anyway,' he said, 'and he had no faith in any of them.'"

"Did he say so?" asked Edith, and Grace replied, "Well, not exactly that. He did make a few exceptions, of which you are one. Mrs. Johnson must have told him that you refused to enter. What harm was there, any way, and what's the room for? I'm beginning to grow curious. Here, he's dismissed Mrs. Johnson and her daughter, telling her if he could not trust her in small matters he could not in those of greater importance, and the good soul has taken the afternoon express for Boston, where she formerly lived. She says he paid her three months' extra wages, so he was liberal in that respect; but the strangest part of all is that he is going to Florida, where he has some claim to or owns a plantation of negroes, and he intends to bring a whole cargo of them to Grassy Spring--housekeeper, cook, chambermaid, coachman, gardener, and all. Don't you think he's crazy?"

Edith thought the facts would warrant such a conclusion, and Grace went on. "I offered to take charge of his house, telling him it ought not to be shut up for several weeks, but he declined so haughtily, saying he should leave the keys with someone less curious than myself, and asked if I supposed YOU would be offended if he offered them to you. I told him no, and I dare say he will send them here, if indeed, he has not already done so. Has he?" she asked, quickly, as she saw a peculiar smile on Edith's lip.

"Yes," Edith answered, feeling the while SO glad that Richard had prevented her from sending that insulting note.

She knew now why the keys were given to her, and the fact that Arthur St. Claire trusted HER even before his own cousin, left a warm, happy spot in her heart. Upon second thought this act was not displeasing to Grace herself. It evinced a preference in Arthur for Edith Hastings, and on her way home she busied herself in building castles of the future, when Edith, as the wife of Arthur and mistress of

Grassy Spring, would cease to be her rival. As Grace had said, Mrs. Johnson and Rose, her daughter, were dismissed, the house was shut up, the owner gone, the keys in Edith's possession, and for many days the leaves of crimson and of gold drifted down upon the walks and lay piled beneath the windows and upon the marble steps, where they rested undisturbed, save when the evening wind whirled them in fantastic circles and then sent them back again to their first lodging place.

Occasionally Edith, on her spirited Bedouin, rode slowly by, glancing at the grounds and garden, where so many flowers were blossoming for naught, and then gazing curiously at the latticed windows looking out toward Collingwood. She knew which ones they were, though the blinds were closed tightly over them, and she wondered if the mystery of that room would ever be revealed to her. Once, as she was riding by, she saw a stranger standing upon the steps of the front door and pulling vehemently at the silver knob which brought him no response. Reining Bedouin at the gate the waited until the gentleman, tired of ringing, came slowly down the walk, apparently absorbed in some perplexing thought. He did not see her until almost upon her, when, bowing politely, he said, "I beg your pardon, Miss, can you tell me where Mr. St. Claire's to be found?"

"He has gone to Florida," she answered, "and will not return for some weeks."

"Gone to Florida, and I not know it! That's very queer," and the stranger bit his lip with vexation.

"Did you wish particularly to see him?" asked Edith, and he replied,

"Yes, a friend lies very sick in the--" he paused a moment, looked searchingly at Edith, and added, "in Worcester. We can do nothing with her, and I have come for him."

Edith thought of NINA, thought of the Den, thought of everything, except that the man seemed waiting for her to speak.

"Won't be home for some weeks," he said at last, as she continued silent, "And you don't know where a letter would reach him?"

"No, sir, but I will deliver any message from you as soon as he returns."

The stranger scrutinized her closely a second time ere he replied,

"Tell him Griswold has been here and wishes him to come to Worcester at once."

Edith was mortal, nay more, was a genuine descendant of mother Eve, and with a feeling akin to what that fair matron must have felt when she wondered how those apples did taste, she said to the man, "Who shall I say is sick?"

"A friend," was the laconic reply, as he walked rapidly away, muttering to himself, "A pretty scrape St. Claire is getting himself into. Poor Arthur, poor Arthur."

It would seen that Edith, too, was imbued with something of the spirit which prompted him to say, "Poor Arthur," for she involuntarily sighed, and casting another glance at the windows of the den, gave loose rein to Bedouin and galloped swiftly down the road.

The next morning was clear and bright, and as Richard felt the bracing air, he said to her, "We will visit Grassy Spring to-day. It's time you gave it a little air."

The carriage was accordingly brought out, and in half an hour's time Richard and Edith were treading the deserted rooms, into which they let the warm sunlight by opening wide the windows, all save those of one chamber. Edith did not go near the Den, and she marvelled that Arthur should have given her its key, indicating which it was. She did not know that the rather peculiar young man had lain for her a snare, by which means he would surely know how far her curiosity had led her. He might have spared himself the trouble, for Edith was the soul of honor, and nothing could have induced her to cross the proscribed threshold.

"It's very pleasant here, isn't it?" Richard asked, as they went from one room to another, and he felt the soft carpets yield to his tread.

"Yes," she answered; "but not as pleasant as Collingwood. I like my own home best," and she looked into his face in time to catch the expression she loved so well--an expression of trusting, childlike happiness, touching to behold in a strong man.

He liked to know that Edith was contented with Collingwood; contented with him; and he hoped it would be so always. He could not bear the thought that he had suffered every fibre of his heart to twine and intertwine themselves around her, only to be one day broken and cast bleeding at his feet. But somehow, here at Grassy Spring, in the home of Arthur St. Claire, he felt oppressed with a dread lest this thing should be; and to Edith, when she asked what made him so pale, he said,

"It's close in here, I think. Let's hurry out into the open air."

She led him to an iron chair beneath a forest maple, and leaving him there alone went back to close the windows she had opened. One of those in the drawing-room resisted all her efforts for a time, but came down at last with a bang, causing her to start, and hit her foot against a frame which she had not before observed, but which she now saw was a portrait standing in the dark corner with its face against the wall.

"Truly there can be no harm in looking at this," she thought, and turning it to the light she stepped back to examine it.

'Twas the picture of a black-eyed, black-haired child--a little girl, scarcely three years old, judging from the baby face, and the fat, dimpled hands turning so earnestly the leaves of a picture book. One tiny foot was bare, and one encased in a red morocco shoe.

"Dear, darling baby," she said aloud, feeling an irresistible desire to hug the little creature to her bosom. "Who are you, baby? Where are you now? and how came you with Mr. St. Claire?"

She asked these questions aloud, and was answered by Richard calling from his seat beneath the maple to know why she tarried so long. With one more lingering glance at the infant, she locked the doors and hastened out to her blind charge. On three or four other occasions she came alone to Grassy Spring, opening the doors and windows, and feasting her eyes upon the beautiful little child. Edith was wonderfully in love with that picture, and many a theory she built as to the original. Grace had told her that Arthur had no sister, and this, while it tended to deepen the mystery, increased her interest.

"I'll ask him about her when he gets home," she thought; and she waited anxiously for his return, which occurred much sooner than she anticipated.

It was a cold, raw November day, and the rain was beating against the windows of the little room she called her boudoir, and where she now sat sewing, when Victor, who had been sent to Grassy Spring to see that the storm did not penetrate the western blinds, appeared before her, ejaculating, "Mon Dieu, Miss Hastings. What do you think there is over yonder at Grassy Spring? A whole swarm of niggers, and Guinea niggers at that, I do believe. Such outlandish specimens! There they sit bent up double with the cold and hovering round the kitchen fire, some on the floor, some on chairs, and one has actually taken the tin dish pan and turned it bottom side up for a stool. They come from Florida, they say, and they sorter 'long to Marsa St. Claire. They called me MARSA, too, and when Mr. St. Claire asked me how my MASTER and young lady were, the old she one who sat smoking in the corner, with a turban on her head as high as a church steeple, took the pipe from her month and actually SWORE.

"Swore, Victor!" exclaimed Edith, who had listened in amazement to his story.

"I don't know what you call it but swearing; says she, 'A white nigger, Lor'-a-mighty,' and the whole bevy of them opened their ranks for time to sit down in their circle--kind of a fellow feeling, you know," and Victor endeavored to hide the shock his pride had received by laughing loudly at the negroes' mistake.

"How did you get in?" asked Edith. "He must have been there before you."

"He had a key to the back door," returned Victor, "and I gave him up mine. He wants you to send the others. Shall I take them over?"

"Yes--no--I will go myself," said Edith, remembering Mr. Griswold, from Worcester, and the message she was to deliver.

"YOU go in this rain! Mr. Harrington won't let you," said Victor, and Edith rejoined, "I shan't ask him. I've been out in worse storms than this. Bring up Bedouin."

Victor was never happier than when obeying Edith, and in an inconceivably short space of time Bedouin stood at the back piazza, where his mistress mounted him and rode away. It was not until she had left the Collingwood grounds and was out upon the main road, that she began to feel any doubts as to the propriety of what she was doing. She had not seen Arthur St. Claire for eight years. She must, of course, introduce herself and would he not marvel to see her there in that rain, when a servant could have brought the keys its well. And the message, too--Victor might have delivered that had she been willing to trust him with it, but she was not. Arthur St. Claire had a secret of some kind; Mr. Griswold was concerned in it, and it was to guard this secret from all curious ears that she was doing what she was. Having thus settled the matter to her mind, Edith rode on, unmindful of the rain, which had partially subsided, but still dripped from her black plumes and glanced off from her velvet habit. A slight nervous trepidation seized her, however, as she drew near to Grassy Spring, and noticed the look of surprise with which a stalwart African, standing by the gate, regarded her. Riding up to him she said, good-naturedly, "How d'ye, uncle?" having learned so much of negro dialect from Rachel, who was a native of Georgia.

Immediately the ivories of the darkie became visible, and with a not ungraceful bow, he answered, "Jest tolable, thankee;" while his eyes wandered up the road, as if in quest of something they evidently did not find, for bending forward helooked curiously behind Edith, saying by way of apology, "I'se huntin' for yer little black boy; whar is he?"

"Where's who?" and in her fright, lest some one of the little "Guinea niggers" about whom Victor had told her, might be seated behind her, Edith leaped with on bound form the saddle, nearly upsetting the young man hastening out to meet her.

Southern bred as the negro was he could not conceive of a white lady's riding without an escort, and failing to see said escort, he fancied it must be some diminutive child perched upon the horse, and was looking to find him, feeling naturally curious to know how the negroes of Yankee land differed from those of Florida. All this Edith understood afterward, but she was too much excited now to thing of any thing except that she had probably made herself ridiculous in the eyes of Arthur St. Claire, who adroitly rescued her from a fall in the mud, by catching her about the waist and clasping one of her hands.

"Miss Hastings, I believe," he said, when he saw that she had regained her equilibrium, "This is a pleasure I hardly expected in this storm,--but come in. You are drenched with rain;" and still holding her hand, he led her into the library, where a cheerful fire was blazing.

Drawing a chair before it he made her sit down, while he untied and removed her hat, brushing the drops of rain from her hair, and doing it in so quiet, familiar, and withal so womanly a manner that Edith began to feel quite at home with him, and to think she had not done so foolish a thing, after all, in coming there. When sure she was comfortable, he drew a chair opposite to her, and for the first time since they met, she had a chance to see what changes eight years had wrought in one she thought so handsome, as a youth. He was larger, more fully developed than when she parted from him in Albany, and it seemed to her as if he were taller, too. He was certainly manlier in his appearance, and the incipient mustache at which her nose was once contemptuously elevated, was now rich, brown beard, adding, as some would think, to the beauty of his face, the pride of his barber, and the envy of his less fortunate comrades. He was a remarkably fine looking man, handsomer even than Richard Harrington, inasmuch as he had not about him the air of helplessness which characterized the blind man. The same old mischievous twinkle lurked in the soft brown eyes, and the corners of the mouth curved just as they used to do. But his smile was not as frequent or as joyous as of old, while on his brow there was a shadow resting--an expression of sad disquiet, as if thus early he had drank deeply from the cup of sorrow. Amid his wavy hair a line of silver was now and then discernible, and Edith thought how much faster he had grown old than Richard Harrington. And well be might, for Richard, in his blindness was happier far than Arthur St. Claire, blessed with health, and riches, and eyesight, and youth. He had no secret eating to his very heart's core, and with every succeeding year magnifying itself into a greater evil than it really was, as an error concealed is sure to do. Besides that, Richard had Edith, while Arthur, alas, poor Arthur, he had worse than nothing; and as he looked across the hearth to where Edith sat, he ceased to wonder that one who for eight years had basked in the sunshine of her presence, should be as young, as vigorous and happy as Richard had appeared to him. But he must not think of this. He professed to be a woman-hater, he who, in his early boyhood, had counted his conquests by scores; and even if he were not, beautiful Edith Hastings could never be aught to him; and he must not suffer himself for a single moment to think HOW beautiful she was, still he could not help looking at her, and not a movement of her hand or a bund of her head escaped him. But so skillfully did he manage that the deluded girl fancied he never once glanced at her, while he expressed to her his gratitude for having taken so good care of his house.

"There is one room, however, you did not open," and the eyes of brown met now the eyes of black, but were quickly withdrawn, as he continued, "I mean the one at the head of the stairs, leading from my private sitting-room."

"How do you know?" asked Edith, a suspicion of the truth flashing upon her. "Did Blue Beard lay a snare in which to catch Fatima?"

"He did," Arthur answered, "but was nearly as certain then as now that she would not fall into it. Miss Hastings, it gives me more pleasure than I can well express to find one female who is worthy to be trusted--who has no curiosity."

"But I have a heap of curiosity," returned Edith, laughingly. "I'm half crazy to know what that room is for and why you are so particular about it."

"Then you deserve more credit than I have given you," he replied, a dark shadow stealing over his handsome face.

Edith was about to ask him of the portrait in the drawing room, when he prevented her by making some playful allusion to the circumstances of their first acquaintance.

"I began to think you had forgotten me," said Edith, "though I knew you could not well forget the theft unjustly charged to me."

She hoped he would now speak of Nina, but he did not, and as she for the first time remembered Mr. Griswold, she said, after a moment's pause,

"I came near forgetting my principal errand here. I could have sent your keys, but I would rather deliver Mr. Griswold's message myself."

She expected Arthur to start, but she was not prepared for him to spring from his chair as suddenly as he did.

"Mr. Griswold!" he repeated. "Where did you see him? Has HE been here? What did he say? Tell me, Edith--Miss Hastings--I beg your pardon--tell me his errand."

He stood close to her now, and his eyes did not leave her face for an instant while she repeated the particulars of her interview with the stranger.

"And this is all--you've told me all that passed between you?" he asked, eagerly.

"Yes, all," she answered, pitying him, he looked so frightened, so disturbed.

Consulting his watch, he continued, "There's time, I see, if I am expeditious, I must take the next train east though I would so much rather stay and talk with you. I shall see you again, Miss Hastings. You'll come often to Grassy Spring, won't you? I need the sight of a face like yours to keep me from going MAD."

He wrung her hand and stepped into the hall just as one of the black women he had brought from Florida appeared.

"Aunt Phillis," he said, "I wish to speak with you," and going with her to the extremity of the hall, they conversed together in low, earnest tones, as if talking of some great sorrow in which both were interested.

Once Edith heard Aunt Phillis say, "Blessed lamb, that I've done toted so many tunes in these old arms. Go, Marser Arthur; never you mind old Phillis, she'll get on somehow. Mebby the young lady in thar kin show me the things and tell me the names of yer Yankee gimcracks."

"I have no doubt she will," returned Arthur, adding something in a whisper which Edith could not hear.

A moment more and Arthur passed the door, equipped with overcoat and umbrella, and she heard his rapid steps upon the back piazza as he went towards the carriage house. Aunt Phillis now re-entered the library, curtesying low to Edith, who saw upon her old black face the trace of recent tears.

"Is Mr. St. Claire's friend very sick?" Edith ventured to ask, and instantly the round bright eyes shot at her a glance of alarm, while the negress replied, "Dunno, misses. He keeps his 'fars mostly to hisself, and Phillis has done larnt not to pry."

Thus rebuked, Edith arose and began to tie on her hat preparatory to leaving.

"Come in dis way a minute, Miss," said Phillis. "We're from Floridy, and dunno more'n the dead what to do in such a shiny kitchen as Marster St. Claire done keeps."

Edith followed her to the kitchen, in which she found several dusky forms crouched before the fire, and gazing about them with a wondering look. To Edith they were exceedingly polite, and taking a seat in their midst she soon learned from a loquacious old lady, who seemed to be superannuated, that "they were all one family, she being the grandmother, Ike and Phillis the father and mother, and 'tothers the children. We're all Ber-NARDS," she said, "case that was ole marster's name, but now I dunno who we does 'long to. Some says to Marster St. Claire and some says to Miss---"

"Mother!" and Phillis bustled up to the old lady, who, uttering a loud outcry, exclaimed,

"The Lord, Phillis; you needn't done trod on my fetched corns. I warn't a gwine to tell," and she loudly bewailed her aching foot, encased in a shoe of most wonderful make.

When the pain had partially subsided, the talkative Judy continued,

"There wasn't no sense, so I tole 'em, in 'totin' us way off here in the dead o' winter. I'se kotched a misery in my back, and got the shivers all over me. I'se too old any way to leave my cabin thar in Floridy, and I'd a heap sight rather of stayed and died on de old plantation. We has good times thar, me and Uncle Abe-- that's an old colored gentleman that lives jinin', and does nothin', just as I do. He lost his wife nex Christmas'll be a year; and, bein' lonesome like, he used to come over o' nights to talk about her, and tell how mizzable it was to be alone."

"You are a widow, I presume," said Edith, her black eyes brimming with fun.

"Yes, chile, I'se been a widdy thirty year, an' Uncle Abe was such a well-to-do nigger, a trifle shaky in the legs, I know; but it don't matter. Marster St. Claire wouldn't part the family, he said, and nothin' to do but I must come. Uncle Abe's cabin was comfable enough, and thar was a hull chest of Rhody's things, a doin' nobody no good."

Aunt Judy paused, and looked into the fire as if seeing there images of the absent Abel, while Edith regarded her intently, pressing her hands twice upon her forehead, as if trying to retain a confused, blurred idea which flitted across her mind.

"Judy," she said, at last, "it seems to me I must have seen YOU somewhere before, though where, I don't know."

"Like enough, honey," returned Judy. "Your voice sounds mighty nateral, and them black eyes shine an' glisten like some oder eyes I seen somewhar. Has you been in Floridy, chile?"

"No," returned Edith; "I was born in New York City, I believe."

"Then 'taint likely we's met afore," said Judy, "though you do grow on me 'mazin'ly. You're the very spawn o' somebody. Phillis, who does the young lady look like?"

Phillis, who had been rummaging the closets and cupboards, now came forward, and scrutinizing Edith's features, said, "She favors Master Ber-nard's last wife, only she's taller and plumper."

But with the querulousness of old age Judy scouted the idea.

"Reckoned she knowed how Marster Bernard's last wife looked. 'Twan't no more like the young lady than 'twas like Uncle Abe," and with her mind thus brought back to Abel, she commenced an eulogy upon him, to which Edith did not care to listen, and she gladly followed Phillis into the pantry, explaining to her the use of such conveniences as she did not fully understand.

"Two o'clock!" she exclaimed, as she heard the silver bell from the library clock. "Richard'll think I'm lost," and bidding her new acquaintances good bye, she hurried to the gate, having first given orders for Bedouin to be brought from the stable.

"Shan't I go home wid you, Miss?" asked the negro, who held the pony; "it's hardly fittin' for you to go alone."

But Edith assured him she was not afraid, and galloped swiftly down the road, while the negro John looked admiringly after, declaring to his father, who joined him, that "she rode mighty well for a Yankee girl."

CHAPTER XII.
LESSONS.

Arthur St. Claire had returned from Worcester, but it was several days ere he presented himself at Collingwood; and Edith was beginning to think he had forgotten her and the promised drawing lessons, when he one evening was ushered by Victor into the parlor, where she was singing to Richard his favorite songs. He was paler than when she saw him before, and she fancied that he seemed weary and worn, as if sleep and himself had been for a long time strangers.

"Did you leave your friend better?" she asked.

"Yes, better," he answered hurriedly, changing the conversation to topics evidently more agreeable.

One could not be very unhappy in Edith's presence. She possessed so much life, vivacity and vigor, that her companions were sure to become more or less imbued with her cheerful spirit; and as the evening advanced, Arthur became much like the Arthur of Brier Hill memory, and even laughed aloud on several occasions.

"I wish I was sure of finding at Grassy Spring somebody just like you," he said to Edith when at last he arose to go. "Yon have driven away a whole army of blues. I almost believe I'd be willing to be blind, if, by that means, I could be cared for as Mr. Harrington is."

"And crazy, too?" slily interrupted Edith, who was standing near him as he leaned against the marble mantel.

"No, no--oh, heavens, no! anything but that," and the hand he placed in Edith's shook nervously, but soon grew still between her soft, warm palms.

There was something life-giving in Edith's touch, as well as soul-giving in her presence, and standing there with his cold, nervous hand in hers, the young man felt himself grow strong again, and full of courage to hope for a happier future than the past had been. He knew SHE could not share the future with him--but he would have as much of her as possible, and just as she was wondering if he would remember the lessons, he spoke of them and asked when she could come.

"Just when Mr. Harrington thinks best," she replied, and thus appealed to, Richard, guided by Edith's voice, came forward and joined them.

"Any time," he said. "To-morrow, if you like," adding that he believed he, too, was to be always present.

Edith's eyes sought those of Arthur, reading there a reflection of her own secret thoughts, to wit, that THREE would he one too many, but they could not tell him so and Arthur responded at once, "Certainly, I shall expect you both, say to-morrow at ten o'clock; I am most at leisure then."

The next morning, at the appointed time, Richard and Edith appeared at Grassy Spring, where they found Arthur waiting for them, his portfolio upon the table, and his pencils lying near, ready to be used.

"I am afraid you'll find it tiresome, Mr. Harrington," he said, as he assigned his visitor a chair, and then went back to Edith.

"I shall do very well," answered Richard, and so he did for that lesson, and the next, and the next, but at last, in spite of his assertion to the contrary, he found it dull business going to Grassy Spring twice each week, and sitting alone with nothing to occupy his mind, except, indeed, to wonder how NEAR Arthur was to Edith, and if he bent over her as he remembered seeing drawing teachers do at school.

Richard was getting very tired of it--very weary of listening to Arthur's directions, and to Edith's merry laughs at her awkward blunders, and he was not sorry when one lesson-day, the fifth since they began, Grace Atherton's voice was heard in the hall without asking for admission. He had long since forgiven Grace for jilting him, and they were the best of friends; so when she suggested their going into the adjoining room, where it was pleasanter and she could play to him if he liked, he readily assented, and while listening to her lively conversation and fine playing, he forgot the lapse of time, and was surprised when Edith came to him with the news that it was 12 o'clock.

"Pray, don't go yet," said Arthur, who was loth to part with his pupil. "You surely do not dine till three, and I have already ordered lunch. Here it comes," and he pointed to the door where Phillis stood, bearing a huge silver salver, on which were wine and cake and fruit of various kinds.

"Grapes," screamed Edith, as she saw the rich purple clusters, which had been put up for winter use by poor, discarded Mrs. Johnson. "I really cannot go till I have some of them," and as there was no alternative Richard sat down to wait the little lady's pleasure.

He did not care for lunch, but joined in the conversation, which turned upon matrimony.

"It must be a very delightful state," said Edith, "provided one were well matched and loved her husband, as I am sure I should do."

"Supposing you didn't love him," asked Grace, "but had married him from force of circumstances, what then?"

"I'd kill him and the circumstances too," answered Edith. "Wouldn't you, Mr. St. Claire?"

"I can hardly tell," he replied, "not having matrimony in my mind. *I* shall never marry."

"Never marry!" and the pang at Edith's heart was discernible in her soft, black eyes, turned so quickly toward this candidate for celibacy.

"How long since you came to that decision?" asked Grace; and in tones which indicated truth, Arthur replied,

"Several years at least, and I have never for a moment changed my mind."

"Because the right one has not come, perhaps," put in Richard, growing very much interested in the conversation.

"The right one will never come," and Arthur spoke earnestly. "The girl does not live, who can ever be to me a wife, were she graceful as a fawn and beautiful as---" he glanced at Edith as if he would call her name, but added instead--"as a Hebe, it could make no difference. That matter is fixed, and is as changeless as the laws of the Medes and Persians."

"I am sorry for you, young man," said Richard, whose face, notwithstanding this assertion, indicated anything but sorrow.

He could now trust Edith alone at Grassy Spring--he need not always be bored with coming there, and he was glad Arthur had so freely expressed his sentiments, as it relieved him of a great burden; so, at parting, when Arthur said to him as usual,

"I'll see you again on Friday," he replied,

"I don't know, I'm getting so worried with these abominably tedious lessons, that for once I'll let her come alone."

Alas, poor, deluded Richard! He did not know that to attain this very object, Arthur had said what he did. It is true, he meant every word he uttered. Matrimony and Edith Hastings must not be thought of together. That were worse than madness, and his better judgment warned him not to see too much of her--told him it was better far to have that sightless man beside them when they met together in a relation so intimate as the teacher bears to his pupil. But Arthur would not listen; Edith was the first who for years had really touched a human chord in his palsied heart, and the vibration would not cease without a fiercer struggle than he cared to make. It could do no harm, he said. He had been so unhappy--was so unhappy now. Edith would, of course, be Richard's wife; he had foreseen that from the very first--had predicted it long ago, but ere the sacrifice was made, he was surely pardonable if, for a little while, he gave himself to the bewildering intoxication of basking in the sunshine of her eyes, of bending so near to her that he could feel her fragrant breath, feel the warm glow of her cheek, of holding those little hands a moment in his own after he had ceased to teach her fingers how to guide the pencil.

All this passed in rapid review before his mind while his lips uttered the words which had so delighted Richard, and when he saw the shadow on Edith's face, his poor, aching heart throbbed with a joy as wild and intense as it was hopeless and insane. This was Arthur St. Claire with Edith present, but with Edith gone, he was quite another man. Eagerly he watched her till she disappeared from view, then returning to the library he sat down where she had sat--laid his head upon the table where her hands had lain, and cursed himself for daring to dream of love in connection with Edith Hastings. It would be happiness for a time, he knew, to hang upon her smile, to watch the lights and shadows of her speaking face, to look into her eyes--those clear, truthful eyes which had in them no guile. All this would be perfect bliss, were it not that the end must come at last--the terrible end--remorse bitterer than death for him, and for her--the pure, unsullied, trusting Edith--ruin, desolation, and madness, it might be.

"Yes, MADNESS!" he exclaimed aloud, "hateful as the word may sound." And he gnashed his teeth as it dropped from between them. "No, Edith, no. Heaven helping me, I will not subject you to this temptation. I will not drag you down with me, and yet, save Griswold, there lives not the person who knows my secret. May be he could be bought. Oh, the maddening thought. Am I a demon or a brute?" And he leaped from his chair, cursing himself again and again for having fallen so low as to dream of an act fraught with so much wrong to Edith, and so much treachery to one as fair, as beautiful as she, and far, far more to be pitied.

Arthur St. Claire was, at heart, a noble, upright, honorable man, and sure, at last, to choose the right, however rugged were the road. For years he had groped in a darkness deeper, more hopeless than that which enshrouded the blind man, and in all that time there had shone upon his pathway not a single ray of daylight. The past, at which he dared not look, lay behind him a dreary waste, and the black future stretched out before him, years on years it might be, in which there would be always the same old cankering wound festering in his soul. He could NOT forget this plague spot. He never had forgotten it for a single moment until he met with Edith Hatings, who possessed for him a powerful mesmeric charm, causing him in her presence to forget everything but her. This fascination was sudden but not less powerful for that. Arthur's was an impulsive nature, and it seemed to him that he had known Edith all his life, that she was a part of his very being. But he must forget her now, she must not come there any more, he could not resist her if she did; and seizing his pen he dashed off a few lines to the effect that, for certain reasons, the drawing lessons must henceforth be discontinued.

Arthur though himself very strong to do so much, but when he arose to ring for the servant who was to take this note to Collingwood, his courage all forsook him. Why need he cast her off entirely? Why throw away the only chance for happiness there was left for him? 'Twas Arthur's weaker manhood which spoke, and he listened, for Edith Hastings was in the scale, a mighty, overwhelming weight. She might come just once more, he said, and his heart swelled within his throat as he thought of being alone with her, no jealous Richard hovering near, like a dark, brooding cloud, his blind eyes shielding her from harm even more than they could have done had they been imbued with sight. The next time she came, the restraint would be removed. She would be alone, and the hot blood poured swiftly through his veins as he thought how for one brief moment he would be happy. He WOULD wind his arm around that girlish waist, where no other manly arm save that of

Richard had ever been; he WOULD hug her to his bosom, where no other head than hers could ever lie; he would imprint one burning kiss upon her lips; would tell her how dear she was to him; and then--his brain reeled and grew dizzy as he thought that THEN he must bid her leave him forever, for an interview like that must not he repeated. But for once, just once, he would taste of the forbidden fruit, and so the good angel Arthur St. Claire wept over the wayward man and then flew sadly away, leaving him to revel in anticipations of what the next Friday would bring him.

CHAPTER XIII.
FRIDAY.

It was just beginning to be light when Edith opened her eyes, and lifting up her head, looked about the room to see if Lulu had been in to make her fire. She always awoke earlier on lesson day, so as to have a good long time TO THINK, and now as she counted the hours, one, two, three and a half, which must intervene before she saw Arthur St. Claire again, she hid her blushing face in the pillow, as if ashamed to let the gray daylight see just how happy she was. These lessons had become the most important incidents in her life, and this morning there was good cause why she should anticipate the interview. She believed Richard was not going, and though she was of course very sorry to leave him behind, she tried hard to be reconciled, succeeding so well that when at 8 o'clock she descended to the breakfast room, Victor asked what made her look so unusually bright and happy.

"I don't know," she replied, "unless it is because we are going to ride," and she glanced inquiringly at Richard, seating himself at the table.

Victor shrugged his shoulders. HE knew more than Edith thought he did, and waited like herself for Richard's answer. Richard HAD intended to remain at home, but it seemed that Edith expected him to go, by her saying WE, and rather than disappoint her he began to think seriously of martyring himself again. Something like this he said, adding that he found it vastly tedious, but was willing to endure it for Edith's sake.

"Pardonnez moi, Monsieur," said Victor, who for the sake of Edith, would sometimes stretch the truth, "I saw Mr. Floyd yesterday, and he is coming here this morning to talk with you about the west wood lot you offered for sale. Hadn't you better stay home for once and let Miss Edith go alone."

Edith gave a most grateful look t Victor, who had only substituted "this morning" for "some time to-day," the latter being what Mr. Floyd had really said.

"Perhaps I had," returned Richard. "I want so much to sell that lot, but if Edith---"

"Never mind me, Mr. Harrington," she cried; "I have not been on Bedouin's back in so long a time that he is getting quite unmanageable, they say, and I shall be delighted to discipline him this morning; the roads are quite fine for winter, are they not Victor?"

"Never were better," returned the Frenchman; smooth and hard as a rock. "You'll enjoy it amazingly, I know. I'll tell Jake not to get out the carriage," and without waiting for an answer the politic victor left the room.

Richard had many misgivings as to the propriety of letting Edith go without him, and he was several times on the point of changing his mind, but Edith did not give him any chance, and at just a quarter before ten she came down equipped in her riding habit, and asking if he had any message for Mr. St. Claire.

"None in particular," he answered, adding that she might come back through the village and bring the mail.

Once on the back of Bedouin, who danced for a few moments like a playful kitten, Edith felt sure she was going alone, and abandoning herself to her delight she flew down the carriage road at a terrific speed, which startled even Victor, great as was his faith in his young lady's skill. But Edith had the utmost confidence in Bedouin, while Bedouin had the utmost confidence in Edith, and by the time they were out upon the main road they had come to a most amicable understanding.

"I mean to gallop round to the office now," thought Edith; "and then I shall not be obliged to hurry away from Grassy Spring."

Accordingly Bedouin was turned toward the village, and in an inconceivably short space of time she stood before the door of the post-office.

"Give me Mr. Harrington's mail, please," Edith said to the clerk who came out to meet her; "and--and Mr. St. Claire's too, I'm going up there, and can take it as well as not."

The clerk withdrew, and soon returned with papers for Richard, and a letter for Arthur. It was post-marked at Worcester, and Edith thought of Mr. Griswold, as she thrust it into her pocket, and started for Grassy Spring, where Arthur was anxiously awaiting her. Hastening out to meet her, he held her hand in his, while he led her up the walk, telling her by his manner, if by nothing else, how glad he was to see her.

"It has seemed an age since Tuesday," he said. "I only live on lesson-days. I wish it was lesson-day always."

"So do I," said Edith, impulsively, repenting her words the moment she met the peculiar glance of Arthur's eyes.

She was beginning to be afraid of him, and half wished Richard was there. Remembering his letter at last, she gave it to him, explaining how she came by it, and marvelling at the sudden whiteness of his face.

"I will wait till she is gone," he thought, as he recognized Dr. Griswold's writing, and knew well what it was about. "I won't let anything mar the bliss of the next two hours," and he laid it upon the table.

"Ain't you going to read it?" asked Edith, as earnestly as if she knew the contents of that letter would save her from much future pain. "Read it," she persisted, declaring, with pretty willfulness that she would not touch a pencil until he complied with her request.

"I suppose I must yield then," he said, withdrawing into the adjoining room, where he broke the seal and read--once--twice-- three times--lingering longest over the sentences which we subjoin.

* * * "To-day, for the first time since you were here, our poor little girl spoke of you of her own accord, asking where you were and why you left her so long alone. I really think it would be better for you to take her home. She is generally quiet with you, and latterly she has a fancy that you are threatened with some danger, for she keeps whispering to herself, 'Keep Arthur from temptation. Keep him from temptation, and don't let any harm come to little MIGGIE.' Who is Miggie? I don't think I ever heard her name until within the last few days." * * *

And this it was which kept Arthur St. Claire from falling. Slowly the tears, such as strong men only shed, gathered in his eyes and dropped upon the paper. Then his pale lips moved, and he whispered sadly, "Heaven bless you, NINA, poor unfortunate Nina. Your prayer SHALL save me, and henceforth Edith shall be to me just what your darling Miggie would have been were she living. God help me to do right," he murmured, as he thought of Edith Hastings, and remembered how weak he was. That prayer of anguish was not breathed in vain, and when the words were uttered he felt himself growing strong again--strong to withstand the charms of the young girl waiting impatiently for him in the adjoining room.

There were many things she meant to say to him in Richard's absence. She would ask him about NINA, and the baby picture which had so interested her. It had disappeared from the drawing room and as yet she had found no good opportunity to question him about it, but she would do so to-day. She would begin at once so as not to forget, and she was just wondering how long it took a man to read a letter, when he came in. She saw at a glance that something had affected him, and knowing intuitively that it was not the time for idle questionings, she refrained from all remark, and the lesson both had so much anticipated, proceeded in almost unbroken silence. It was very dull indeed, she thought, not half so nice as when Richard was there, and in her pet at Arthur's coolness and silence, she made so many blunders that at last throwing pencil and paper across the room, she declared herself too stupid for any thing.

"You, too, are out of humor," she said, looking archly into Arthur's face, "and I won't stay here any longer. I mean to go away and talk with Judy about Abel."

So saying, she ran off to the kitchen where she was now a great favorite, and sitting down at Judy's feet, began to ask her of Florida and Sunnybank, her former home.

"Tell me more of the magnolias," she said, "It almost seems to me as if I had seen those beautiful white blossoms and that old house with its wide hall."

"Whar was you raised?" asked Judy, and Edith replied,

"I told you once, in New York, but I have such queer fancies, as if I had lived before I came into this world."

"Jest the way Miss Nina used to go on, muttered the old woman, looking steadily into the fire.

"Nina!" and Edith started quickly. "DID you know Nina, Aunt Judy? Do you know her now? Where is she? Who is she, and that black-eyed baby in the frame? Tell me all about them."

"All about what?" I asked Phillis, suddenly appearing and casting a warning glance at her mother, who replied, "'Bout marster's last wife, the one you say she done favors." Then, in an aside to Edith, she added, "I kin pull de wool over her eyes. Bimeby mabby I'll done tell you how that ar is de likeness of Miss Nina's half sister what is dead, and 'bout Miss Nina, too, the sweetest, most misfortinest human de Lord ever bornd."

"She isn't a great ways from here, is she?" whispered Edith, as Phillis bustled into the pantry, hurrying back ere Judy could more than shake her head significantly.

"Dear Aunt Phillis, won't you please tell Ike to bring up Bedouin," Edith said coaxingly, hoping by this ruse to get rid of the old negress; but Phillis was too cunning, and throwing up the window sash, she called to Ike, delivering the message.

Edith, however, managed slily to whisper, "In Worcester, isn't she?" while Judy as slily nodded affirmatively, ere Phillis' sharp eyes were turned again upon them. Edith's curiosity concerning the mysterious Nina was thoroughly roused, and determining to ferret out the whole affair by dint of quizzing Judith whenever an opportunity should occur, she took her leave.

"Mother," said Phillis, the moment Edith was out of hearing, "havn't you no sense, or what possessed you to talk of Miss Nina to her? Havn't you no family pride, and has you done forgot that Marster Arthur forbade our talkin' of her to strangers?"

Old Judy at first received the rebuke in silence, then bridling up in her own defense, she replied, "Needn't tell me that any good will ever come out o' this kiverin' up an' hidin', and keeping whist. It'll come out bimeby, an' then folks'll wonder what 'twas all did for. Ole marster didn't act so by Miss Nina's mother, an' I believe thar's somethin' behind, some carrying on that we don't know; but it's boun' to come out fust or last. That ar Miss Edith is a nice trim gal. I wish to goodness Marster Arthur'd done set to her. I'd like her for a mistress mighty well. I really b'lieve he has a hankerin' notion after her, too, an' it's nater that he should have. It's better for the young to marry, and the old, too, for that matter. Poor Uncle Abe! Do you s'pose, Phillis, that he goes over o' nights to Aunt Dilsey's cabin sen' we've come away. Dilsey's an onery nigger, anyhow," and with her mind upon Uncle Abel, and her possible rival Dilsey, old Judy forgot Edith Hastings, who, without bidding Arthur good morning, had gallopped home to Collingwood, where she found poor, deluded Richard, waiting and wondering at the non-appearance of Mr. Floyd, who was to buy his western wood lot.

CHAPTER XIV.
THE MYSTERY AT GRASSY SPRING.

For several weeks longer Edith continued taking lessons of Arthur, going sometimes with Richard, but oftener alone, and feeling always that a change had gradually come over her teacher. He was as kind to her as ever, took quite as much pains with her, and she was sensible of a greater degree of improvement than had marked the days when she trembled every time he touched her hands. Still there was a change. He did not bend over her now as he used to do; did not lay his arm across the back of her chair, letting it some times fall by accident upon her shoulders; did not look into her eyes with a glance which made her blush and turn away; in short, he did not look at her at all, if he could help it, and in this very self-denial lay his strength. He was waging a mighty battle with himself, and inch by inch he was gaining the victory, for victory it would be when he brought himself to think of Edith Hastings without a pang--to listen to her voice and look into her face without a feeling that she must be his. He could not do this yet, but he kept himself from telling her of his love by assuming a reserved, studied manner, which led her at last to think he might be angry, and one day, toward the first of March, when he had been more than usually silent, she asked him abruptly how she had offended, her soft eyes filling with tears as she expressed her sorrow if by any thoughtless act she had caused him pain.

"You could not offend me, Edith," he said; "that would be impossible, and if I am sometimes could an abstracted, it is because I have just cause for being so. I am very unhappy, Edith, and your visits here to me are like oases to the weary traveller. Were it not for you I should wish to die; and yet, strange as it may seem, I have prayed to die oftener since I knew you as you now are than I ever did before, I committed a fatal error once and it has embittered my whole existence. It was early in life, to, before I ever say you, Edith."

"Why Mr. St. Claire," she exclaimed, "you were nothing but a boy when you came to Brier Hill."

"Yes, a boy," he exclaimed, "or I had never done what I did; but it cannot be helped, and I must abide the consequences. Now let us talk of something else. I am going away to-morrow, and you need not come again until I send for you; but whatever occurs, don't think I am offended."

She could not think so when she met the olden look she ahs missed so long, and wondering where he could be going, she arose to take her leave. He went with her to the door, and wrung her hand nervously, bidding her in heart a final farewell, for when they met again a great gulf would be between them,--a gulf he had helped to dig, and which he could not ass. Edith had intended to ask old Judy where Arthur was going, without, however, having much hope of success: for, since the conversation concerning Nina, Judy had been wholly non-committal, plainly showing that she had been trained for the occasion, but changed her mind, and rode leisurely away, going round by Brier Hill to call upon Grace whom she had not seen for some little time. Grace, as usual, was full of complaints against Arthur for being so misanthropical, so cross- grained and so queer, shutting himself up like a hermit and refusing to see any one but herself and Edith.

"What is he going to Worcester for?" she asked, adding that one of the negroes had told old Rachel, who was there the previous night.

But Edith did not know, unless it was to be married, and laughing at her own joke, she bade Grace good-bye, having learned by accident what she so much desired to know.

The next morning she arose quite early, and looking in the direction of Grassy Spring, which, when the leaves were fallen, was plainly discernible, she saw Arthur's carriage driving from his gate. There was no train due at that hour, and she stood wondering until the carriage, which, for a moment, had been hidden from her view, appeared a second time in sight, and as it passed the house she saw Aunt Phillis's dusky face peering from the window. She did not see Arthur, but she was sure he was inside; and when the horses were turned into the road, which, before the day of cars, was the great thoroughfare between Shannondale and Worcester, she knew he had started for the latter place in his carriage.

"What can it be for?" she said; "and why has he taken Phillis?"

But puzzle her brain as she might, she could not fathom the mystery, and she waited for what would next occur.

In the course of the day Victor, who, without being really meddlesome, managed to keep himself posted with regard to the affairs at Grassy Spring, told her that Mr. St. Claire, preferring his carriage to the cars, had gone in it to Worcester, and taken Phillis with him; that he would be absent some days; and that Sophy, Phillis's daughter, when questioned as to his business, had answered evasively,

"Gone to fetch his wife home for what I know."

"Maybe it is so," said Victor, looking Edith steadily in the face, "Soph didn't mean me to believe it; but there's many a truth spoken in jest."

Edith knew that, but she would not hearken for a moment to Victor's suggestion. It made her too unhappy, and for three days she had a fair opportunity of ascertaining the nature of her feelings toward Arthur St. Claire, for nothing is more conducive to the rapid development of love, than a spice of jealousy lest another has won the heart we so much covet.

The next day, the fourth after Arthur's departure, she asked Victor to ride with her on horseback, saying the fresh March wind would do her good. It was nearly sunset when they started, and, as there was a splendid moon, they continued their excursion to quite a distance, so that it was seven ere they found themselves at the foot of the long hill which wound past Collingwood and on to Grassy Spring. Half way up the hill, moving very slowly, as if the horses were jaded and tired, was a traveling carriage, which both Edith and Victor recognized at once as belonging to Arthur St. Claire.

"Let's overtake them," said Edith, and chirruping to Bedouin, she was soon so near to the carriage that her quick ear caught the sound of a low, sweet voice singing a German air, with which she herself had always been familiar, though when she first learned it she could not tell.

It was one of those old songs which Rachel had called weird and wild, and now, as she listened to the plaintive tones, they thrilled on every nerve with a strange power as if it were a requiem sung by the dead over their own buried hopes. Nearer and nearer Bedouin pressed to the slowly moving vehicle, until at last she was nearly even with it.

"Look, Miss Edith!" and Victor grasped her bridle rein, directing her attention to the arms folded upon the window and the girlish head resting upon the arms, in the attitude of a weary child.

One little ringless, blue-veined hand was plainly discernible in the bright moonlight, and Edith thought how small and white and delicate it was.

"Let's go on," she whispered, and they dashed past the carriage just as Arthur leaned forward to see who they were.

"That was a young lady," said Victor coming up with Edith, who was riding at a headlong speed.

"Yes, I knew it," and Edith again touched Bedouin with her whip as if the fast riding suited well her tumultuous emotions.

"His bride?" said Victor, interrogatively, and Edith replied, "Very likely, Victor," and she stopped Bedouin short. "Victor, don't tell any one of the lady in the carriage until it's known for certain that there is one at Grassy Spring."

Victor could see no reason for this request, but it was sufficient for him that Edith had made it, and he promised readily all that she desired. They were at home by this time, and complaining of a headache Edith excused herself earlier than usual and stole up to her chamber where she could he alone to wonder WHO was the visitor at Grassy Spring. It might be a bride, and it might be NINA. Starting to her feet as the last mentioned individual came into her mind, she walked to the window and saw just what she more than half expected to see--a light shining through the iron lattice of the DEN--a bright, cheerful light--and as she gazed, there crept over her a faint, sick feeling, as if she knew of the ruin, the desolation, the blighted hopes and beautiful wreck embodied in the mystery at Grassy Spring. Covering her eyes with her hands the tears trickled through her fingers, falling not so much for Arthur St. Claire as for the plaintive singing girl shrouded in so dark a mystery. Drying her eyes she looked again across the meadow, but the blinds of the Den were closed, and only the moonbeams fell where the blaze of the lamp had been.

A week went by, and though Grace came twice to Collingwood, while Victor feigned several errands to Grassy Spring, nothing was known of the stranger. Grace evidently had no suspicion of her existence, while Victor declared there was no trace of a white woman any where about the premises. Mr. St. Claire, he said, sat in the library, his feet crossed in a chair and his hands on top of his head as if in a brown study, while Aunt Phillis appeared far more impatient than usual and had intimated to him plainly that "in her 'pinion white niggers had better be at home tendin' to thar own business, of they had any, and not pryin' into thar neighbor's affairs."

At last Edith was surprised at receiving a note from Arthur, saying he was ready to resume their lessons at any time. Highly delighted with the plan Edith answered immediately that she would come on the morrow, which was Friday. Richard did not offer to go, owing in a great measure to the skillful management of Victor, who, though he did not suggest Mr. Floyd and the western wood lot, found some equally good excuse why his master's presence would, that day of all others, be necessary at home.

The wild March winds by this time had given place to the warmer, balmier air of April. The winter snow had melted from the hillside, and here and there tufts of fresh young grass were seen starting into life. It was just such a morning, in short, as is most grateful to the young, and Edith felt its inspiring influence as she rode along the rather muddy road. Another there was, too, who felt it; and as Edith sauntered slowly up the path, entering this time upon the rear piazza instead of the front, she heard again the soft, low voice which had sounded so mournful and sweet when heard in the still moonlight. Looking up she saw that a window of the Den was open, and through the lattice work a little hand was thrust, as if beckoning her to come. Stepping bank she tried to obtain a view of the person, but failed to do so, though the hand continued beckoning, and from the height there floated down to her the single word, "MIGGIE." That was all; but it brought her hand to her head as if she had received a sudden blow.

"Miggie--Miggie," she repeated. "I HAVE heard that name before. It must have belonged to some one in the Asylum."

A confused murmur as if of expostulation and remonstrance was now heard--the childish hand disappeared and scarcely knowing what she was about, Edith stepped into the hall and advanced into the library, where she sat down to wait for Arthur. It was not long ere he appeared, locking the door as he came in and thus cutting off all communication between that room and the stairway leading to the Den. Matters were, in Edith's estimation, assuming a serious aspect, and remembering how pleadingly the name "Miggie" had been uttered, she half-resolved to demand of Arthur the immediate release of the helpless creature thus held in durance vile. But he looked so unhappy, so hopelessly wretched that her sympathy was soon enlisted for him rather than his fair captive. Still she would try him a little and when they were fairly at work she said to him jestingly,

"I heard it hinted that you would bring home a wife, but I do not see her. Where is she, pray?"

Arthur uttered no sound save a stifled moan, and when Edith dared to steal a look at him she saw that his brown hair was moist with perspiration, which stood also in drops about his lips.

"Mr. St. Claire," she said, throwing down her pencil and leaning back in her chair, "I can endure this no longer. What IS the matter? Tell me. You have some great mental sorrow, I know, and I long to share it with you--may I? Who have you up stairs and why this mystery concerning her?"

She laid her hand upon his arm, and looked imploringly into the face, which turned away from her, as if afraid to meet her truthful glance. Once he thought to tell her all, but when he remembered how beautiful she was, how much he loved her, and how dear her society was to him, he refrained, for he vainly fancied that a confession would drive her from him forever. He did not know Edith Hastings; he had not yet fathomed the depths of her womanly nature, and he could not guess how tenderly, even while her own heart was breaking, she would have soothed his grief and been like an angel of mercy to the innocent cause of all his woe.

"I dare not tell you," he said. "You would hate me if I did, and that I could not endure. It may not be pleasant for you to come here any more, and perhaps you had better not."

For a moment Edith sat motionless. She had not expected this from Arthur, and it roused within her a feeling of resentment.

"And so you only sent for me to give me my dismissal," she said, in a cold, icy tone. "Be it as you like. I draw tolerably well, you say. I have no doubt I can get along alone. Send your bill at once to Mr. Harrington. He does not like to be in debt."

She spoke proudly, haughtily, and her eyes, usually so soft in their expression, had in them a black look of anger, which pierced Arthur's very soul. He could not part with her THUS, and grasping the hand reached out to take its gauntlet, he held it fast, while he said, "What are we doing, Edith? Quarrelling? It must not be. I suggested your giving up the lessons because I thought the arrangement might be satisfactory to you, and not because *I* wished it, for I do not; I cannot give up the only source of happiness left to me. Forget what I said. Remain my pupil and I'll try to be more cheerful in your presence. You shall NOT help to bear my burden as you bear that of Collingwood's unfortunate inmates."

Edith never liked to hear her relations to Richard referred to in this manner, and she answered quickly,

"You are mistaken, Mr. St. Claire, in thinking I bear any burden either here or elsewhere. No one ever had a happier home than I, and there's nothing on earth I would not do for Richard."

"Would you marry him, Edith?" and Arthur scanned her closely. "Would you be his wife if he demanded it as his right? and I think he will do this sometime."

Edith trembled from head to foot, as she answered,

"Not if he demanded it as a right, though he might well do that, for I owe him everything. But if he loved me, and I loved him."

She paused, and in the silence which ensued the tumultuous beating of her heart was plainly audible. No one before had suggested to her the possibility of her being Richard's wife, and the idea was terrible to her. She loved him, but not as a wife should love her husband. He loved her, too; and now, as she remembered many things in the past, she was half convinced that she to him was dearer than a sister, child, or friend. He had forgotten the Swedish baby's mother. She knew he had by his always checking her when she attempted to speak of Eloise. Out of the ashes of this early love a later love had sprung, and SHE was possibly its object. The thought was a crushing one, and unmindful of Arthur's presence she laid her head upon the table and sobbed,

"It cannot be. Richard will never ask me to be his wife. Never, oh never."

"But if he does, Edith, you will not tell him NO. Promise me that. It's my only hope of salvation from total ruin!" and Arthur drew so near to her that his arm found its way around her slender waist.

Had he struck her with a glittering dagger he could not have hurt her more than by pleading with her to be another's wife. But she would not let him know it. He did not love her as she had sometimes foolishly fancied he did; and lifting up her head she answered him proudly,

"Yes, Arthur St. Claire, when Richard Harrington asks me to be his bride I will not tell him no. Are you satisfied?"

"I am," he said, though his white lips gave the lie to the words he uttered, and his heart smote him cruelly for his selfishness in wishing to save himself by sacrificing Edith; and it would be a sacrifice, he knew--a fearful sacrifice, the giving her to a blind man, old enough to be her sire, noble, generous and good, though he were.

It was a little singular that Arthur's arm should still linger about the waist of one who had promised to be another's wife, provided she were asked, but so it was; it staid there, while he persuaded her to come again to Grassy Spring, and not to give up the lessons so pleasant to them both.

He was bending very near to her when a sound upon the stairs caught his ear. It was the same German air Edith had heard in the yard, and she listened breathlessly while it came nearer to the door. Suddenly the singer seemed to change her mind, for the music began slowly to recede and was soon lost to hearing within the four walls of the Den. Not a word was spoken by either Arthur or Edith, until the latter said,

"It is time I was at home," and she arose to go.

He offered no remonstrance, but accompanying her to the gate, placed her in the saddle, and then stood watching her as she galloped away.

CHAPTER XV.
NINA.

Three or four times Edith went to Grassy Spring, seeing nothing of the mysterious occupant of the Den, hearing nothing of her, and she began to think she might have returned to Worcester. Many times she was on the point of questioning Arthur, but from what had passed, she knew how disagreeable the subject was to him, and she generously forbore.

"I think he might tell me, anyway," she said to herself, half poutingly, when, one morning near the latter part of April, she rode slowly toward Grassy Spring.

Their quarrel, if quarrel it could be called, had been made up, or, rather, tacitly forgotten, and Arthur more than once had cursed himself for having, in a moment of excitement, asked her to marry Richard Harrington. While praying to be delivered from temptation he was constantly keeping his eyes fixed upon the forbidden fruit, longing for it more and move, and feeling how worthless life would be to him without it. Still, by a mighty effort, he restrained himself from doing or saying aught which could be constrained into expressions of love, and their interviews were much like those which had preceded his last visit to Worcester. People were beginning to talk about him and his beautiful pupil, but leading the isolated life he did, it came not to his ears. Grace indeed, might have enlightened both himself and Edith with regard to the village gossip, but looking upon the latter as her rival, and desiring greatly that she should marry Arthur, she forebore from communicating to either of them anything which would be likely to retard an affair she fancied was progressing famously. Thus without a counsellor or friend was Edith left to follow the bent of her inclinations; and on this April morning, as she rode along, mentally chiding Arthur for not entrusting his secret to her, she wondered how she had ever managed to be happy without him, and if the time would ever come when her visits to Grassy Spring would cease.

Leaving Bedouin at the rear gate she walked slowly to the house, glancing often in the direction of the DEN, the windows of which were open this morning, and as she came near she saw a pair of soft blue eyes peering at her through the lattice, then a little hand was thrust outside, beckoning to her as it did once before.

"Wait, Miggie, while I write," came next to her ear, in a voice as sweet and plaintive as a broken lute.

Instantly Edith stopped, and at last a tiny note came fluttering to her feet. Grasping it eagerly she read, in a pretty, girlish hand:

"DARLING MIGGIE:--Nina has been SO sick this great long while, and her head is so full of pain. Why don't you come to me, Miggie? I sit and wait and listen till my forehead thumps and thumps, just as a bad nurse thumped it once down in the Asylum.

"Let's run away--you and I; run back to the magnolias, where it's always summer, with no asylums full of wicked people.

"I'm so lonely, Miggie. Come up stairs, won't you? They say I rave and tear my clothes, but I won't any more if you'll come. Tell Arthur so. He's good. He'll do what you ask him."

"Poor little Nina," and Edith's tears fell fast upon the bit of paper. "I WILL see you to-day. Perhaps I may do you some good. Dear, unfortunate Nina!"

There was a step upon the grass, and thrusting the note into her pocket, Edith turned to meet Arthur, who seemed this morning unusually cheerful and greeted her with something like his olden tenderness. But Edith was too intent upon Nina to think much of him, and after the lesson commenced, she appeared so abstracted that it was Arthur's turn to ask if she were offended. She had made herself believe she was, for notwithstanding Nina's assertion that "Arthur was good," she thought it a sin and a shame for him to keep any thing but a raving lunatic hidden away up stairs; and after a moment's hesitation she answered, "Yes, I am offended, and I don't mean to come here any more, unless---"

"Edith," and the tone of Arthur's voice was fraught with pain so exquisite that Edith paused and looked into his face, where various emotions were plainly visible. Love, fear, remorse, apprehension, all were blended together in the look he fixed upon her. "You won't leave me," he said. "Any thing but that. Tell me my error, and how I can atone."

Edith was about to speak, when, on the stairs without,--the stairs leading from the den--there was the patter of little feet, and a gentle, timid knock was heard upon the door.

"It's locked--go back;" and Arthur's voice had in it a tone of command.

"Mr. St. Claire," and Edith sprang from her chair, "I can unlock that door, and I will."

Like a block of marble Arthur stood while Edith opened the oak-paneled door. Another moment and Nina stood before her, as she stands now first before our readers.

Edith knew her in a moment from the resemblance to the daguerreotype seen more than eight years before, and as she now scanned her features it seemed to her they had scarcely changed at all. Arthur had said of her then that she was not quite sixteen, consequently she was now nearly twenty-five, but she did not look as old as Edith, so slight was her form, so delicate her limbs, and so childlike and simple the expression of her face. She was very, very fair, and Edith felt that never before had she looked upon a face so exquisitely beautiful. Her hair was of a reddish-yellow hue, and rippled in short silken rings all over her head, curling softly in her neck, but was not nearly as long as it had been in the picture. Alas, the murderous shears had more than once strayed roughly among those golden locks, to keep the little white, fat hands, now clasped so harmlessly together, from tearing them out with frantic violence. Edith thought of this and sighed, while her heart yearned toward the helpless young creature, who stood regarding her with a scrutinizing glance, as one studies a beautiful picture. The face was very white--indeed, it seemed as if it were long since the blood had visited the cheeks, which, nevertheless, were round and plump, as were the finely moulded arms, displayed to good advantage by the loose sleeves of the crimson cashmere wrapper. The eyes were deeply, darkly blue, and the strangely gleaming light which shone from them, betrayed at once the terrible truth that Nina was crazed.

It was a novel sight, those two young girls watching each other so intently, both so beautiful and yet so unlike--the one, tall, stately, and almost queen-like in her proportions, with dark, brilliant complexion; eyes of midnight blackness, and masses of raven hair, bound around her head in many a heavy braid--the other, fairy-like in size, with golden curls and soft blue eyes, which filled with tears at last as some undefinable emotion swept over her. In the rich, dark beauty of Edith's face there was a wonderful fascination, which riveted the crazy girl to the spot where she had stopped when first she crossed the threshold, and when at last, sinking upon the sofa, Edith extended her arms, as a mother to her child, poor little Nina went forward, and with a low, gasping sob, fell upon her bosom, weeping passionately, her whole frame trembling and her sobs so violent that Edith became alarmed, and tried by kisses and soft endearing words to soothe her grief and check the tears raining in torrents from her eyes.

"It's nice to cry. It takes the heavy pain away," and Nina made a gesture that Edith must not stop her, while Arthur, roused from his apathy, also said,

"She has not wept before in years. It will be a great relief."

At the sound of HIS voice Nina lifted up her head, and turned toward the corner whence it came, but Edith saw that in the glance there was neither reproach nor fear, nothing save trusting confidence, and her heart insensibly softened toward him.

"Poor Arthur," Nina murmured, and laying her head again on Edith's bosom, she said, "Every body is sad where I am, but I can't help it. Oh, I can't help it. Nina's crazy, Miggie, Nina is. Poor Nina," and the voice which uttered these words was so sadly touching that Edith's tears mingled with those of the young creature she hugged the closer to her, whispering,

"I know it, darling, and I pity you so much. Maybe you'll get well, now that you know me."

"Yea, if you'll stay here always," said Nina. "What made you gone so long? I wanted you so much when the nights were dark and lonesome, and little bits of faces bent over me like yours used to be, Miggie--yours in the picture, when you wore the red morocco shoe and I led you on the high verandah."

"What does she mean?" asked Edith, who had listened to the words as to something not wholly new to her.

"I don't know," returned Arthur, "unless she has confounded you with her sister, MARGUERITE, who died many years ago, I have heard that Nina, failing to speak the real name, always called her MIGGIE. Possibly you resemble Miggie's mother. I think Aunt Phillis said you did."

Edith, too, remembered Phillis' saying that she looked like "Master Bernard's" wife, and Arthur's explanations seemed highly probable.

"Dear, darling Nina," she said, kissing the pure white forehead, "I WILL be a sister to you."

"And stay with me?" persisted Nina. "Sleep with me nights with your arms round my neck, just like yon used to do? I hate to sleep alone, with Soph coiled up on the floor, she scares me so, and won't answer when I call her. Then, when I'm put in the recess, it's terrible. DON'T let me go in there again, will you?"

Edith had not like Grace, looked into the large closet adjoining the Den, and she did not know what Nina meant, but at a venture she replied,

"No, darling. You'll be so good that they will not wish to put you there."

"I CAN'T," returned Nina, with the manner of one who distrusted herself. "I try, because it will please Arthur, but I must sing and dance and pull my hair when my head feels so big and heavy, and once, Miggie, when it was big as the house, and I pulled my hair till they shaved it off, I tore my clothes in pieces and threw them into the fire. Then, when Arthur came--Dr. Griswold sent for him, you see--I buried my fingers in HIS hair, so," and she was about to clutch her own golden locks when Edith shudderingly caught her hands and held them tightly lest they should harm the tresses she thought so beautiful.

"Arthur cried," continued Nina--"cried so hard that my brain grew cool at once. It's dreadful to see a man cry, Miggie--a great, strong man like Arthur. Poor Arthur, didn't you cry and call me your lost Nina?"

A suppressed moan was Arthur's answer, and Nina, when she heard it, slid from Edith's arms and crossing over to where she sat, climbed into his lap with all the freedom of a little child, and winding her arms about his neck, said to him softly,

"Don't be so sorry, Arthur, Nina'll be good. Nina is good now. He's crying again. Make him stop, wont you? It hurts Nina so. There, poor boy," and the little waxen hands wiped away the tears falling so fast over Arthur's face.

Holding one upon the end of her finger and watching it until it dropped upon the carpet, she said with a smile, "Look, Miggie, MEN'S tears are bigger than girls."

Oh, how Edith's heart ached for the strange couple opposite her-- the strong man and the crazy young girl who clung to him as confidingly, as if his bosom were her rightful resting place. She pitied them both, but her sympathies were enlisted for Arthur, and coming to his side she laid her hand upon the damp brown locks, which Nina once had torn in her insane fury, and in a voice which spoke volumes of sympathy, whispered, "I am sorry for you."

This was too much for Arthur, and he sobbed aloud, while Edith, forgetting all proprieties in her grief for him, bowed her face upon his head, and he could feel her hot tears dropping on his hair.

For a moment Nina looked from one to the other in silence, then standing upon her feet and bending over both, she said,

"Don't cry, Miggie, don't cry, Arthur. Nina ain't very bad to day. She wont be bad any more. Don't. It will all come right some time. It surely will. Nina won't be here always, and there'll be no need to cry when she is gone."

She seemed to think the distress was all on her account, and in her childish way she sought to comfort them until hope whispered to both that, as she said, "It would come right sometime."

Edith was the first to be comforted, for she did not, like Arthur, know what coming right involved. She only thought that possibly Nina's shattered intellect might be restored, and she longed to ask the history of one, thoughts of whom had in a measure been blended with her whole life, during the last eight years. There was a mystery connected with her, she knew, and she was about to question Arthur, who had dried his tears and was winding Nina's short curls around his fingers, when Phillis appeared in the library, starting with surprise when she saw the trio assembled there.

"Marster Arthur," she began, glancing furtively at Edith, "how came Miss Nina here? Let me take her back. Come, honey," and she reached out her hand to Nina, who, jumping again upon Arthur's knee, clung to him closely, exclaiming, "No, no, old Phillis; Nina's good--Nina'll stay with Miggie!" and as if fancying that Edith would be a surer protector than Arthur, she slid from his lap and running to the sofa where Edith sat, half hid herself behind her, whispering, "Send her off--send her off. Let me stay with you!"

Edith was fearful that Nina's presence might interfere with the story she meant to hear, but she could not find it in her heart to send away the little girl clinging so fondly to her, and to Phillis she said, "She may stay this once, I am sure. I will answer for her good behavior."

"'Taint that--'taint that," muttered Phillis, jerking herself from the room, "but how's the disgrace to be kep' ef everybody sees her."

"Disgrace!" and Edith glanced inquiringly at Arthur.

She could not believe that Nina was any disgrace, and she asked what Phillis meant. Crossing the room Arthur sat down upon the sofa with Nina between himself and Edith, who was pleased to see that he wound his arm around the young girl as if she were dear to him, notwithstanding her disgrace. Like a child Nina played with his watch chain, his coat buttons, and his fingers, apparently oblivious to what was passing about her. She only felt that she was where she wished to be, and knowing that he could say before her what he pleased without the least danger of her comprehending a word, Arthur, much to Edith's surprise, began:

"You have seen Nina, Miss Hastings. You know what is the mystery at Grassy Spring--the mystery about which the villagers are beginning to gossip, so Phillis says, but now that you have seen, now that you know she is here, I care not for the rest. The keenest pang is over and I am beginning already to feel better. Concealment is not in accordance with my nature, and it has worn on me terribly. Years ago you knew OF Nina; it is due to you now that you know WHO she is, and why her destiny is linked to mine. Listen, then, while I tell you her sad story."

"But SHE," interrupted Edith, pointing to Nina, whose blue eyes were turned to Arthur. "Will it not be better to wait? Won't she understand?"

"Not a word," he replied. "She's amusing herself, you see, with my buttons, and when these fail, I'll give her my drawing pencil, or some one of the numerous playthings I always keep in my pocket for her. She seldom comprehends what we say and never remembers it. This is one of the peculiar phases of her insanity."

"Poor child," said Edith, involuntarily caressing Nina, who smiled up in her face, and leaning her head upon her shoulder, continued her play with the buttons.

Meanwhile Arthur sat lost in thought, determining in his own mind how much he should tell Edith of Nina, and how much withhold. He could not tell her all, even though he knew that by keeping back a part, much of his past conduct would seem wholly inexplicable, but he could not help it, and when at last he saw that Edith was waiting for him, he pressed his hands a moment against his heart to stop its violent beating, and drawing a long, long sigh, began the story.

CHAPTER XVI.
ARTHUR'S STORY.

"I must commence at the beginning," he said, "and tell you first of Nina's father--Ernest Bernard, of Florida. I was a load of fourteen when I met him in Richmond, Virginia, which you know as my former home. He was spending a few weeks there, and dined one day with my guardian, with whom I was then living. I did not fancy him at all. He seemed even to me, a boy, like a bad, unprincipled man, and I afterward learned that such had been his former character, though at the time I knew him he had reformed in a great measure. He was very kind indeed to me, and as I became better acquainted with him my prejudices gradually wore away, until at last I liked him very much, and used to listen with delight to the stories he told of his Florida home, and of his little, golden-haired Nina, always finishing his remarks concerning he with, 'But you can't have her, boy. Nobody can marry Nina. Had little Miggie lived you might, perhaps, have been my son-in-law, but you can't as 'tis, for Nina will never marry.'"

"No, Nina can never marry;" and the golden curls shook decidedly, as the Nina in question repeated the words, "Miggie can marry Arthur, but not Nina, no--no!"

Edith blushed painfully, and averted her eyes, while Arthur continued:

"During Mr. Bernard's stay in Richmond he was attacked with that loathsome disease the small pox, and deserted by all his friends, was in a most deplorable condition, when I, who had had the varioloid, begged and obtained permission to nurse him, which I did as well as I was able, staying by him until the danger was over. How far I was instrumental to his recovery I cannot say. He professed to think I saved his life, and was profuse in his protestations of gratitude. He was very impulsive and conceived for me a friendship which ended only with his death. At all events he proved as much by the great trust eventually reposed in me," and he nodded toward Nina, who having tired of the buttons and the chain, was busy now with the bunch of keys she had purloined from his pocket.

"I was in delicate health," said Arthur, "and as the cold weather was coming on, he insisted upon taking me home with him, and I accordingly accompanied him to Florida--to Sunny-bank, his country seat. It was a grand old place, shaded by magnolias and surrounded by a profusion of vines and flowering shrubs, but the most beautiful flower of all was NINA, then eleven years age."

Nina knew that he was praising her--that Edith sanctioned the praise, and with the same feeling the little child experiences when told that it is good, she smiled upon Arthur, who, smoothing her round white check, went on:

"My sweet Florida rose, I called her, and many a romping frolic we had together during the winter months, and many a serious talk, too, we had of her second mother; her own she did not remember, and of her sister Miggie whose grave we often visited, strewing it with flowers and watering it with tears, for Nina's attention for her lost sister was so touching that I often wept with her over Miggie's grave."

"Miggie ISN'T dead," said Nina. "She's here, ain't you Miggie?" and she nestled closer to Edith, who was growing strangely interested in that old house, shaded with magnolias, and in the grave of that little child.

"I came home in the spring," said Arthur, going on with the story Nina had interrupted, "but I kept up a boyish correspondence with Nina, though my affection for her gradually weakened. After becoming a pupil in Geneva Academy, I was exceedingly ambitious, and to stand first in my class occupied more of my thoughts than Nina Bernard. Still, when immediately after I entered Geneva College as a sophomore, I learned that her father intended sending her to the seminary in that village, I was glad, and when I saw her again all my old affection for her returned with ten-fold vigor, and the ardor of my passion was greatly increased from the fact that other youths of my age worshipped her too, toasting the Florida rose, and quoting her on all occasions. GRISWOLD was one of these. Dr. Griswold. How deep his feelings were, I cannot tell. I only know that he has never married, and he is three years older than myself. We were room-mates in college, and when he saw that Nina's preference was for me, he acted the part of a noble, disinterested friend. Few know Griswold as he is."

Arthur paused, and Edith fancied he was living over the past when Nina was not as she was now, but alas, he was thinking what to tell her next. Up to this point he had narrated the facts just as they had occurred, but he could do so no longer. He must leave out now--evade, go round the truth, and it was hard for him to do so.

"We were engaged," he began at last. "I was eighteen, she fifteen. But she looked quite as old as she does now. Indeed, she was almost as far in advance of her years as she is now behind them. Still we had no idea of marriage until I had been graduated, although Nina's confidential friend, who was quite romantic, suggested that we should run away. But from this I shrank as a most foolish act, which, if divulged, would result in my being expelled, and this disgrace I could not endure. In order, however, to make the matter sure, I wrote to her father, asking for his daughter when I became of age. Very impatiently I waited for his answer, which, when it came, was a positive refusal, yet couched in language so kind that none save a fool would have been angry.

"'Nina could not marry,' he said, 'and I must break the engagement at once. Sometime he would tell me why, but not then--not till I was older.'"

Accompanying this was a note to Nina, in which he used rather severer terms, forbidding her to think of marriage, and telling her he was coming immediately to take her to Europe, whither he had long contemplated going.

There was another pause, and a long blank was made in the story, which Arthur at last resumed, as follows:

"He came for her sooner than we anticipated, following close upon the receipt of his letter, and in spite of Nina's tears took her with him to New York, from whence early in May they started for Europe. That was nine years ago next month, and during the vacation following I came to Shannondale and saw you, Edith, while you saw Nina's picture."

Nina was apparently listening now, and turning to him she said, "Tell her about the night when I stepped on your back and so got out of the window."

Arthur's face was crimson, but he answered laughingly "I fear Miggie will not think us very dignified, if I tell her of all our stolen interviews and the means used to procure them."

Taking a new toy from his pocket he gave it to Nina, who, while examining it, forgot THAT NIGHT, and he went on.

"I come now to the saddest part of my story. Nina and I continued to write, for her father did not forbid that, stipulating, however, that he should see the letters which passed between us. He had placed her in a school at Paris, where she remained until after I was graduated and of age. Edith," and Arthur's voice trembled, "I was too much a boy to know the nature of my feelings toward Nina when we were engaged, and as the time wore on my love began to wane."

Edith's heart beat more naturally now than it had before since the narrative commenced, but she could not forbear from saying to him, reproachfully, "Oh, Arthur."

"It was wrong, I know," he replied, "and I struggled against it with all my strength, particularly when I heard that she was coming home. Griswold knew everything, and he suggested that a sight of her might awaken the olden feeling, and with a feverish anxiety I waited in Boston for the steamer which I supposed was to bring her home. After many delays she came in a sailing vessel, but came alone. Her father had died upon the voyage and been buried in the sea, leaving her with no friend save a Mr. Hudson, whose acquaintance they had made in Paris."

At the mention of Mr. Hudson the toy dropped from Nina's fingers and the blue eyes flashed up into Edith's face with a more rational expression than she had heretofore observed in them.

"What is it, darling?" she asked, as she saw there was something Nina would say.

The lip quivered like that of a grieved child, while Nina answered softly, "I did love Charlie better than Arthur, and it was so wicked."

"Yes," rejoined Arthur quickly, "Nina's love for me had died away, and centered itself upon another. Charlie Hudson had sought her for his wife, and while confessing her love for him she insisted that she could not be his, because she was bound to me. This, however, did not prevent his seeking an interview with her father, who told him frankly the terrible impediment to Nina's marriage with any one. It was a crushing blow to young Hudson, but he still clung to her with all a brother's devotion, soothing her grief upon the sea, and caring for her tenderly until Boston was reached, and he placed her in my hands, together with a letter, which her father wrote a few days before he died."

"He's married now," interrupted Nina, "Charlie's married, but he came to see me once, down at the old Asylum, and I saw him through the grates, for I was shut up in a TANTRUM. He cried, Miggie, just as Arthur does sometimes, and called me POOR LOST NINA. He held an angel in his arms with blue eyes like mine, and he said she was his child and Margaret's! Her name was Nina, too. Wasn't it nice?" And she smiled upon Edith, who involuntarily groaned as she thought how dreadful it must have been for Mr. Hudson to gaze through iron bars upon the wreck of his early love.

"Poor man," she sighed, turning to Arthur. "Is he happy with his Margaret!"

"He seems to be," said Arthur, "People can outlive their first affection, you know. He resides in New York now, and is to all appearance a prosperous, happy man. The curse has fallen alone on me, who alone deserve it."

He spoke bitterly, and for a moment sat apparently thinking; then, resuming his story, said,

"I did not open Mr. Bernard's letter until we reached the Revere House, and I was alone in my room. Then I broke the seal and read, while my blood curdled within my veins and every hair pricked at its roots. The old man knew he was about to die, and confessed to me in part his manifold transgressions, particularly his inhuman treatment of his last wife, the mother of little Miggie, but as this cannot, of course, be interesting to you, I will not repeat it."

"Oh, do," exclaimed Edith, feeling somehow that anything concerning the mother of Miggie Bernard would interest her.

"Well, then," returned Arthur, "he did not tell me all the circumstances of his marriage. I only know that she was a foreigner and very beautiful--a governess, too, I think in some German family, and that he married her under an assumed name."

"An assumed name!" Edith cried. "Why was that, pray?"

"I hardly know," returned Arthur, "but believe he became in some way implicated in a fight or gambling brawl in Paris, and being threatened with arrest took another name than his own, and fled to Germany or Switzerland, where he found his wife. They were married privately, and after two or three years he brought her to his Florida home, where his proud mother and maiden sister affected to despise her because of her poverty. He was at that time given to drinking, and almost every day became beastly intoxicated, abusing his young wife so shamefully that her life became intolerable, and at last when he was once absent from home for a few weeks, he resolved upon going back to Europe, and leaving him forever. This plan she confided to a maid servant who had accompanied her from England, a resolute, determined woman, who arranged the whole so skillfully that no one suspected their designs until they were far on their way to New York. The old mother, who was then living, would not suffer them to be pursued, and more than a week went by ere Mr. Bernard learned what had occurred. He followed them of course. He was man enough for that, but falling in with some of his boon companions, almost as soon as he reached the city, he drank so deeply that for several days he was unable to search for them, and in that time both his wife and Miggie died."

"Oh, Mr. St. Claire," and Edith's eyes filled with tears.

"Yes, both of them died," he continued. "Mrs. Bernard's health was greatly undermined by sorrow, and when a prevailing epidemic fastened itself upon her, it found an easy prey. The waiting-maid wrote immediately to Florida, and her letter was sent back to Mr. Bernard, who, having become sobered, hastened at once to find her place of abode. She was a very intelligent woman for one of her class, and had taken the precaution to have the remains of her late mistress and child deposited in such a manner that they could easily be removed if Mr. Bernard should so desire it. He did desire it, and the bodies were taken undisturbed to Florida, where they now rest quietly, side by side with the proud mother and sister, since deceased. After this Mr. Bernard became a changed and better man, weeping often over the fate of his young girl-wife and his infant daughter, whom he greatly loved. Other troubles he had, too, secret troubles which he confided to me in the letter brought by Mr. Hudson. After assuring me of his esteem and telling me how much he should prefer me for his son-in-law to Charlie Hudson, he added that in justice to us both he must now speak of the horrible cloud hanging over his beautiful Nina, and which was sure at last to envelop her in darkness. You can guess it, Edith. You have guessed it already--hereditary insanity--reaching far back into the past, and with each successive generation developing itself earlier and in a more violent form. He knew nothing of it when he married Nina's mother, a famous New Orleans belle, for her father purposely kept it from him, hoping thus to get her off his hands ere the malady manifested itself.

"In her case it came on with the birth of Nina, and from that day to her death she was a raving, disgusting maniac, as her mother and grandmother had been before her. This was exceedingly mortifying to the proud Bernards, negroes and all, and the utmost care was taken of Nina, who, nevertheless, was too much like her mother to hope for escape. There was the same peculiar look in the eye--the same restless, nervous motions, and from her babyhood up he knew his child was doomed to chains, straight jackets and narrow cells, while the man who married her was domed to a still more horrible fate. These were his very words, and my heart stopped its beating as I read, while I involuntarily thanked Heaven, who had changed her feelings towards me. She told me with many tears that she had ceased to love me, and asked to be released for the fulfillment of her vow. I knew then she would one day be just what she is, and did not think it my duty to insist. But I did not forsake her, though my affection for her then was more like a brother's than a lover's. In his will, which was duly made and witnessed, Mr. Bernard appointed me the guardian of his child, empowering me to do for her as if she were my sister, and bidding me when the calamity should overtake her, care for her to the last.

"'They don't usually survive ling,' he wrote, and he made me his next heir after Nina's death. It was a great charge for one just twenty-two, a young, helpless girly and an immense fortune to look after; but Griswold, my tied friend, came to my aid, and pointed out means by which a large portion of the Bernard estate could be turned into money, and thus save me much trouble. I followed his advice, and then old homestead is all the landed property there is for me to attend to now, and as this is under the supervision of a competent overseer, it give me no uneasiness. I suggested to Nina that she should accompany me to Florida soon after her arrival in Boston, but she preferred remaining for a time in some boarding school, and I made arrangements for her to be received as a boarder in Charlestown Seminary, leaving her there while I went South to transact business incumbent upon me as her guardian.

"How it happened I never knew, but by some accident her father's letter to me became mixed up with her papers, and while I was gone she read it, learning for the first time what the mystery was which hung over her mother's fate, and also of the doom awaiting her. She fainted, it was said, and during the illness which followed raved in frantic fury, suffering no one to approach her save Griswold, who, being at that time a physician in the Lunatic Asylum at Worcester, hastened to her side, acquiring over her a singular power. It is strange that in her fits of violence she never speaks of me, nor yet of Charlie Hudson. Indeed, the past seems all a blank to her, save as she refers to it incidentally as she has to-day."

"But did she stay crazy?" asked Edith.

"Not wholly so," returned Arthur, "but from that time her reason began to fail, until now she is hopelessly insane, and has not known a rational moment for more than three years."

"Nor been home in all that time?" said Edith, while Arthur replied,

"She would not go. She seemed to shrink from meeting her former friends; and at last, acting upon Griswold's advice, I placed her in the Asylum, going myself hither and thither like a feather tossed about by the gale. Griswold was my ballast, my polar star, and when he said to me, buy a house and have a home, I answered that I would; and when he told me of Grassy Spring, bidding me purchase it, I did so, although I dreaded coming to this neighborhood of all others. I had carefully kept everything from Grace, who, while hearing that I was in some way interested in a Florida estate, knew none of the particulars, and I became morbidly jealous lest she or anyone else should hear of Nina's misfortune, or what she was to me.

"It was a favorite idea of Griswold's that Nina might be benefited by a change of place, and when I first came here I knew that she, too, would follow me in due time. She has hitherto been subject to violent attacks of frenzy, during which nothing within her reach was safe; and, knowing this, Griswold advised me to prepare a room, where, at such times, she could be kept by herself, for the sight of people always made her worse. The Den, with the large closet adjoining, was the result of this suggestion, and as I have a great dread of neighborhood gossip, I resolved to say nothing of her until compelled to do so by her presence in the house. I fancied that Mrs. Johnson was a discreet woman, and my purpose was to tell her of Nina as soon as I was fairly settled; but she abused her trust by letting Grace into the room. You refused to enter, and my respect for you from that moment was unbounded."

She looked at him in much surprise, and he added,

"You wonder, I suppose, how I know this. I was here at the time, was in the next room when you came into the library to wait for Grace. I watched you through the glass door, wondering who you were, until my cousin appeared and I overheard the whole."

"And that is why you chose me instead of Grace to take charge of your keys," interrupted Edith, beginning to comprehend what had heretofore been strange to her. "But, Mr. St. Claire, I don't understand it at all--don't see why there was any need for so much secrecy. Supposing you did dread neighborhood gossip, you could not help being chosen Nina's guardian. She could not help being crazy. Why not have told at once that there was such a person under your charge? Wouldn't it have been better? It was no disgrace to you that you have kept the father's trust, and cared for his poor child," and she glanced lovingly at the pretty face nestled against her arm, for Nina had fallen asleep.

Arthur did not answer immediately, and when he did, his voice trembled with emotion.

"It would have been better," he said; "but when she first became insane, I shrank from having it generally known, and the longer I hugged the secret the harder I found it to divulge the whole. It would look queerly, I thought, for a young man like me to be tramelled with a crazy girl. Nobody would believe she was my ward, and nothing more, and I became a sort of monomaniac upon the subject. Had I never loved her--" he paused, and leaned his head upon his hands, while Edith, bending upon him a most searching look, startled him with the words, "Mr. St. Claire, you have not told me all. There is something behind, something mightier than pride or a dread of gossip."

"Yes, Edith, there is something behind, but I can't tell YOU what it is, you of all others."

He was pacing the floor hurriedly now, but stopped suddenly, and standing before Edith, said: "Edith Hastings, you are somewhat to blame in this matter. Before I knew you I only shrank from having people talk of my matters sooner than was absolutely necessary. But after you became my pupil, the desire that you should never see Nina as she is, grew into a species of madness, and I have bent every energy to keeping you apart. I did not listen to reason, which told me you must know of it sooner or later, but plunged deeper and deeper into a labyrinth of attempted concealment. When I found it necessary to dismiss Mrs. Johnson, if I would keep my affairs to myself, I thought of the old family servants at Sunnybank. I knew they loved and pitied Nina, and were very sensitive with regard to her misfortune. It touches Phillis' pride to think her young mistress is crazy, and as hers is the ruling mind, she keeps the others in subjection, though old Judy came near disclosing the whole to you at one time, I believe. You know her sad story now, but you do not know how like an iron weight it hangs upon me, crushing me to the earth, wearing my life away, and making me old before my time. See here," and lifting his brown locks, he showed her many a line of silver. "If I loved Nina Bernard, my burden would be easier to bear."

"Oh, Mr. St. Claire," interrupted Edith, "You surely do love her. You cannot help loving her, and she so beautiful, so innocent."

"Yes," he answered, "as a brother loves an unfortunate sister. I feel towards her, I think, as a mother does towards a helpless child, a tender pity which prompts me to bear with her even when she tries me almost beyond endurance. She is not always as mild as you see her now, though her frenzied moods do not occur as frequently as they did. She loves me, I think, as an infant loves its mother, and is better when I am with her. At all events, since coming to Grassy Spring, she has been unusually quiet, until within the last two weeks, when a nervous fever has confined her to her room and made her somewhat unmanagable. Griswold said she would be better here, and though I had not much faith in the experiment, I see now that he was right. Griswold is always right, and had I followed his advice years ago, much of my trouble might have been averted. Edith, never conceal a single act, if you wish to be happy. A little fault, if covered up, grows into a mountain; and the longer it is hidden, the harder it is to be confessed. This is my experience. There was a false step at first, and it lies too far back in the past to be remedied now. No one knows of it but myself, Griswold, Nina, and my God. Yes, there IS one more whose memory might be refreshed, but I now have no fear of him."

Edith did not ask who this other was, neither did she dream that Richard Harrington was in any way connected with the mystery. She thought of him, however, wondering if she might tell him of Nina, and asking if she could.

Arthur's face was very white, as he replied, "Tell him if you like, or any one else. It is needless to keep it longer, but, Edith, you'll come again, won't you? come to see Nina if nothing more. I am glad you have seen her, provided you do not desert me wholly."

"Of course I shall not," she said, as she laid the golden head of the sleeping girl upon the cushion of the sofa, preparatory to leaving, "I'll come again, and forgive you, too, for anything you may have done, except a wrong to her," and she carefully kissed the poor, crazy Nina.

Then, offering her hand to Arthur she tried to bid him good-bye as of old, but he missed something in her manner, and with feelings sadly depressed he watched her from the window, as, assisted by Ike, she mounted her pony and galloped swiftly away.

"She's lost to me forever, and there's nothing worth living for now," he said, just as a little hand pressed his arm, and a sweet childish voice murmured, "Yes, there is, Arthur. Live for Nina, poor Nina," and the snowy fingers, which, for a moment, had rested lightly on his arm, began to play with the buttons of his coat, while the soft blue eyes looted pleadingly into his.

"Yes, darling; he said, caressing her flowing curls, and pushing them back from her forehead, "I will live for you, hereafter. I will love no one else."

"No one but Miggie. You MAY love her. You must love her, Arthur. She's so beautiful, so grand, why has she gone from Nina, I want her here, want her all the time;" and Nina's mood began to change.

Tears filled her eyes, and burying her face in Arthur's bosom she begged him to go after Miggie, to bring her. back and keep her there always, threatening that if he did'nt "Nina would be bad."

Tenderly, but firmly, as a parent soothes a refractory child, did Arthur soothe the excitable Nina, telling her Miggie should come again, or if she did not, they'd go up and see her.

CHAPTER XVII.
NINA AND MIGGIE.

It would be impossible to describe Edith's feelings as she rode toward home. She knew Arthur had not told her the whole, and that the part omitted was the most important of all. What could it be? She thought of a thousand different things, but dismissed them one after another from her mind as too preposterous to be cherished for a moment. The terrible reality never once occurred to her, else her heart had not beaten as lightly as it did, in spite of the strange story she had heard. She was glad that she had met with Nina--glad that every obstacle to their future intercourse was removed--and while she censured Arthur much she pitied him the more and scolded herself heartily for feeling so comfortable and satisfied because he had ceased to love the unfortunate Nina.

"I can't blame him for not wishing to be talked about," she said. "Shannondale IS a horribly gossipping place, and people would have surmised everything; but the sooner they know it now the sooner it will die away. Let me think. Who will be likely to spread the news most industriously?"

Suddenly remembering Mrs. Eliakim Rogers, the busiest gossip in town, she turned Bedouin in the direction of the low brown house, standing at a little distance from the road, and was soon seated in Mrs. Eliakim's kitchen, her ostensible errand being to inquire about some plain sewing the good lady was doing for her, while her real object was to communicate as much of Arthur's story as she thought proper. Incidentally she spoke of Mr. St. Claire, and when the widow asked "What under the sun possessed him to live as he did," she replied by telling of NINA, his ward, who, she said, had recently come to Grassy Spring from the Asylum, adding a few items as to how Arthur chanced to be her guardian, talking as if she had known of it all the time, and saying she did not wonder that a young man like him should shrink from having it generally understood that he had a crazy girl upon his hands. He was very kind to her indeed, and no brother could treat his sister more tenderly than he treated Nina.

To every thing she said, Mrs. Eliakim smilingly assented, drawing her own conclusions the while and feeling vastly relieved when, at last, her visitor departed, leaving her at liberty to don her green calash and start for the neighbors with this precious morsel of gossip. Turning back, Edith saw her hurrying across the fields, and knew it would not be long ere all Shannondale were talking of Arthur's ward.

Arrived at home she found the dinner waiting for her, and when asked by Richard what had kept her she replied by repeating to him in substance what she had already told Mrs. Eliakim Rogers. There was this difference however, between the two stories--the one told to Richard was longer and contained more of the particulars. She did not, however, tell him of Arthur's love for Nina, or of the neglected wife, the mother of little Miggie, though why she withheld that part of the story she could not tell. She felt a strange interest in that young mother dying alone in the noisome city, and in the little child buried upon her bosom, but she had far rather talk of Nina and her marvellous beauty, feeling sure that she had at least one interested auditor, Victor, who was perfectly delighted to have the mystery of Grassy Spring unravelled, though he felt a little disappointed that it should amount to nothing more than a crazy girl, to whom Mr. St. Claire was guardian.

This feeling of Victor was in a great measure shared by the villagers, and, indeed, after a day or two of talking and wondering, the general opinion seemed to be that Arthur had magnified the evil and been altogether too much afraid of Madam Rumor, who was inclined to be rather lenient toward him, particularly as Edith Hastings took pains to tell how kind he was to Nina, who gave him oftentimes so much trouble. The tide of popular feeling was in his favor, and the sympathy which many openly expressed for him was like a dagger to the young man, who knew he did not deserve it. Still he was relieved of a great burden, and was far happier than he had been before, and even signified to Grace his willingness to mingle in society and see company at his own house. The consequence of this was throngs of visitors at Grassy Spring, said visitors always asking for Mr. St. Claire, but caring really to see Nina, who shrank from their advances, and hiding herself in her room refused at last to go down unless Miggie were there.

MIGGIE had purposely absented herself from Grassy Spring more than two whole weeks, and when Richard asked the cause of it she answered that she did not know, and, indeed, she could not to herself define the reason of her staying so long from a place where she wished so much to be, unless it were that she had not quite recovered from the shock it gave her to know that Arthur had once been engaged, even though he had wearied of the engagement. It seemed to her that he had built between them a barrier which she determined he should be the first to cross. So she studiously avoided him, and thus unconsciously plunged him deeper and deeper into the mire, where he was already foundering. Her apparent indifference only increased the ardor of his affection, and though he struggled against it as against a deadly sin, he could not overcome it, and at last urged on by Nina, who begged so hard for Miggie, he resolved upon going to Collingwood and taking Nina with him.

It was a warm, pleasant afternoon in May, and Nina had never looked more beautiful than when seated in the open carriage, and on her way to Collingwood, talking incessantly of Miggie, whom she espied long before they reached the house. It was a most joyful meeting between the two young girls, Nina clinging to Edith as if fearful of losing her again, if by chance she should release her hold.

Arthur did not tell Edith how much he had missed her, but Nina did, and when she saw the color deepen on Edith's cheeks she added, "You love him, don't you, Miggie?"

"I love every body, I hope," returned the blushing Edith, as she led her guests into the room where Richard was sitting.

At sight of the blind man Nina started, and clasping her hands together, stood regarding him fixedly, while a look of perplexity deepened upon her face.

"Speak to her, Edith," whispered Arthur, but ere Edith could comply with his request, Nina's lips parted and she said, "YOU DID DO IT, DIDN'T YOU?"

"Whose voice was that?" and Richard started forward.

It's Nina, Mr. Harrington; pretty Nina Bernard; and Edith came to the rescue.

"She has a sweet, familiar voice," said Richard, "Come to me, little one, will you?"

He evidently thought her a child, for in her statement Edith had not mentioned her age, and Richard had somehow received the impression that she was very young. It suited Nina to be thus addressed, and she went readily to Richard, who pressed her soft, warm hands, and then telling her playfully that he wished to know how she looked, passed his own hand slowly over her face and hair, caressing the latter and twining one of the curls around his fingers; then, winding his arm about her slender waist, he asked how old she was.

"FIFTEEN YEARS AND A HALF," was her prompt reply.'

Richard never thought of doubting her word. She was very slight indeed. "A little morsel," he called her, and as neither Arthur nor Edith corrected the mistake, he was suffered to think of Nina Bernard as one, who, were she rational, would be a mere school-girl yet.

She puzzled him greatly, and more than once he started at some peculiar intonation of her voice.

"Little Snowdrop," he said, at last, "it seems to me I have known you all my life. Look at me, and say if we have met before?"

Edith was too intent upon Nina's answer to notice Arthur, and she failed to see the spasm of pain and fear which passed over his face, leaving it paler than its wont. Bending over Nina he waited like Edith while she scanned Richard curiously, and then replied, "Never, UNLESS YOU ARE THE ONE THAT DID IT--are you?"

"Did what?" asked Richard, and while Nina hesitated, Arthur replied, "She has a fancy that somebody made her crazy."

"Not I, oh, no, not I, poor little dove. I did not do it, sure," and Richard smoothed the yellow curls resting on his knee.

"Who was it, then?" persisted Nina. "He was tall, like you, and dark and handsome, wasn't he Arthur? You know--you were there?" and she turned appealingly to the young man, whose heart beat so loudly as to be plainly audible to himself.

"It was Charlie Hudson, perhaps," suggested Edith, and Arthur mentally blessed her for a remark which turned the channel of Nina's thoughts, and set her to telling Richard how Charlie cried when he saw her through the iron bars, wearing that queer-looking gown.

"I danced for him with all my might," she said, "and sang so loud, for I thought it would make him laugh as it did the folks around me, but he only cried the harder. What made him?" and she looked up wistfully in Richard's face. "YOU are crying, too!" she exclaimed. "Everybody cries where I am. Why do they? I wish they wouldn't. I'm good to-day--there, please don't, Mr. Big-man, THAT DID DO IT,"?

and raising her waxen hand she brushed away the tear trembling on Richard's long eyelashes.

Edith now sought to divert her by asking if she were fond of music, and would like to hear her play,

"Nina'll play," returned the little maiden, and going to the piano she dashed off a wild, impassioned, mixed-up impromptu, resembling now the soft notes of the lute or the plaintive sob of the winter wind, and then swelling into a full, rich, harmonious melody, which made the blood chill in Edith's veins, and caused both Richard and Arthur to hold their breath.

This music ceased, and rising from the stool Nina expressed a desire to go home, insisting that Edith should go with her and stay all night.

"I want to sleep with my arms around your neck just like you used to do," she said; and when Arthur, too, joined in the request, Edith answered that she would if Richard were willing.

"And sleep with a lunatic,--is it quite safe?" he asked.

"Perfectly so," returned Arthur, adding that the house was large enough, and Edith could act her own pleasure with regard to sleeping apartments.

"Then it's settled that I may go," chimed in Edith, quite as much delighted at the prospect of a long evening with Arthur, as with the idea of seeing more of Nina.

She knew she was leaving Richard very lonely, but she promised to be home early on the morrow, and bidding good-bye, followed Arthur and Nina to the carriage.

Nina was delighted to have Edith with her, and after their arrival at Grassy Spring, danced and skipped about the house like a gay butterfly, pausing every few moments to wind her arms around the neck of her guest, whom she kissed repeatedly, calling her always MIGGIE, and telling her how much she loved her.

"Don't you want to see YOU as you used to be?" she asked suddenly. "If you do, come up,--come to my room. She may?" and she turned toward Arthur, who answered, "certainly, I will go myself," and the three soon stood at the door of the DEN.

It was Edith's first visit there, and a feeling of awe came over her as she crossed the threshold of the mysterious room. Then a cry of joyful surprise burst from her lips as she saw how pleasant it was in there, and how tastefully the chamber was fitted up. Not another apartment in the house could compare with it, and Edith felt that she could be happy there all her life, were it not for the iron lattice, which gave it somewhat the appearance of a prison.

"Here you are," cried Nina, dragging her across the floor to the portrait of the little child which had so interested her during Arthur's absence. "This is she--this is you,--this is Miggie," and Nina jumped up and down, while Edith gazed again upon the sweet baby face she had once seen in the drawing-room.

"There is a slight resemblance between you," said Arthur, glancing from one to the other, "Had she lived, her eyes must have been like yours; but look, this was Nina's father."

Edith did not answer him. Indeed, she scarcely knew what he was saying, for a nameless fascination chained her to the spot, a feeling as if she were beholding her other self, as if she had leaped backward many years, and was seated again upon the nursery floor like the child before her. Like gleams of lightning, confused memories of the past came rushing over her only to pass away, leaving her in deeper darkness. One thought, however, like a blinding flash caused her brain to reel, while she grasped Arthur's arm, exclaiming, "Are you sure the baby died--sure she was buried with her mother?"

"Yes, perfectly sure," was Arthur's reply, and with the sensation of disappointment, Edith turned at last from Miggie to the contemplation of the father; the Mr. Bernard whom she was not greatly disposed to like.

He was a portly, handsome man, but his face showed traces of early debauchery and later dissipation. Still, Edith was far more interested in him than in the portrait of Nina's mother, the light-haired, blue-eyed woman, so much like the daughter that the one could easily be recognized from it a resemblance to the other.

"Where is the second Mrs. Bernard's picture?" she asked, and Arthur answered, "It was never taken, but Phillis declares YOU are like her, and this accounts for Nina's pertinacity in calling you Miggie."

The pictures were by this time duly examined, and then Nina, still playing the part of hostess, showed to Edith every thing of the least interest until she came to the door, leading into the large square closet.

"Open it, please," she whispered to Arthur. "Let Miggie see where Nina stays when she tears."

Arthur unlocked the door, and Edith stepped with a shudder into the solitary cell which had witnessed more than one wild revel, and echoed to more than one delirious shriek.

"Is it necessary?" she asked, and Arthur replied: "We think so; otherwise she would demolish every thing within her reach, and throw herself from the window it may be."

"THAT'S SO," said Nina, nodding approvingly. "When I'm bad, I have to tear. It cures my head, and I'm so strong then, that it takes Phillis and Arthur both to put that gown on me. I can't tear that," and she pointed to a loose sacque-like garment, made of the heaviest possible material, and hanging upon a nail near the door of the cell.

"Have you been shut up since you came here?" Edith inquired, and Nina rejoined. "Once; didn't you hear me scream?" Phillis tried to make me quit, but I told her I wouldn't unless they'd let you come. I saw you on the walk, you know. I'm better with you, Miggie; a heap better since you made me cry. It took a world of hardness and pain away, and my head has not ached a single time since then. I'm most well; ain't I, Arthur."

"Miss Hastings certainly has a wonderful influence over you," returned Arthur, and as the evening wore away, Edith began to think so, too.

Even the servants commented upon the change in Nina, who appeared so natural and lady-like, that once there darted across Arthur's mind the question, "what if her reason SHOULD be restored! I will do right, Heaven helping me," he moaned mentally, for well he knew that Nina sane would require of him far different treatment from what Nina crazy did. It was late that night when they parted, he to his lonely room where for hours he paced the floor with feverish disquiet, while Edith went from choice with Nina to the DEN, determined to share her single bed, and smiling at her own foolishness when once a shadow of fear crept into her heart. How could she be afraid of the gentle creature, who, in her snowy night dress, with her golden hair falling about her face and neck, looked like some beautiful angel flitting about the room, pretending to arrange this and that, casting half bashful glances at Edith, who was longer in disrobing and at last, as if summoning all her courage for the act, stepping behind the thin lace window curtains, which she drew around her, saying softly, "don't look at me, Miggie, will you, 'cause I'm going to pray."

Instantly the brush which Edith held was stayed amid her raven hair, and the hot tears rained over her face as she listened to that prayer, that God would keep Nina from TEARING any more, and not let Arthur cry, but make it all come right some time with him and Miggie, too. Then followed that simple petition, "now I lay me down to sleep," learned at the mother's knee by so many thousand children whose graves like hillocks in the church-yard lie, and when she arose and came from behind the gauzy screen where she fancied she had been hidden from view, Edith was not wrong in thinking that something like the glory of Heaven shone upon her pure white brow. All dread of her was gone, and when Sophy came in, offering to sleep upon the floor as was her usual custom, she promptly declined, for she would rather be alone with Nina.

Edith had never been intimate with any girl of her own age, and to her it was a happiness entirely new, she nestling down in the narrow bed with a loved companion whose arms wound themselves caressingly around her neck, and whose lips touched hers many times, whispering, "Bless you, Miggie, bless you, precious sister, you can't begin to guess how much I love you. Neither can I tell you. Why, it would take me till morning."

It became rather tiresome after a time being kept awake, and fearing lest she WOULD talk till morning, Edith said to her,

"I shall go home if you are not more quiet."

There was something in Edith's voice which prompted the crazy girl to obey, and with one more assurance of love she turned to her pillow, and Edith knew by her soft, regular breathing, that her troubles were forgotten.

"I hardly think you'll care to repeat the experiment again," Arthur said to Edith next morning, when he met her at the table, and saw that she looked rather weary. "Nina, I fear, was troublesome, as Sophy tells me she often is."

Edith denied Nina's having troubled her much. Still she felt that she preferred her own cozy bed-chamber to Nina's larger, handsomer room, and would not promise to spend another night at Grassy Spring, although she expressed her willingness to resume her drawing lessons, and suggested that Nina, too, should become a pupil. Arthur would much rather have had Edith all to himself, for he knew that Nina's presence would be a restraint upon him, but it was right, and he consented as the only means of having Edith back again in her old place, fancying that when he had her there it would be the same as before. But he was mistaken, for when the lessons were resumed, he found there was something between them,-- something which absorbed Edith's mind, and was to him a constant warning and rebuke. Did he bend so near Edith at her task, that his brown locks touched her blacker braids, a shower of golden curls was sure to mingle with the twain, as Nina also bent her down to see what he was looking at. Did the hand which sometimes guided Edith's pencil ever retain the fingers longer than necessary, a pair of deep blue eyes looked into his, not reproachfully, for Nina could not fathom the meaning of what she saw, but with an expression of childlike trust and confidence far more potent than frowns and jealous tears would have been. Nina was in Arthur's way, but not in Edith's, and half the pleasure she experienced now in going to Grassy Spring, was derived from the fact that she thus saw more of Nina than she would otherwise have done. It was a rare and beautiful sight, the perfect love existing between these two young girls, Edith seeming the elder, inasmuch as she was the taller and more self-reliant of the two. As a mother watches over and loves her maimed infant, so did Edith guard and cherish Nina, possessing over her so much power that a single look from her black eyes was sufficient to quiet at once the little lady, who, under the daily influence of her society visibly improved both in health and spirits.

CHAPTER XVIII.
DR. GRISWOLD.

Still Nina's mind was enshrouded in as deep a gloom as ever, and Dr. Griswold, who, toward the latter part of June, came to see her, said it would be so always. There was no hope of her recovery, and with his olden tenderness of manner he caressed his former patient, sighing as he thought of the weary life before her. For two days Dr. Griswold remained at Grassy Spring, learning in that time much how matters stood. He saw Edith Hastings,-- scanned with his clear, far-reaching eye every action of Arthur St. Claire, and when at last his visit was ended, and Arthur was walking with him to the depot, he said abruptly, "I am sorry for you, St. Claire; more sorry than I ever was before, but you know the path of duty and you must walk in it, letting your eyes stray to neither side, lest they fall upon forbidden fruit."

Arthur made no reply save to kick the gnarled roots of the tree under which they had stopped for a few moments.

"Edith Hastings is very beautiful!" Dr. Griswold remarked suddenly, and as if SHE had just entered his mind. "Does she come often to Grassy Spring?"

"Every day," and Arthur tried to look his friend fully in the face, but could not, and his brown eyes fell as he added hastily, "she comes to see Nina; they are greatly attached."

"She HAS a wonderful power over her, I think," returned Dr. Griswold; "and I am not surprised that you esteem her highly on that account, but how will it be hereafter when other duties, other relations claim her attention. Will she not cease to visit you and so Nina made worse?"

"What new duties? What relations do you mean," Arthur asked quickly, trembling in every joint as he anticipated the answer.

"I have a fancy that Miss Hastings will reward that blind man for all his kindness with her heart and hand."

"Her hand it may be, but her heart, NEVER," interrupted Arthur, betraying by his agitation what Dr. Griswold had already guessed.

"Poor Arthur," he said, "I know what is in your mind and pity you so much, but you can resist temptation and you MUST. There's no alternative. You chose your destiny years ago--abide by it, then. Hope and pray, as I do, that Edith Hastings will be the blind man's bride."

"Oh, Griswold," and Arthur groaned aloud, "you cannot wish to sacrifice her thus!"

"I can--I do--it will save you both from ruin."

"Then you think--you DO think she loves me," and Arthur looked eagerly at his friend, who answered, "I think nothing, save that she will marry Mr. Harrington. Your cousin told me there was a rumor to that effect. She is often at Collingwood, and ought to be posted."

"Griswold, I wish I were dead," exclaimed Arthur. "Yes, I wish I were dead, and were it not that I dread the hereafter, I would end my existence at once in yonder river," and he pointed to the Chicopee, winding its slow way to the westward.

Dr. Griswold gazed at him a moment in silence, and then replied somewhat sternly, "Rather be a man and wait patiently for the future."

"I would, but for the fear that Edith will be lost to me forever," Arthur answered faintly, and Dr. Griswold replied, "Better so than lost herself. Why not be candid with her; tell her everything; go over the entire past, and if she truly loves you, she will wait, years and years if need be. She's young yet, too young to be a wife. Will you tell her?"

"I can't, I can't," and Arthur shook his head despairingly. "I have hidden the secret too long to tell it now. It might have been easy at first, but now--it's too late. Oh, Griswold, you do not understand what I suffer, for you never knew what it was to love as I love Edith Hastings." For a moment Dr. Griswold looked at him in silence. He knew how fierce a storm had gathered round him, and how bravely he had met it. He knew, too, how impetuous and ardent was his disposition, how much one of his temperament must love Edith Hastings, and he longed to speak to him a word of comfort. Smoothing the brown hair of the bowed head, and sighing to see how many threads of silver were woven in it, he said,

"I pity you so much, and can feel for you more than you suspect. You say I know not what it is to love. Oh, Arthur, Arthur. You little guessed what it cost me, years ago, to give up NINA BERNARD. It almost broke my heart, and the wound is bleeding yet! Could the past be undone; could we stand where we did that night which both remember so well, I would hold you back; and Nina, crazy as she is, should this moment be mine--mine to love, to cherish, to care for and weep over when she is dead. Poor little unfortunate Nina--my darling--my idol--my clipped-wing bird!"

It was Dr. Griswold's voice which trembled now, and Arthur's which essayed to comfort him.

"I never dreamed of this," he said. "I knew you, with others, had a liking for her, but you relinquished her so willingly, I could not guess you loved her so well," and in his efforts to soothe his friend, Arthur forgot his own sorrow in part.

It was time now for the Dr. to go, as the smoke of the coming train was visible over the hills. "You need not accompany me further," he said, offering his hand to Arthur, who pressed it in silence, and then walked slowly back to Grassy Spring.

Those were terrible days which followed the visit of Dr. Griswold, for to see Edith Hastings often was a danger he dared not incur, while to avoid her altogether was utterly impossible, and at last resolving upon a change of scene as his only hope, he one morning astonished Grace with the announcement that he was going South, and it might be many weeks ere he returned.

Since coming to that neighborhood, Arthur had been a puzzle to Grace, and she watched him now in amazement, as he paced the floor, giving her sundry directions with regard to Nina, and telling her where a letter would find him in case she should be sick, and require his personal attention. It was in vain that Grace expostulated with him upon what seemed to her a foolish and uncalled-for journey. He was resolved, and saying he should not probably see Edith ere his departure, he left his farewell with her.

Once he thought of bidding her encourage Edith to marry the blind man, but he could not quite bring himself to this. Edith was dearer to him now than when she promised him that if Richard sought her hand she would not tell him no, and he felt that he would rather she should die than be thus sacrificed. Anxiously Grace looked after him as he walked rapidly away, thinking within herself that long association with Nina had impaired his reason. And Arthur was more than half insane. Not until now had he been wholly roused to the reality of his position. Dr. Griswold had rent asunder the flimsy veil, showing him how hopeless was his love for Edith, and so, because he could not have her, he must go away. It was a wise decision, and he was strengthened to keep it in spite of Nina's tears that he should stay.

"Nina'll die, or somebody'll die, I know," and the little girl clung sobbing to his neck, when the hour of parting came.

Very gently he unclasped her clinging arms; very tenderly he kissed her lips, bidding her give one to Miggie, and then he left her, turning back ere he reached the gate, as a new idea struck him. Would NINA go with him; go to her Florida home, if so he would defer his journey a day or so. He wondered he had not thought of this before. It would save him effectually, and he anxiously waited her answer.

"If Miggie goes I will, but not without."

This was Nina's reply, and Arthur turned a second time away.

In much surprise, Edith, who came that afternoon, heard of Arthur's departure.

"Why did he go without bidding me good-bye?" she asked.

"I don't know, but he left a kiss for you right on my lips," said Nina, putting up her rosebud mouth for Edith to take what was unquestionably her own.

While they were thus talking together, the door bell rang, and Soph, who answered the ring, admitted Dr. Griswold.

"Dr. Griswold here again so soon!" exclaimed Edith, a suspicion crossing her mind that Arthur had arranged for him to take charge of Nina during his absence. "But it shall not be," she thought, "I can prevent her returning to the Asylum, and I will."

She might have spared herself all uneasiness, for Dr. Griswold knew nothing of Arthur's absence, and seemed more surprised than she had been.

"I am so glad, so glad," he said; and when Edith looked inquiringly at him, he answered, "I am glad because it is right that he should go."

Edith did not in the least comprehend his meaning, and as he manifested no intention to explain, the conversation soon turned upon other topics than Arthur and his sudden journey. Since Arthur's visit to Worcester, Dr. Griswold had heard nothing from him, and impelled by one of those strange influences which will sometimes lead a person on to his fate, he had come up to Shannondale partly to see how matters stood and partly to whisper a word of encouragement to one who needed it so much. He had never been very robust or strong; the secret which none save Arthur knew had gradually undermined his health, and he was subject to frequent attacks of what he called his nervous headaches. The slightest cause would sometimes induce one of these, and when on the morning after his arrival at Grassy Spring he awoke from a troubled sleep he knew by certain unmistakable signs that a day of suffering was in store for him. This on his own account he would not have minded particularly, for he was accustomed to it, but his presence was needed at home; and the knowledge of this added to the intensity of his pain, which became so great that to rise from his pillow was impossible, and Soph, when sent to his room to announce that breakfast was waiting, reported him to her mother as "mighty sick with blood in the face."

All the day long he lay in the darkened room, sometimes dreaming, sometimes moaning, and watching through his closed eyes the movements of Nina, who had constituted herself his nurse, treading on tiptoe across the floor, whispering to herself, and apparently carrying on an animated conversation with some imaginary personage. Softly, she bathed his aching head, asking every moment if he were better, and going once behind the door where he heard her praying that "God would make the good doctor well."

Blessed Nina, there was far more need for this prayer than she supposed, for when the next day came, the pain and heat about the eyes and head were not in the least abated, and a physician was called, who pronounced the symptoms to be those of typhoid fever. With a stifled moan, Dr. Griswold turned upon his pillow, while his great, unselfish heart went out after his poor patients in the Asylum, who would miss him so much. Three days passed away, and it was generally known in the village that a stranger lay sick of typhus fever at Grassy Spring, which with common consent was shunned as if the deadly plague had been rioting there. Years before the disease had raged with fearful violence in the town, and many a fresh mound was reared in the graveyard, and many a hearth-stone desolated. This it was which struck a panic to the hearts of the inhabitants when they knew the scourge was again in their midst, and save the inmates of the house, and Edith Hastings, none came to Dr. Griswold's aid. At first Richard refused to let the latter put herself in the way of danger, but for once Edith asserted her right to do as she pleased, and declared that she WOULD share Nina's labors. So for many weary days and nights those two young girls hovered like angels of mercy around the bed where the sick man tossed from side to side, while the fever burned more and more fiercely in his veins until his reason was dethroned, and a secret told which otherwise would have died with him. Gradually the long hidden love for Nina showed itself, and Edith, who alone could comprehend the meaning of what he said and did, saw how a strong, determined man can love, even when there is no hope.

"Little wounded dove," he called the golden-haired maiden, who bent so constantly over him, caressing his burning face with her cool, soft hands, passing her snowy fingers through his disordered hair, and suffering him to kiss her as he often did, but insisting always that MIGGIE should be kissed also, and Edith, knowing that what was like healing to the sick man would be withheld unless she, too, submitted, would sometimes bow her graceful head and receive upon her brow the token of affection.

"You must hug Miggie, too," Nina said to him one day, when he had held her slight form for a moment to his bosom. "She's just as good to you as I am."

"Nina," said Edith, "Dr. Griswold does not love me as he does you, and you must not worry him so. Don't you see it makes him worse?" and lifting the hair she pointed to the drops of perspiration standing upon his forehead.

This seemed to satisfy Nina, while at the same time her darkened mind must have caught a glimmer of the truth, for her manner changed perceptibly, and for a day or so she was rather shy of Dr. Griswold. Then the mood changed again, and to the poor dying man was vouchsafed a glimpse of what it might have been to be loved by Nina Bernard.

"Little sunbeam--little clipped-winged bird--little pearl," were the terms of endearment he lavished upon her, as, with his feeble arm about her, he told her one night how he loved her. "Don't go Edith," he said, as he saw her stealing from the room; "sit down here beside me and listen to what I have to say."

Edith obeyed, and taking her hand and Nina's in his, as if the touch of them both would make him strong to unburden his mind, he began:

"Let me call you Edith, while I'm talking, for the sake of one who loves you even as I love Nina,"

Edith started, and very foolishly replied,

"Do you mean Mr. Harrington?"

She knew he didn't, but her heart was so sore on the subject of Arthur's absence that she longed to be reassured in some way, and so said what she did.

"No, Edith, it is not Mr. Harrington, I mean," and Dr. Griswold's bright eyes fastened themselves upon the trembling girl as if to read her inmost soul, and see how far her feelings were enlisted.

"It's Arthur," said Nina, nodding knowingly at both.

"Arthur," Edith repeated bitterly. "Fine proof he gives of his love. Going from home for an indefinite length of time without one word for me. He hates me, I know," and bursting into tears she buried her face in the lap of Nina, who sat upon the bed.

"Poor Edith!" and another hand than Nina's smoothed her bands of shining hair. "By this one act you have confessed that Arthur's love is not unrequited. I hoped it might be otherwise. God help you, Edith. God help you."

He spoke earnestly, and a thrill of fear ran through Edith's veins. Lifting up her head, she said,

"You talk as if it were a certainty that Arthur St. Claire loves me. He has never told me so--never."

She could not add that he had never given her reason to think so, for he had, and her whole frame quivered with joy as she heard her suspicions confirmed by Dr. Griswold.

"He does love you, Edith Hastings. He has confessed as much to me, and this is why he has gone from home. He would forget you, and it is right. He must forget you; he must not love. It would be a wicked, wicked thing; and Edith--are you listening--do you hear all I say?"

"Yes," came faintly from Nina's lap, where Edith had laid her face again.

"Then promise not to marry him, so long--so long--Oh, Nina, how can I say it? Edith, swear you'll never marry Arthur. Swear, Edith, swear."

His voice was raised to a shriek, and by the dim light of the lamp, which fell upon his pallid features, both Edith and Nina saw the wild delirium flashing from his eye. Nina was the first to detect it, and wringing Edith's hand she whispered, imploringly,

"Swear, Miggie, once. Say THUNDER, or something like that as softly as you can. It won't be so very bad, and he wants you to so much."

Frightened as Edith was at Dr. Griswold's manner she could not repress a smile at Nina's mistaken idea. Still she did NOT swear, and all that night he continued talking incoherently of Arthur, of Edith, of Nina, Geneva, Richard Harrington, and a thousand other matters, mingling them together in such a manner that nothing clear or connected could be made of what he said. In the morning he was more quiet, but there was little hope of his life, the physician said. From the first he had greatly desired to see Arthur once more, and when his danger became apparent a telegram had been forwarded to the wanderer, but brought back no response. Another was sent, and another, the third one, in the form of a letter, finding him far up the Red river, where in that sultry season the air was rife with pestilence, which held with death many a wanton revel, and would surely have claimed him for its victim, but for the timely note which called him away.

Night and day, day and night, as fast as the steam-god could take him, he traveled, his heart swelling with alternate hope and fear as he neared the north-land, seeing from afar the tall heads of the New England mountains, and knowing by that token that he was almost home.

* * * * * *

It was night, dark night at Grassy Spring, and the summer rain, which all the day had fallen in heavy showers, beat drearily against the windows of the room where a fair young girl was keeping watch over the white-faced man whose life was fast ebbing away. They were alone,--Dr. Griswold and Nina--for both would have it so. He, because he felt how infinitely precious to him would be his last few hours with her, when there was no curious ear to listen; and she, because she would have Miggie sleep. Nina knew no languor from wakefulness. She was accustomed to it, and as if imbued with supernatural strength, she had sat night after night in that close room, ministering to the sick man as no one else could have done, and by her faithfulness and tender care repaying him in part for the love which for long, weary years had known no change, and which, as life draw near its close, manifested itself in a desire to have her constantly at his side, where he could look into her eyes, and hear the murmurings of her bird-like voice.

Thus far Edith and the servants had shared her vigils, but this night she preferred to be alone, insisting that Edith, who began to show signs of weariness, should occupy the little room, adjoining, where she could be called, if necessary. Not apprehending death so soon the physician acquiesced in this arrangement, stipulating, however, that Phillis should sleep upon the lounge in Dr. Griswold's chamber, but the care, the responsibility, should all be Nina's, he said, and with childish alacrity she hastened to her post. It was the first time she had kept the watch alone, but from past experience the physician believed she could be trusted, and he left her without a moment's hesitation.

Slowly the hours went by, and Nina heard no sound save the low breathing of the sleepers near, the dropping of the rain, and the mournful sighing of the wind through the maple trees. Midnight came, and then the eyes of the sick man opened wide and wandered about the room as if in quest of some one.

"Nina," he said, faintly, "Are you here? Why has the lamp gone out? It's so dark that I can't see your face."

Bending over him, Nina replied,

"I'm here, doctor. Nina's here. Shall I get more light so you CAN see?"

"Yes, darling, more light--more light;" and swift as a fawn Nina ran noiselessly from room to room, gathering up lamp after lamp, and candle after candle, and bringing them to the sick chamber, which blazed as if on fire, while the musical laugh of the lunatic echoed through the room as she whispered to herself, "Twenty sperm candles and fifteen lamps! 'Tis a glorious watch I keep to-night."

Once she thought of wakening Edith to share in her transports, but was withheld from doing so by a feeling that "Miggie" would not approve her work.

"It's light as noonday," she said, seating herself upon the bedside. "Can't you see me now?"

"No, Nina, I shall never look on your dear face again until we meet in Heaven. There you will be my own. No one can come between us," and the feeble arms wound themselves lovingly around the maiden, who laid her cheek against his feverish one, while her little fingers strayed once more amid the mass of disordered hair, pushing it back from the damp forehead, which she touched with her sweet lips.

"Nina," and the voice was so low that Nina bent her down to catch the sound, "I am dying, darling. You are not afraid to stay with me till the last?"

"No," she answered, "not afraid, but I do so wish you could see the splendid illumination. Twenty candles and fifteen lamps--the wicks of them all an inch in height. Oh, it's grand!" and again Nina chuckled as she saw how the lurid blaze lit up the window panes with a sheet of flame which, flashing backward, danced upon the wall in many a grotesque form, and cast a reddish glow even upon the white face of the dying.

He was growing very restless now, for the last great struggle had commenced; the soul was waging a mighty battle with the body, and the conflict was a terrible one, wringing groans of agony from him and great tears from Nina, who forgot her bonfire in her grief. Once when the fever had scorched her veins and she had raved in mad delirium, Dr. Griswold had rocked her in his arms as he would have rocked a little child, and remembering this the insane desire seized on Nina to rock him, too, to sleep. But she could not lift him up, though she bent every energy to the task, and at last, passing one arm beneath his neck she managed to sit behind him, holding him in such a position that he rested easier, and his convulsive movements ceased entirely. With his head upon her bosom she rocked to and fro, uttering a low, cooing sound, as if soothing him to sleep.

"Sing, Nina, sing," he whispered, and on the night air a mournful cadence rose, swelling sometimes so high that Edith moved uneasily upon her pillow, while even Phillis stretched out a hand as if about to awaken.

Then the music changed to a plaintive German song, and Edith dreamed of Bingen on the Rhine, while Dr. Griswold listened eagerly, whispering at intervals,

"Precious Nina, blessed dove, sing on--sing till I am at rest."

This was sufficient for Nina, and one after another she warbled the wild songs she knew he loved the best, while the lamps upon the table and the candles upon the floor flickered and flamed and cast their light far out into the yard, where the August rain was falling, and where more than one bird, startled from its slumbers, looked up to see whence came the fitful glare, wondering, it may be, at the solemn dirge, floating out into the darkness far beyond the light.

The gray dawn broke at last, and up the graveled walk rapid footsteps came--Arthur St. Claire hastening home. From a distant hill he had caught the blaze of

Nina's bonfire, and trembling with fear and dread, he hurried on to learn what it could mean. There was no stir about the house--no sign of life, only the crimson blaze shining across the fields, and the sound of a voice, feeble now, and sunk almost to a whisper, for Nina's strength was giving way. For hours she had sung, while the head upon her bosom pressed more and more heavily--the hand which clasped hers unloosed its hold--the eyes which had fastened themselves upon her with a look of unutterable love, closed wearily--the lips, which, so long as there was life in them, ceased not to bless her, were still, and poor, tired, crazy Nina, fancying that he slept at last, still swayed back and forth, singing to the cold senseless clay, an infant lullaby.

"Hushaby, my baby--go to sleep, my child."

HE had sung it once to her. SHE sang it now to him, and the strange words fell on Arthur's ear, even before he stepped across the threshold, where he stood appalled at the unwonted spectacle which met his view. Nina manifested no surprise whatever, but holding up her finger, motioned him to tread cautiously, if he would come near where she was.

"He couldn't see," she whispered, "and I made him a famous light. Isn't it glorious here, smoke, and fire and all? He is sleeping quietly now, only his head is very heavy. It makes my arm ache so hard, and his hands are growing cold, I cannot kiss them warm," and she held the stiffening fingers against her burning cheek, shuddering at the chill they gave her, just as Arthur shuddered at the sight, for it needed nothing more to tell him that Dr. Griswold was dead!

CHAPTER XIX.
EX-OFFICIO.

The spacious rooms at Grassy Spring had been filled to their utmost capacity by those of the villagers, who, having recovered from their panic, came to join in the funeral obsequies of Dr. Griswold. In the yard without the grass was trampled down and the flowers broken from their stalks by the crowds, who, failing to gain admittance to the interior of the house, hovered about the door, struggling for a sight of the young girl, whose strange death watch and stranger bonfire was the theme of every tongue. Solemnly the voice of God's ambassador was heard, proclaiming, "I am the resurrection and the life, saith the Lord; he that believeth in me, though he were dead, yet shall he live," and then a song was sung, the voices of the singers faltering, all but one, which, rising clear and sweet above the rest, sang of the better world, where the bright eternal noonday ever reigns, and the assembled throng without held their breath to listen, whispering to each other, "It is Nina, the crazy girl. She was the doctor's betrothed."

Down the gravelled walk,--along the highway,--over the river, and up the hill to the village churchyard the long procession moved, and when it backward turned, one of the number was left behind, and the August sunset fell softly upon his early grave. Sadly the mourners, Arthur, Edith and Nina, went to their respective homes, Edith seeking the rest she so much needed, Nina subdued and awed into perfect quiet, sitting with folded hands in the room where her truest friend had died, while Arthur, alone in his chamber, held as it were communion with the dead, who seemed this night to be so near to him.

Swiftly, silently, one by one, the days came and went until it was weeks since Dr. Griswold died, and things at Grassy Spring assumed their former routine. At first Nina was inclined to be melancholy, talking much of the deceased, and appearing at times so depressed that Arthur trembled, lest she should again become unmanageable, wondering what he should do with her now the Dr. was gone. Gradually, however, she recovered her usual health and spirits, appearing outwardly the same; but not so with Arthur, whose thoughts and feelings no one could fathom. It was as if he had locked himself within a wall of ice, which nothing had power to thaw. He saw but little of Edith now; the lessons had been tacitly given up, and, after what she had heard from Dr. Griswold, she could not come to Grassy Spring just as she used to do, so she remained at home, marvelling at the change in Arthur, and wondering if he really loved her, why he did not tell her so. Much of what Dr. Griswold had said she imputed to delirium, and with the certainty that she was beloved, she would not dwell upon anything which made her unhappy, and she waited for the end, now hastening on with rapid strides.

Behind the icy wall which Arthur had built around himself, a fierce storm was blowing, and notwithstanding the many midnight watches kept over Dr. Griswold's grave, the tempest still raged fearfully, threatening to burst its barriers and carry all before it. But it reached its height at last, and wishing to test his strength, Arthur asked Nina one pleasant night to go with him to Collingwood. She consented readily, and in a few moments they were on their way. They found the family assembled upon the broad piazza, where the full moon shone upon them through the broad leaves of woodbine twining about the massive pillars. Edith sat as usual upon a stool at Richard's feet, and her face wore a look of disappointment. Thoughts of Eloise Temple had been in her mind the entire day, and sitting there with Richard, she had ventured to ask him again of the young girl in whom she was so much interested. But Richard shook his head. He was reserving Eloise Temple for a future day, and he said to Edith,

"I cannot tell you of her yet, or where she is."

"When will you then?" and Edith spoke pettishly. "You always put me off, and I don't see either why you need to be so much afraid of telling me about her, unless her mother was bad, or something."

"Edith," Richard replied, "I do not wish to explain to you now. By and by I'll tell you, it may be, though even that will depend on circumstances;" and he sighed as he thought what the circumstances must be which would keep from Edith any further knowledge of Eloise than she already possessed.

Edith did not hear the sigh. She only knew that it was useless to question him, and beating her little foot impatiently, she muttered, "More mystery. If there's any thing I hate it's mystery.--"

She did not finish what she meant to say, for at that moment she spied Arthur and Nina coming through the garden gate as the nearest route.

Edith was not in the best of humors. She was vexed at Richard, because he wouldn't tell and at Arthur for "acting so," as she termed it,--this acting so implying the studied indifference with which he had treated her of late. But she was not vexed with Nina, and running out to meet her, she laid her arm across her neck, and led her with many words of welcome to the stool she had just vacated, saying laughingly: "I know Mr. Harrington would rather you should sit here than a cross patch like me! I'm ill-natured to-night, Mr. St. Claire," and she bit her words off with playful spitefulness.

"Your face cannot be an index to your feelings, then," returned Arthur, retaining her offered hand a moment, and looking into her eyes, just to see if he could do it without flinching.

It was a dangerous experiment, for Edith's soul looked through her eyes, and Arthur read therein that which sent feverish heats and icy chills alternately through his veins. Releasing her hand he sat down upon the upper step of the piazza, and leaning against one of the pillars, began to pluck the leaves within his reach, and mechanically tear them in pieces.

Meantime Richard had signified to Edith his wish that she should bring another stool, and sit beside him just as Nina was doing.

"I can then rest my hands upon the heads of you both," he said, smoothing the while Nina's golden curls,

"Now tell us a story, please," said Nina; and when Richard asked what it should be, she replied,

"Oh, tell us about the years ago when you were over the sea, and why you have never married. Maybe you have, though. You are old enough, I reckon. Did you ever marry anybody?"

"YES, *I* DID," returned Richard; "a little girl with hair like yours, I think, though my eyesight then was almost gone, and I saw nothing distinctly."

"Wha-a-at!" exclaimed Edith, at the same time asking Arthur if he was hurt as he started suddenly,

"There it goes. It was a BEE, I guess;" and Nina pointed to an insect flitting by, but so far from Arthur as to render a sting from the diminutive creature impossible. Still it served as an excuse, and blessing Nina in his heart for the suggestion, Arthur talked rapidly of various matters, hoping in this way to change the conversation. But Edith was not to be put off, even if Nina were. She was too much interested to know what Richard meant, and as soon as politeness would permit, she said to him,

"Please go on, and tell us of the girl you married. Who was the bridegroom, and where did it occur?"

There was no longer a shadow of hope that the story would not be told, and folding his arms like one resigned to his fate, Arthur listened, while Richard related to the two girls how, soon after his removal to Geneva, he had been elected Justice of the Peace in place of one resigned. "I did not wish for the office." he said, "although I was seldom called upon to act, and after my sight began to fail so fast, people never came to me except on trivial matters. One night, however, as many as--let me see--as many as ten years ago, my house keeper told me there were in the parlor four young people desirous of seeing me, adding that she believed a wedding was in contemplation."

"Splendid!" cried Edith; "and you married them, didn't you? Tell us all about it; how the bride looked, and every thing."

"I cannot gratify you in that respect," returned Richard. "There was a veil of darkness between us, and I could see nothing distinctly, but I knew she was very slight, so much so, indeed, that I was sorry afterward that I did not question her age."

"A runaway match from the Seminary, perhaps," suggested Arthur, in tones so steady as to astonish himself.

"I have sometimes thought so since," was Richard's reply, "but as nothing of the kind was ever known to have occurred, I may have been mistaken."

"But the names?" cried Edith, eagerly, "you could surely tell by that, unless they were feigned."

"Which is hardly probable," Richard rejoined, "though they might as well have been for any good they do me now. I was too unhappy then, too much wrapped up in my own misfortunes to care for what was passing around me, and though I gave them a certificate, keeping myself a memorandum of the same, I soon forgot their names entirely."

"But the copy," chimed in Edith, "that will tell. Let's hunt it up. I'm so interested in these people, and it seems so funny that you should have married them. I wonder where they are. Have you never heard a word from them?"

"Never, since that night," said Richard; "and what is more unfortunate still for an inquisitive mother Eve, like you, the copy which I kept was burned by a servant who destroyed it with sundry other business papers, on one of her cleaning house days."

"Ah-h," and Arthur drew a long, long breath, which prompted Edith to ask if be were tired.

"You're not as much interested as I am," she said. "I do wish I knew who the young bride was--so small and so fair. Was she as tall as Nina?" and she turned to Richard, who replied,

"I can hardly judge the height of either. Stand up, Snow Drop, and let me feel if you are as tall as the bride of ten years ago."

"Yes, Nina is the taller of the two," said Richard, as he complied with his request and stood under his hand. "I have often thought of this girl-wife and her handsome boy-husband, doubting whether I did right to marry them, but the young man who accompanied them went far toward reassuring me that all was right. They were residents of the village, he said, and having seen me often in town, had taken a fancy to have me perform the ceremony, just for the novelty of the thing."

"It's queer you never heard of them afterward," said Edith; while Nina, looking up in the blind man's face, rejoined,

"YOU DID IT THEN?"

"Nina," said Arthur ere Richard could reply, "it is time we were going home; there is Sophy with the shawl which you forgot." And he pointed toward Sophy coming through the garden, with a warm shawl tucked under her arm, for the dew was heavy that night and she feared lest Nina should take cold.

"Nina won't go yet; she isn't ready," persisted the capricious maiden. "Go till I call you," and having thus summarily dismissed Soph, the little lady resumed the seat from which she had arisen, and laying her head on Richard's, whispered to him softly, "CAN'T YOU SCRATCH IT OUT?"

"Scratch what out?" he asked; and Nina replied,

"Why, IT; what you've been talking about. Nothing ever came of it but despair and darkness."

"I do not know what you mean," Richard said, and as Arthur did not volunteer any information, but sat carelessly scraping his thumb nail with a pen-knife, Edith made some trivial remark which turned the channel of Nina's thoughts, and she forgot to urge the request that "it should be scratched out."

"Nina'll go now," she said, after ten minutes had elapsed, and calling Soph, Arthur was soon on his way home, hardly knowing whether he was glad or sorry that every proof of his early error was forever destroyed.

CHAPTER XX.
THE DECISION.

The summer was over and gone; its last breath had died away amid the New England hills, and the mellow October days had come, when in the words of America's sweetest poetess,

"The woods stand bare and brown,
And into the lap of the South land,
The flowers are blowing down."

Over all there was that dreamy, languid haze, so common to the Autumn time, when the distant hills are bathed in a smoky light and all things give token of decay. The sun, round and red, as the October sun is wont to be, shone brightly upon Collingwood, and looked cheerily into the room where Edith Hastings sat, waiting apparently for some one whose tardy appearance filled her with impatience. In her hand she held a tiny note received the previous night, and as she read for the twentieth time the few lines contained therein, her blushes deepened on her cheek, and her blank eyes grew softer and more subdued in their expression.

"Edith," the note began, "I must see you alone. I have something to say to you which a third person cannot hear. May I come to Collingwood to-morrow at three o'clock, P.M.? In haste, Arthur St. Claire."

The words were very cold, but to Edith they contained a world of meaning. She knew she was beloved by Arthur St. Claire. Dr. Griswold had told her so. Grace had told her so. Nina had told her so, while more than all his manner had told her so repeatedly, and now HE would tell her so himself and had chosen a time when Richard and Victor were both in Boston, as the one best adapted to the interview.

Edith was like all other maidens of eighteen, and her girlish heart fluttered with joy as she thought what her answer would be, but not at first,--not at once, lest she seem too anxious. She'd make him wait a whole week, then see how he felt. He deserved it all for his weak vacillation. If he loved her why hadn't he told her before! She didn't believe there was such a terrible impediment in the way. Probably he had sworn never to marry any one save Nina, but her insanity was certainly a sufficient reason for his not keeping the oath. Dr. Griswold was peculiar,--over-nice in some points, and Arthur had been wholly under his control, becoming morbidly sensitive to the past, and magnifying every trivial circumstance into a mountain too great to be moved.

This was Edith's reasoning as she sat waiting that October afternoon for Arthur, who came ere long, looking happier, more like himself than she had seen him since the memorable day when she first met Nina. Arthur had determined to do right, to tell without reserve the whole of his past history to Edith Hastings, and the moment he reached this decision half his burden was lifted from his mind. It cost him a bitter struggle thus to decide, and lest his courage should give way, he had asked for an early interview. It was granted, and without giving himself time to repent he came at once and stood before the woman who was dearer to him than his life. Gladly would he have died could he thus have blotted out the past and made Edith his wife, but he could not, and he had come to tell her so.

Never had she been more beautiful than she was that afternoon. Her dress of crimson merino contrasted well with her clear dark complexion. Her magnificent hair, arranged with far more care than usual, was wound in many a heavy braid around her head, while, half-hidden amid the silken bands, and drooping gracefully behind one ear, was a single white rose-bud, mingled with scarlet blossoms of verbena; the effect adding greatly to her beauty. Excitement lent a brighter sparkle to her brilliant eyes, and a richer bloom to her glowing cheeks, and thus she sat waiting for Arthur St. Claire, who felt his heart grow cold and faint as he looked upon her, and knew her charms were not for him. She detected his agitation, and as a kitten plays with a captured mouse, torturing it almost to madness, so she played with him ere suffering him to reach the point. Rapidly she went from one subject to another, dragging him with her whether he would or not, until at last as if suddenly remembering herself, she turned her shining eyes upon him, and said, "I have talked myself out, and will now give you a chance. You wrote that you wished to see me."

But for this direct allusion to his note, Arthur would assuredly have gone away, leaving his errand untold. But he could not do so now. She was waiting for him to speak, and undoubtedly wondering at his silence. Thrice he attempted to articulate, but his tongue seemed paralyzed, and reeking with perspiration, he sat unable to move until she said again, "Is it of Nina you would tell me?"

Then the spell was broken, Nina was the sesame which unlocked his powers of speech; and wiping the large drops from his forehead, he answered,

"Yes, Edith, of Nina, of myself, of you. Edith, you know how much I love you, don't you, darling?"

The words were apparently wrung from him greatly against his will. They were not what he intended to say, and he would have given worlds to have recalled them, but they were beyond his reach, and the very walls of the room seemed to echo in thunder tones,

"You know how much I love you, don't you, darling?"

Yes, she did know; he knew she did by the glance she gave him back, and laying his head upon the table, he neither moved nor spoke until a footstep glided to his side, and a soft hand pressed his burning brow, while a voice, whose tones drifted him far, far back to the sea of darkness and doubt where he had so long been bravely buffeting the billows, whispered to him,

"Arthur, I DO know, or rather believe you love me. You would not tell me an untruth, but I do not understand why it should make you so unhappy."

He did not answer her at once, but retained within his own the little hand which trembled for a moment like an imprisoned bird and then grew warm and full of vigorous life just as Edith was, standing there before him. What should he do? What could he do? Surely, never so dark an hour had gathered round him, or one so fraught with peril. Like lightning his mind took in once more the whole matter as it was. Griswold was dead. On his grave the autumn leaves were falling and the nightly vigils by that grave had been of no avail. Nina could never comprehend, the written proof was burned, Richard had forgotten, there was nothing in the way save his CONSCIENCE and that would not be silent. Loudly it whispered to the anguished man that happiness could not be secured by trampling on Nina's rights;

that remorse would mix itself with every joy and at the last would drive him mad.

"You mistake me, I cannot," he began to say, but Edith did not heed it, for a sound without had caught her ear, telling her that Richard had unexpectedly returned, and Victor was coming for her.

There was an expression of impatience on Edith's face, as to Victor's summons she replied, "Yes, yes, in a moment;" but Arthur breathed more freely as, rising to his feet, he said, "I cannot now say all I wish to say, but meet me, to-morrow at this hour in the Deering Woods, near the spot where the mill brook falls over those old stones. You know the place. We went there once with-- NINA."

He wrung her hand, pitying her more than he did himself, for he knew how little she suspected the true nature of what he intended to tell her.

"God help us both, me to do right, and her to bear it," was his mental prayer, as he left her at the door of the room where Richard was waiting for her.

There were good and bad angels lugging at Arthur's heart as he hastened across the fields where the night was falling, darker, gloomier, than ever it fell before. Would it be a deadly sin to marry Edith Hastings? Would Nina be wronged if he did? were questions which the bad spirits kept whispering in his ear, and each time that he listened to these questionings, he drifted further and farther away from the right, until by the time his home was reached he hardly knew himself what his intentions were.

Very bright were the lights shining in the windows of his home, and the fire blazed cheerfully in the library, where Nina, pale and fair as a white pond lily, had ordered the supper table to be set, because she thought it would please him, and where, with her golden curls tucked behind her ears, and a huge white apron on, she knelt before the glowing coals, making the nicely-buttered toast he liked so well. Turning toward him her childish face as he came in, she said,

"See--Nina's a nice little housekeeper. Wouldn't it be famous if we could live alone, you and I?"

Arthur groaned inwardly, but made her no reply. Sitting down in his armchair, he watched her intently as she made his tea, removed her apron, brushed her curls, and then look her seat at the table, bidding him do the same. Mechanically he obeyed, affecting to eat for her sake, while his eyes were constantly fastened upon her face. Supper being over and the table removed, he continued watching her intently as she flitted about the room, now perching herself upon his knee, calling him "her good boy," now holding a whispered conversation with Miggie, who, she fancied, was there, and again singing to herself a plaintive song she had sung to Dr. Griswold. When it drew near her bedtime she went to the window, from which the curtain was thrown back, and looking out upon the blackness of the night, said to Arthur,

"The darkness is very dark. I should think poor Dr. Griswold would be afraid lying there alone in that narrow grave. What made him die, Arthur? I didn't want him to. It had better been I, hadn't it?"

She came close to him now, and sitting on his knee held his bearded chin in her hand, while she continued,

"Would my poor boy be very lonesome, knowing that Nina wasn't here, nor up stairs, nor in the Asylum, nor over at Miggie's, nor anywhere? Would you miss me a bit?"

"YES, YES, YES!"

The words came with quiet, gasping sobs, for in his hour of bitterest anguish, Arthur had never for an instant wished HER gone--the little blue-eyed creature clinging so confidingly to him and asking if he would miss her when she was dead.

"Nina's would be a little grave," she said, "not as large as Miggie's, and perhaps it won't be long before they dig it. I can wait. You can wait; can't you, boy?"

What was it which prompted her thus to speak to him? What was it which made him see Griswold's glance in the eyes looking so earnestly to his own? Surely there was something more than mere chance in all this. Nina would save him. She had grasped his conscience, and she stirred it with no gentle hand, until the awakened man writhed in agony, such as the drowning are said to feel when slowly restored to life, and bowing his head on Nina's, he cried,

"What shall I do? Tell me, Nina, what to do!"

Once before, when thus appealed to, she had answered him, "Do right," and she now said the same to the weeping man, who sobbed aloud, "I will. I will tell her all to-morrow. I wish it were to- morrow now, but the long night must intervene, and a weak, vacillating fool like me may waver in that time. Nina," and he held her closer to him, "stay here with me till morning. I am stronger where you are. The sight of you does me good. Phillis will fix you a bed upon the sofa and make you comfortable; will you stay?"

Every novelty was pleasing to Nina and she assented readily, stipulating, however, that he should not look at her while she said her prayers.

In much surprise Phillis heard of this arrangement, but offered no objection, thinking that Arthur had probably detected signs of a frenzied attack and chose to keep her with him where he could watch her. Alas! they little dreamed that 'twas to save himself he kept her there, kneeling oftentimes beside her as she slept, and from the sight of her helpless innocence gathering strength for the morrow's duty. How slowly the hours of that never-to-be- forgotten night dragged on, and when at last the grey dawn came creeping up the east, how short they seemed, looked back upon. Through them all Nina had slept quietly, moving only once, and that when Arthur's tears dropped upon her face. Then, unconsciously, she put her arms around his neck and murmured, "It will all be right sometime."

"Whether it is or not, I will do right to-day," Arthur said aloud, and when the sun came stealing into the room, it found him firm as a granite rock.

Nina's presence saved him, and when the clock pointed to three, he said to her, "Miggie is waiting for me in the Deering woods, where the mill-brook falls over the stones. You called it Niagara, you know, when you went there once with us. Go to Miggie, Nina. Tell her I'm coming soon. Tell her that I sent you."

"And that you will do right?" interrupted Nina, retaining a confused remembrance of last night's conversation.

"Yes, tell her I'll do right. Poor Edith, she will need your sympathy so much;" and with trembling hands Arthur himself wrapped Nina's shawl around her, taking more care than usual to see that she was shielded from the possibility of taking cold; then, leading her to the door and pointing in the direction of the miniature Niagara he bade her go, watching her with a beating heart as she bounded across the fields toward the Deering woods.

CHAPTER XXI.
THE DEERING WOODS.

Edith had been in a state of feverish excitement all the day, so happy had she been made by the certainty that Arthur loved her. She had not doubted it before, but having it told her in so many words was delightful, and she could scarcely wait for the hour when she was to hear the continuation of a story abruptly terminated by the return of Richard. Poor Richard! He was sitting in his library now, looking so lonely, when on her way through the hall she glanced in at him, that she almost cried to think how desolate he would be when she was gone.

"I'll coax Arthur to come here and live," she said to herself, thinking how nice it would be to have Arthur and Nina and Richard all in one house.

The hands of her watch were pointing to three, as, stepping out upon the piazza she passed hurriedly through the grounds and turned in the direction of the Deering Woods. Onward, onward, over the hill and across the fields she flew, until the woods were reached--the silent, leafless woods, where not a sound was heard save the occasional dropping of a nut, the rustle of a leaf, or the ripple of the millbrook falling over the stones. The warm sun had dried the withered grass, and she sat down beneath a forest tree, watching, waiting, wondering, and trembling violently at last as in the distance she heard the cracking of the brittle twigs and fancied he was coming.

"I'll pretend I don't hear him," she said, and humming a simple air she was industriously pulling the bark from the tree when NINA stood before her, exclaiming,

"You ARE here just as Arthur said you'd be. The woods were so still and smoky that I was most afraid."

Ordinarily Edith would have been delighted at this meeting, but now she could not forbear wishing Nina away, and she said to her somewhat sternly,

"What made you come?"

"He sent me," and Nina crouched down at Edith's feet, like a frightened spaniel. "Arthur is coming, too, and going to do right. He said he was, bending right over me last night, and when I woke this morning there was a great tear on my face. 'Twasn't mine, Miggie. It was too big for that. It was Arthur's."

"How came he in your room?" Edith asked, a little sharply, and Nina replied,

"I was in the library. We both staid there all night. It wasn't in my room, though Arthur has a right, Miggie. IT NEVER WAS SCRATCHED OUT!"

Edith was puzzled, and was about to question Nina as to her meaning, when another step was heard, a manly, heavy tread, precluding all possibility of a mistake this time. Arthur St. Claire had come!

"It's quite pleasant since yesterday," he said, trying to force a smile, but it was a sickly effort, and only made more ghastly and wan his pallid features, over which ages seemed to have passed since the previous day, leaving them scarred, and battered, and worn.

Edith had never noticed so great a change in so short a time, for there was scarcely a vestige left of the once handsome, merry- hearted Arthur in the stooping, haggard man, who stood before her, with blood-shot eyes, and an humble, deprecating manner, as if imploring her forgiveness for the pain he had come to inflict. Nothing could prevent it now. Her matchless beauty was naught to him. He did not even see it. He thought of her only as a being for whose sake he would gladly die the most torturing death that human ingenuity could devise, if by this means, he could rescue her unscathed from the fire he had kindled around her. But this could not be; he had fallen, dragging her down with him, and now he must restore her even though it broke her heart just as his was broken. He had felt the fibres snapping, one by one; knew his life blood was oozing out, drop by drop, and this it was which made him hesitate so long. It was painful for him to speak, his throat was so parched and dry, his tongue so heavy and thick.

"What is it, Arthur?" Edith said at last, as Nina, uttering a cry of fear, hid her face in the grass to shut out Arthur from her sight, "Tell me, what is it?"

Seating himself upon a log near by, and clasping his hands together with a gesture of abject misery, Arthur replied.

"Edith, I am not worthy to look into your face; unless you take your eyes from mine--oh, take them away, or I cannot tell you what I must."

Had her very life depended upon it, Edith could not have removed her eyes from his. An undefinable fear was curdling her blood--a fear augmented by the position of her two companions--Nina, with her head upon the grass, and that strange, white-faced being on the log. Could THAT be Arthur St. Claire, or was she laboring under some horrible delusion? No, the lips moved; it was Arthur, and leaning forward she listened to what he was saying,

"Edith, when yesterday I was with you, some words which I uttered and which were wrung from me, I know not how, gave you reason to believe that I was then asking you to become my wife, while something in your manner told me that to such asking you would not answer no. The temptation then to take you to my arms, defying earth and heaven, was a terrible one, and for a time I wavered, I forgot everything but my love for you; but that is past and I come now to the hardest part of all, the deliberate surrender of one dearer than life itself. Edith, do you remember the obstacle, the hindrance which I always said existed to my marrying any one?"

She did not answer; only the eyes grew larger as they watched him; and he continued,

"I made myself forgot it for a time, but Heaven was kinder far than I deserved, and will not suffer me longer. Edith, you CANNOT be my wife."

She made a movement as if she would go to him, but his swaying arms kept her off, and he went on;

"There IS an obstacle, Edith--a mighty obstacle, I could trample it down if I would, and there is none to question the act; but, Edith, I dare not do you this wrong."

His voice was more natural now, and Nina, lifting up her head, crept closely to him, whispering softly, "Good boy, you will do right."

His long, white fingers threaded her sunny hair, and this was all the token he gave that he was conscious of her presence.

"Don't you know now, Edith, what it is which stands between us?" he asked; and Edith answered, "It is Nina, but how I do not understand."

Arthur groaned a sharp, bitter groan, and rocking to and fro replied, "Must I tell you? Won't you ever guess until I do? Oh, Edith, Edith--put the past and present together--remember the picture found in my room when you were a little girl, the picture of Nina Bernard; think of all that has happened; my dread to meet with Richard, though that you possibly did not know; my foolish fear, lest you should know of Nina; her clinging devotion to me; my brotherly care for her; Richard's story of the one single marriage ceremony he ever performed, where the bride's curls were like these," and he lifted Nina's golden ringlets. "You hear me, don't you?"

He knew she did, for her bosom was heaving with choking sobs as if her soul were parting from the body; her breath came heavily from between her quivering lips, and her eyes were riveted upon him like coals of living fire. Yes, he knew she heard, and he only questioned her to give himself another moment ere he cut asunder the last chord and sent her drifting out upon the dark sea of despair.

"Edith--Edith--Edith," and with each word he hugged Nina closer to him, so close that she gave a cry of pain, but he did not heed it; he hardly knew he held her--his thoughts were all for the poor, wretched girl, rising slowly to her feet. "Edith, you surely understand me now. The obstacle between us is---; oh, Nina, say it for me, tell her what you are to me."

"I know," and Edith Hastings stood tall and erect before him, "NINA IS YOUR WIFE."

Nina looked up and smiled, while Edith crossed her arms upon her breast, and waited for him to answer.

"Yes, Edith,--though never before acknowledged as such, Nina is my wife; but, Edith, I swear it before high Heaven, she is only a wife in name. Never for a day, or hour, or moment have I lived with her as such. Were it otherwise, I could not have fallen so low. Her father came the very night we were married, and took her away next morning. Griswold and I must have met him just as we left the yard, after having assisted Nina and her room-mate, Sarah Warren, to reach the window, from which they had adroitly escaped little move than an hour before. No one had missed them,--no one ever suspected the truth, and as Miss Warren died a few months afterward, only Nina, Griswold and myself knew the secret, which I guarded most carefully for fear of expulsion from college. You know the rest. You know it all, Nina is my wife. Nina is my wife,- -my wife,--my wife."

He kept whispering it to himself, as if thus he would impress it the more forcibly upon the unconscious Edith, who lay upon the withered grass just where Nina had lain, rigid and white and free for the present from all suffering. Arthur could not move; the blow had fallen on them both with a mightier force than even he had anticipated, killing her he feared, and so benumbing himself that to act was impossible, and he continued sitting upon the log with his elbows resting on his knees and his face upon his hands. Only Nina had any reason then or judgment. Hastening to Edith she knelt beside her, and lifting up her head pillowed it upon her lap, wiping from her temple the drops of blood slowly trickling from a cut, made by a sharp stone.

"Miggie, Miggie," she cried, "wake up. You scare me, you look so white and stiff. Please open your eyes, darling, just a little ways, so Nina'll know that you ain't dead. Oh, Arthur, she is DEAD!" and Nina shrieked aloud, when, opening herself the lids, she saw the dull, fixed expression of the glassy eye.

Laying her back upon the grass, she crept to Arthur's side, and tried to rouse him, saying imploringly, "Miggie's dead, Arthur; Miggie's dead. There is blood all over her face. It's on me, too, look," and she held before him her fingers, covered with a crimson stain. Even this did not move him; he only kissed the tiny hand wet with Edith's blood, and whispered to her, "Richard."

It was enough. Nina comprehended his meaning at once; and when next he looked about him she was flying like a deer across the fields to Collingwood, leaving him alone with Edith. From where he sat he could see her face, and its corpse-like pallor chilled him with horror. He must go to her. It would be long ere Nina guided the blind man to the spot, and, exerting all his strength, he tottered to the brook, filled his hat with water, and crawling, rather than walking, to Edith's side, dashed it upon her head, washing the stains of blood, away, and forcing back the life so nearly gone. Gradually the eyes unclosed, and looked into his with a glance so full of love. tenderness, reproach, and cruel disappointment, that he turned away, for he could not meet that look.

The blood from the wound upon the forehead was flowing freely now, and faint from its loss, Edith sank again into a state of unconsciousness, while Arthur, scarcely knowing what he did, crept away to a little distance, where, leaning against a tree, he sat insensible as it were, until the sound of footsteps roused him, and he saw Nina coming, holding fast to the blind man's wrist, and saying to him encouragingly,

"We are almost there. I see her dress now by the bank. Wake up, Miggie; we're coming--Richard and I. Don't you hear me, Miggie?"

* * * * * *

Victor had been sent to the village upon an errand for Richard, who was sitting in his arm-chair, just where Edith had left him an hour before, dozing occasionally, as was his custom after dinner, and dreaming of his singing bird.

"Little rose-bud," he whispered to himself. "It's strange no envious, longing eyes have sought her out as yet, and tried to win her from me. There's St. Claire--cannot help admiring her, but thus far he's been very discreet, I'm sure. Victor would tell me if he saw any indications of his making love to Edith."

Deluded Richard! Victor Dupres kept his own counsel with regard to Edith and the proprietor of Grassy Spring; and when questioned by his master, as he sometimes was, he always answered, "Monsieur St. Claire does nothing out of the way."

So Richard, completely blinded, trusted them both, and had no suspicion of the scene enacted that afternoon in the Deering Woods. Hearing a swift footstep coming up the walk, he held his breath to listen, thinking it was Edith, but a moment only sufficed to tell it was Nina. With a rapid, bounding tread she entered the library, and gliding to his side, startled him with, "Come, quick, Miggie's dead--dead in the Deering Woods!"

For an instant Richard's brain reeled, and rings of fire danced before his sightless eyes; then, remembering the nature of the one who had brought to him this news, hope whispered that it might not be so bad, and this it was which buoyed him up and made him strong to follow his strange guide.

* * * * * *

Down the lane, across the road, and over the fields Nina led him, bareheaded as he was, and in his thin-soled, slippers, which were torn against the briers and stones, for in her haste Nina did not stop to choose the smoothest path, and Richard was too intent on Edith to heed the roughness of the way. Many questions be asked her as to the cause of the accident, but she told him nothing save that "Miggie was talking and fell down dead." She did not mention Arthur, for, fancying that he had in some way been the cause of the disaster, she wished to shield him from all censure, consequently Richard had no idea of the crushed, miserable wretch leaning against the sycamore and watching him as he came up. He only heard Nina's cry, "Wake up, Miggie, Richard's here!"

It needed more than that appeal, however, to rouse the unconscious girl, and Richard, as he felt her cold, clammy flesh, wept aloud, fearing lest she were really dead. Eagerly he felt for her heart, knowing then that she still lived.

"Edith, darling, speak to me," and he chafed her nerveless hands, bidding Nina bring him water from the brook.

Spying Arthur's hat Nina caught it up, when the thought entered her mind, "He'll wonder whose this is." Then with a look of subtle cunning, she stole up behind the blind man, and placing the hat suddenly upon his head, withdrew it as quickly, saying, "I'll get it in this, shan't I?"

Richard was too much excited to know whether he had worn one hat or a dozen, and he answered her at once, "Use it of course."

The cold water brought by Nina roused Edith once more, and with a sigh she lay back on Richard's bosom, so trustfully, so confidingly, that Arthur, looking on, foresaw what the future would bring, literally giving her up then and there to the blind man, who, as if accepting the gift, hugged her fondly to him and said aloud, "I thank the good Father for restoring to me my Edith."

She suffered him to caress her as much as he liked, and offered no remonstrance when lifting her in his strong arms, he bade Nina lead him back to Collingwood. Like a weary child Edith rested her head upon his shoulder, looking behind once, and regarding Arthur with a look he never forgot, even when the darkness in which he now was groping had passed away, and the full daylight was shining o'er him. Leading Richard to a safe distance, Nina bade him wait a moment while she went back for something she had forgotten--then hastening to Arthur's side she wound her arms around his neck, smoothed his hair, kissed his lips, and said to him so low that Richard could not hear,

"NINA won't desert you. She'll come to you again, when she gets Miggie home. You did do it, didn't you? but Nina'll never tell."

Kissing him once more, she bounded away, and with feelings of anguish which more than compensated for his error, Arthur looked after them as they moved slowly across the field, Richard sometimes tottering beneath his load, which, nevertheless, he would not release, and Nina, holding to his arm, telling him where to go, and occasionally glancing backward toward the spot where Arthur sat, until the night shadows were falling, and he shivered with the heavy dew. Nina did not return, and thinking that she would not, he started for home, never knowing how he reached there, or when; only this he knew, no one suspected him of being in the Deering Woods when Edith Hastings was attacked with that strange fainting fit. Thanks for this to little Nina, who, returning as she had promised, found the forgotten HAT still dripping with water, and hiding it beneath her shawl, carried it safely to Grassy Spring, where it would betray no one.

CHAPTER XXII.
THE DARKNESS DEEPENS.

Death brooded over Collingwood, and his black wing beat clamorously against the windows of the room to which, on that fearful night, Richard had borne his fainting burden, and where for days and weeks she lay so low that with every coming morning the anxious villagers listened for the first stroke of the bell which should tell that Edith was dead. Various were the rumors concerning the cause of her illness, all agreeing upon one point, to wit, that she had fainted suddenly in the woods with Nina, and in falling, had received a deep gash upon her forehead. This it was which made her crazy, the people said, and the physician humored the belief, although with his experience he knew there was some secret sorrow preying upon that young mind, the nature of which he could not easily guess. It never occurred to him that it was in any way associated with Arthur St. Claire, whose heart-broken expression told how much he suffered, and how dear to him was the delirious girl, who never breathed his name, or gave token that she knew of his existence. Every morning, regularly he rung the Collingwood bell, which was always answered by Victor, between whom and himself there was a tacit understanding, perceptible in the fervent manner with which the faithful valet's hand was pressed whenever the news was favorable. He did not venture into her presence, though repeatedly urged to do so by Grace, who mentally accused him of indifference toward Edith. Alas, she knew not of the nightly vigils kept by the wretched man, when with dim eye and throbbing head he humbled himself before his Maker, praying to be forgiven for the sorrow he had wrought, and again wrestling in agony for the young girl, whose sick room windows he could see, watching the livelong night the flickering of the lamp, and fancying he could tell from its position, if any great change occurred in her.

Richard was completely crushed, and without noticing any one he sat hour after hour, day after day, night after night, always in one place, near the head of the bed, his hands folded submissively together, and his sightless eyes fixed upon the pillow, where he knew Edith was, with a hopeless, subdued expression touching to witness. He did not weep, but his dry, red eyes, fastened always upon the same point, told of sealed fountains where the hot tears were constantly welling up, and failing to find egress without, fell upon the bruised heart, which blistered and burned beneath their touch, but felt no relief. It was in vain they tried to persuade him to leave the room; he turned a deaf ear to their entreaties, and the physician was beginning to fear for his reason, when crazy Nina came to his aid, and laying her moist hand upon his said to him, not imploringly, but commandingly, "Come with me."

There was a moment's hesitation, and then Richard followed her out into the open air, sitting where she bade him sit, and offering no resistance when she perched herself upon his knee and passed her arm around his neck.

"Make him cry, can't you? That will do him good," whispered Victor, who had come out with them.

Nina knew that better than himself. SHE remembered the time when the sight of Edith had wrung from her torrents of tears, cooling her burning brow, and proving a blessed relief, the good effects of which were visible yet. And now it was her task to make the blind man cry. She recognized something familiar in the hard, stony expression of his face, something which brought back the Asylum, with all its dreaded horrors. She had seen strong men there look just as he was looking. Dr. Griswold had called them crazy, and knowing well what that word implied she would save Richard from so sad a fate.

"It will be lonesome for you when Miggie's gone," she said, as a prelude, to the attempt; "lonesomer than it has ever been before; and the nights will be so dark, for when the morning comes there'll be no Miggie here. She will look sweetly in her coffin, but you can't see her, can you? You can FEEL how beautiful she is, perhaps; and I shall braid her hair just as she used to wear it."

There was a perceptible tremor in Richard's frame, and perceiving it, Nina continued quickly,

"We shall never forget her, shall we? and we'll often fancy we hear her singing through the halls, even though we know she's far away heading the choir in Heaven. That will be a pleasanter sound, won't it, than the echo of the bell when the villagers count the eighteen strokes and a half, and know it tolls for Miggie? The hearse wheels, too--how often we shall hear them grinding through the gravel, as they will grind, making a little track when they come up, and a deeper one when they go away, for they'll carry Miggie then."

"Oh, Nina! hush, hush! No, no!" and Richard's voice was choked with tears, which ran over his face like rain.

Nina had achieved her object, and, with a most satisfied expression she watched him as he wept. Her's was a triple task, caring for Richard, caring for Arthur, and caring for Edith, but most faithfully did she perform it. Every day, when the sun was low in the western sky, she stole away to Grassy Spring, speaking blessed words of comfort to the despairing Arthur, who waited for her coming as for the visit of an angel. She was dearer to him now since he had confessed his sin to Edith, and could she have been restored to reason he would have compelled himself to make her his wife in reality as well as in name. She was a sweet creature, he knew; and he always caressed her with unwonted tenderness ere he sent her back to the sick room, where Edith ever bemoaned her absence, missing her at once, asking for pretty Nina, with the golden hair. She apparently did not remember that Nina stood between herself and Arthur St. Claire, or, if she did, she bore no malice for the patient, all-enduring girl who nursed her with so much care, singing to her the plaintive German air once sung to Dr. Griswold, and in which Edith would often join, taking one part, while Nina sang the other; and the members of the household, when they heard the strange melody, now swelling load and full, as some fitful fancy took possession of the crazy vocalists, and now sinking to a plaintive wail, would shudder, and turn aside to weep, for there was that in the music which reminded them of the hearse wheels grinding down the gravel, and of the village bell giving the eighteen strokes. Sometimes, for nearly a whole night those songs of the olden time would echo through the house, and with each note she sang the fever burned more fiercely in Edith's veins, and her glittering black eyes flashed with increased fire, while her fingers clutched at her tangled hair, as if they thus would keep time to the thrilling strain. Her hair troubled her, it was so heavy, so thick, so much in her way, and when she manifested a propensity to relieve herself of the burden by tearing it from the roots the physician commanded them to cut away those beautiful shining braids, Edith's crowning glory.

It was necessary, he said, and the sharp, polished scissors were ready for the task, when Nina, stepping in between them and the blue-black locks, saved the latter from the nurse's barbaric hand. She remembered well when her own curls had fallen one by one beneath the shears of an unrelenting nurse, and she determined at all hazards to spare Edith from a like fancied indignity.

"Miggie's hair shall not be harmed," she said, covering with her apron the wealth of raven tresses. "I can keep her from pulling it. I can manage her;" and the sequel proved that she was right.

It was a singular power that blue-eyed blonde possessed over the dark-eyed brunette, who became at last as obedient to Nina's will as Nina once had been to her's, and it was amusing to watch Nina flitting about Edith, now reasoning with, now coaxing, and again threatening her capricious patient, who was sure eventually to do as she was bidden.

Only once while the delirium lasted did Edith refer to Arthur, and then she said reproachfully, "Oh, Nina, what made him do so?"

They were alone, and bending over her, Nina replied, "I am so sorry, Miggie, and I'll try to have the ugly thing SCRATCHED OUT."

This idea once fixed in Nina's mind could not easily be dislodged, and several times she went to Richard, asking him to SCRATCH IT OUT! Wishing to humor her as far as possible he always answered that he would if he knew what she meant. Nina felt that she must not explain, and with vigilant cunning she studied how to achieve her end without betraying Arthur. It came to her one night, and whispering to Edith, "I am going to get it fixed," she glided from the room and sought the library where she was sure of finding Richard. It was nearly eleven o'clock, but he had not yet retired, and with his head bent forward he sat in his accustomed place, the fire-light shining on his face, which had grown fearfully haggard and white within the last two weeks. He heard Nina's step, and knowing who it was, asked if Edith were worse.

"No," returned Nina, "she'll live, too, If you'll only scratch it out."

He was tired of asking what she meant, and he made no answer. But Nina was too intent upon other matters to heed his silence. Going to his secretary she arranged materials for writing, and then taking his hand, said, in the commanding tone she used toward Edith when at all refractory, "Come and write. 'Tis the only chance of saving her life."

"Write what?" he asked, as he rose from his chair and suffered her to lead him to the desk.

He had written occasionally since his blindness, but it was not a frequent thing, and his fingers closed awkwardly about the pen she placed in his hand. Feeling curious to know the meaning of all this, he felt for the paper and then said to her,

"I am ready for you to dictate."

But dictation was no part of Nina's intentions. The lines traced upon that sheet would contain a secret which Richard must not know; and with a merry laugh, as she thought how she would cheat him, she replied,

"No, SIR. Only Miggie and I can read what you write. Nina will guide your hand and trace the words."

Dipping the pen afresh into the ink, she bade him take it, and grasping his fingers, guided them while they wrote as follows;

"I, THE BLIND MAN, RICHARD HARRINGTON,--

"That last was my name," interrupted Richard, who was rewarded by a slight pull of the hair, as Nina said,

"Hush, be quiet."

A great blot now came after the "Harrington," and wiping it up with the unresisting Richard's coat sleeve, Nina continued:

"--DO HEREBY SOLEMNLY--"

She was not sure whether "swear" or "declare" would be the more proper word, and she questioned Richard, who decided upon "swear" as the stronger of the two, and she went on:

"--SWEAR THAT THE MARRIAGE OF--

"As true as you live you can't SEE?" she asked, looking curiously into the sightless eyes.

"No; I can't see," was the response, and satisfied that she was safe, Nina made him write,

"--ARTHUR ST. CLAIRE AND NINA BERNARD, PERFORMED AT MY HOUSE, IN MY PRESENCE, AND BY ME--"

Nina didn't know what, but remembering a phrase she had often heard used, and thinking it might be just what was needed, she said,

"Does 'NULL AND VOID' mean 'SCRATCHED OUT?'"

"Yes," he answered, smiling in spite of himself, and Nina added with immense capitals,

"--NULL AND VOID," to what she had already written.

"I reckon it will be better to have your name," she said, and the cramped fingers were compelled to add: "RICHARD HARRINGTON, COLLINGWOOD, November 25th 18--"

"There!" and Nina glanced with an unusual amount of satisfaction at the wonderful hieroglyphics which covered nearly an entire page of foolscap, so large were the letters and so far apart the words. "That'll cure her, sure," and folding it up, she hastened back to Edith's chamber.

Old Rachel watched that night, but Nina had no difficulty in coaxing her from the room, telling her she needed sleep, and Miggie was so much more quiet when alone with her. Rachel knew this was true, and after an hour or so withdrew to another apartment, leaving Edith alone with Nina. For a time Edith slept quietly, notwithstanding that Nina rattled the spoons and upset a chair hoping thus to wake her.

Meanwhile Richard's curiosity had been thoroughly roused with regard to the SCRATCHING OUT, and knowing Victor was still up, he summoned him to his presence, repeating to him what had just occurred and saying, "If you find that paper read it. It is surely right for me to know what I have written."

"Certainly," returned Victor, bowing himself from the room.

Rightly guessing that Nina would read it aloud to Edith, he resolved to be within hearing distance, and when he heard Rachel leave the chamber he drew near the door, left ajar for the purpose of admitting fresher air. From his position he saw that Edith was asleep, while Nina, with the paper clasped tightly in her hand, sat watching her. Once the latter thought she heard a suspicious sound, and stealing to the door she looked up and down the hall where a lamp was burning, showing that it was empty.

"It must have been the wind," she said, resuming her seat by the bedside, while Victor Dupres, gliding from the closet where he had taken refuge, stood again at his former post, waiting for that deep slumber to end.

"Nina, are you here?" came at last from the pale lips, and the bright, black eyes unclosed looking wistfully about the room.

Silent and motionless Victor stood, while Nina, bending over Edith, answered, "Yes, Miggie, I am here, and I've brought you something to make you well. HE wrote it--Richard did--just now, in the library. Can you see if I bring the lamp?" and thrusting the paper into Edith's hands she held the lamp close to her eyes.

"You havn't strength, have you?" she continued, as Edith paid no heed. "Let me do it for you," and taking the crumpled sheet, she read in tones distinct and dear:

"I, THE BLIND MAN, RICHARD HARRINGTON, DO HEREBY SOLEMNLY SWEAR THAT THE MARRIAGE OF ARTHUR ST. CLAIRE AND NINA BERNARD, PERFORMED AT MY HOUSE, IN MY PRESENCE, AND BY ME, IS NULL AND VOID. RICHARD HARRINGTON, COLLINGWOOD, NOVEMBER 5TH, 18--"

Slowly a faint color deepened on Edith's cheek, a soft lustre was kindled in her eye, and the great tears dropped from her long lashes. Her intellect was too much clouded for her to reason clearly upon anything, and she did not, for a moment, doubt the validity of what she heard. Richard could annul the marriage if he would, she was sure, and now that he had done so, the bitterness of death was past,--the dark river forded, and she was saved. Nina had steered the foundering bark into a calm, quiet sea, and exulting in her good work, she held Edith's head upon her bosom, and whispered to her of the joyous future when she would live with Arthur.

As a child listens to an exciting tale only comprehends in part, so Edith listened to Nina, a smile playing about her mouth and dancing in her eyes, which at last, as the low voice ceased, closed languidly as did the soft blue orbs above them, and when the grey dawn stole into the room it found them sleeping in each other's arms,--the noble-hearted Nina who had virtually given up her husband and the broken-hearted Edith who had accepted him. They made a beautiful tableau, and Victor for a time stood watching them, wiping the moisture from his own eyes, and muttering to himself, "Poor Edith, I understand it now, and pity you so much. But your secret is safe. Not for worlds would I betray that blessed angel, Nina." Then, crossing the hall with a cautious tread, he entered his own apartment and sat down to THINK. Victor Dupres knew WHAT HAD BEEN SCRATCHED OUT!

CHAPTER XXIII.
PARTING.

It was late the next morning, ere Nina and Edith awoke from that long sleep, which proved so refreshing to the latter, stilling her throbbing pulse, cooling her feverish brow, and subduing the wild look of her eyes, which had in them the clear light of reason. Edith was better. She would live, the physician said, feeling a glow of gratified vanity as he thought how that last dose of medicine, given as an experiment, and about which he had been so doubtful, had really saved her life. She would have died without it, he knew, just as Mrs. Matson, who inclined to homoeopathic principles, knew her patient would have died if she had not slily thrown it in the fire, substituting in its stead sweetened water and pills of bread.

Victor and Nina, too, had their theory with regard to the real cause of Edith's convalescence, but each kept his own counsel, Victor saying to Richard when questioned as to whether he had read the paper or not,

"No, Miss Nina keeps it clutched tightly in her hand, as if suspecting my design."

In the course of the day, however, Nina relaxed her vigilance, and Victor, who was sent up stairs with wood, saw the important document lying upon the hearth rug, where Nina had unconsciously dropped it.

"It's safer with me," he thought, and picking it up, he carried it to his own apartment, locking it in his trunk where he knew no curious eyes would ever find it.

In her delight at Edith's visible improvement, Nina forgot the paper for a day or two, and when at last she did remember it, making anxious inquiries for it, Mrs. Matson, who was not the greatest stickler for the truth, pacified her by saying she had burned up a quantity of waste papers scattered on the floor, and presumed this was among them. As Nina cared for nothing save to keep the SCRATCHING OUT from every one except those whom it directly concerned, she dismissed the subject from her mind, and devoted herself with fresh energy to Edith, who daily grew better.

She had not seen Arthur since that night in the Deering Woods, neither did she wish to see him. She did not love him now, she said; the shock had been so great as to destroy the root of her affections, and no excuse he could offer her would in the least palliate his sin. Edith was very harsh, very severe toward Arthur. She should never go to Grassy Spring again, she thought; never look upon his face unless he came to Collingwood, which she hoped he would not do, for an interview could only be painful to them both. She should tell him how deceved she was in him, and Edith's cheeks grew red, and her eyes unusually bright, as she mentally framed the speech she should make to Arthur St. Claire, if ever they did meet. Her excitement was increasing, when Nina came in, and tossing bonnet and shawl on the floor, threw herself upon the foot of the bed, and began to cry, exclaiming between each sob,

"Nina can't go! Nina won't go, and leave you here alone! I told him so the vile boy, but he wouldn't listen, and Soph is packing my trunks. Oh, Miggie, Miggie! how can I go without you? I shall tear again, and be as bad as ever."

"What do you mean?" asked Edith, "Where are you going, and why?"

Drying her tears, Nina, in her peculiar way, related how "Arthur wouldn't believe it was scratched out; Richard couldn't do such a thing, he said; nobody could do it, but a divorce, and Arthur wouldn't submit to that. He loves me better, than he used to do," she said; "and he talked a heap about how he'd fix up Sunny Bank. Then he asked me how I liked the name of Nina St. Claire. *I* HATE IT!" and the blue eyes flashed as Edith had never seen them flash before. "I won't be his wife! I'd forgotten all what it was that happened that night until he told it to you in the woods. Then it came back to me, and I remembered how we went to Richard, because he was most blind, and did not often come to Geneva. That was Sarah Warren's plan I believe, but my head has ached and whirled so since that I most forget. Only this I know, nothing ever came of it; and over the sea I loved Charlie Hudson, and didn't love Arthur. But, Miggie he's been so good to me so like my mother. He's held me in his arms a heap of nights when the fire was in my brain; and once, Miggie, he held me so long, and I tore so awfully, that he fainted, and Dr. Griswold cried, and said, 'Poor Arthur; poor boy!' That's when *I* BIT HIM!--bit Arthur, Miggie, right on his arm, because he wouldn't let me pull his hair. Dr. Griswold shook me mighty hard, but Arthur never said a word. He only looked at me so sorry, so grieved like, that I came out of my tantrum, and kissed the place. I've kissed it ever so many times since then, and Arthur knows I'm sorry. I ain't a fit wife for him. I don't blame him for wanting you. I can't see the WRONG, but it's because I'm so thick-headed, I suppose! I wish I wasn't!" And fixing her gaze upon the window opposite, Nina seemed to be living over the past, and trying to arrange the events of her life in some clear, tangible form.

Gradually as she talked Edith had softened toward Arthur--poor Arthur, who had borne so much. She might, perhaps, forgive him, but to FORGET was impossible. She had suffered too much at his hands for that, and uttering a faint moan as she thought how all her hopes of happiness were blasted, she turned on her pillow just as Nina, coming out of her abstracted fit, said to her,

"Did I tell you we are going to Florida--Arthur and I--going back to our old home, in two or three days, Arthur says it is better so. Old scenes may cure me."

Alas, for poor human nature. Why did Edith's heart throb so painfully, as she thought of Nina cured, and taken to Arthur's bosom as his wife. She knew SHE could not be that wife, and only half an hour before she had said within herself, "*I* HATE HIM." Now, however, she was conscious of a strong unwillingness to yield to another the love lost to her forever, and covering her head with the sheet, she wept to think how desolate her life would be when she knew that far away, in the land of flowers, Arthur was learning to forget her and bestowing his affection upon restored, rational Nina.

"Why do you cry?" asked Nina, whose quick ear detected the stifled sobs. "Is it because we are going? I told him you would, when he bade me come and ask if you would see him before he goes."

"Did he--did he send me that message?" and the Edith, who wouldn't for the world meet Arthur St. Claire again, uncovered her face eagerly. "Tell him to come to-morrow at ten o'clock. I am the strongest then; and Nina, will you care if I ask you to stay away? I'd rather see him alone."

Edith's voice faltered as she made this request, but Nina received it in perfect good faith, answering that she would remain at home.

"I must go now," she added. "He's waiting for me, and I do so hope you'll coax him to stay here. I hate old Florida."

Edith however felt that it was better for them both to part. She had caught a glimpse of her own heart, and knew that its bleeding fibres still clung to him, and still would cling till time and absence had healed the wound.

"I will be very cold and indifferent to-morrow," she said to herself, when after Nina's departure, she lay, anticipating the dreaded meeting and working herself up to such a pitch of excitement that the physician declared her symptoms worse, asking who had been there, and saying no one must see her, save the family, for several days.

The doctor's word was law at Collingwood, and with sinking spirits Edith heard Richard in the hall without, bidding Mrs. Matson keep every body from the sick room for a week. Even Nina was not to be admitted, for it was clearly proved that her last visit had made Edith worse. What should she do? Arthur would be gone ere the week went by, and she MUST see him. Suddenly Victor came into her mind. She could trust him to manage it, and when that night, while Mrs. Matson was at her tea he came up as usual with wood, she said to him, "Victor, shut the door so no one can hear, and then come close to me."

He obeyed, and standing by her bedside waited for her to speak.

"Victor, Mr. St. Claire is going to Florida in a day or two. I've promised to see him to-morrow at ten o'clock, and Richard says no one can come in here, but I must bid Arthur good-bye and Nina, too. Can't you manage it, Victor?"

"Certainly," returned Victor, who, better than any one else knew his own power over his master. "You shall see Mr. St. Claire, and see him alone."

Victor had not promised more than be felt able to perform, and when at precisely ten o'clock next day the door bell rang, he hastened to answer the summons, admitting Arthur, as he had expected.

"I called to see Miss Hastings," said Arthur, "I start for Florida to-morrow, and would bid her good-bye."

Showing him into the parlor, Victor sought Richard's presence, and by a few masterly strokes of policy and well-worded arguments, obtained his consent for Arthur to see Edith just a few moments.

"It was too bad to send him away without even a good-bye, when she had esteemed him so highly as a teacher," Richard said, unwittingly repeating Victor's very words--that a refusal would do her more injury than his seeing her could possibly do. "I'll go with him. Where is he?" he asked, rising to his feet.

"Now, I wouldn't if I was you. Let him talk with her alone. Two excite her a great deal more than one, and he may wish to say some things concerning Nina which he does not care for any one else to hear. There is a mystery about HER, you know."

Richard did not know, but he suffered himself to be persuaded, and Victor returned to Arthur, whom be conducted in triumph to the door of Edith's chamber. She heard his well known step. She knew that he was coming, and the crimson spots upon her cheeks told how much she was excited. Arthur did not offer to caress her--he dared not do that now--but be knelt by her side, and burying his face in her pillow, said to her,

"I have come for your forgiveness, Edith. I could not go without it. Say that I am forgiven, and it will not be so hard to bid you farewell forever."

Edith meant to be very cold, but her voice was choked as she replied,

"I can forgive you, Arthur, but to forget is harder far. And still even that might be possible were I the only one whom you have wronged; but Nina--how could you prove so faithless to your marriage vow?"

"Edith," and Arthur spoke almost sternly. "You would not have me live with Nina as she is now."

"No, no," she moaned, "not as she is now, but years ago. Why didn't you acknowledge her as your wife, making the best of your misfortune. People would have pitied you so much, and I--oh, Arthur, the world would not then have been so dark, so dreary for me. Why did you deceive me, Arthur? It makes my heart ache so hard."

"Oh, Edith, Edith, you drive me mad," and Arthur took in his the hand which all the time had unconsciously been creeping toward him. "I was a boy, a mere boy, and Nina was a little girl. We thought it would be romantic, and were greatly influenced by Nina's room-mate, who planned the whole affair. I told you once how Nina wept, pleading with her father to let her stay in Geneva, but I have not told you that she begged of me to tell him all, while I unhesitatingly refused. I knew expulsion from College would surely be the result, and I was far too ambitious to submit to this degradation when it could be avoided. You know of the gradual change in our feelings for each other, know what followed her coming home, and you can perhaps understand how I grew so morbidly sensitive to anything concerning her, and so desirous to conceal my marriage from every one. This, of course, prompted me to keep her existence a secret as long as possible, and, in my efforts to do so, I can see now that I oftentimes acted the part of a fool. If I could live over the past again I would proclaim from the housetops that Nina was my wife. I love her with a different love since I told you all. She is growing fast into my heart, and I have hopes that a sight of her old home, together with the effects of her native air, will do her good. Griswold always said it would, and preposterous as it seems, I have even dared to dream of a future, when Nina will be in a great measure restored to reason."

"If she does, Arthur, what then?" and, in her excitement, Edith raised herself in bed, and sat looking at him with eyes which grew each moment rounder, blacker, brighter, but had in them, alas, no expression of joy; and when in answer to her appeal, Arthur said,

"I shall make her my wife," she fell back upon her pillow, uttering a moaning cry, which to the startled Arthur sounded like,

"No, no! no, no! not your wife."

"Edith," and rising to his feet Arthur stood with folded arms, gazing pityingly upon her, himself now the stronger of the two. "Edith, you, of all others, must not tempt me to fall. You surely will counsel me to do right! Help me! oh, help me! I am so weak, and I feel my good resolutions all giving way at sight of your distress! If it will take one iota from your pain to know that Nina shall never be my acknowledged wife, save as she is now, I will swear to you that, were her reason ten times restored, she shall not; But, Edith, don't, don't make me swear it. I am lost, lost if you do. Help me to do right, won't you, Edith?"

He knelt beside her again, pleading with her not to tempt him from the path in which he was beginning to walk; and Edith, as she listened, felt the last link, which bound her to him, snapping asunder. For a moment she HAD wavered; had shrank from the thought that any other could ever stand to him in the relation she once had hoped to stand; but that weakness was over, and while chiding herself for it, she hastened to make amends.

Turning her face toward him, and laying both her hands on his bowed head, she said,

"May the Good Father bless you, Arthur, even as you prove true to Nina. I have loved you, more than you will ever know, or I can ever tell, and my poor, bruised heart clings to you still with a mighty grasp. It is so hard to give you up, but it is right. I shall think of you often in your beautiful Southern home, praying always that God will bless you and forgive you at the last, even as I forgive you. And now farewell, MY Arthur, I once fondly hoped to call you, but mine no longer--NINA'S Arthur--go."

She made a gesture for him to leave her, but did not unclose her eyes. She could not look upon him, find know it was the last, last time, but she offered no remonstrance when he left, upon her lips a kiss so full of hopeless and yearning tenderness that it burned there many a day after he was gone. She heard him turn away, heard him cross the floor, knew he paused upon the threshold, and still her eye-lids never opened, though the hot tears rained over her face in torrents.

"The sweetest joy I have ever known was my love for you, Edith Hastings," he whispered, and then the door was closed between them.

Down the winding stairs he went, Edith counting every step, for until all sound of him had ceased she could not feel that they were parted forever. The sounds did cease at last, he had bidden Richard a calm good-bye, had said good-bye to Victor, and now he was going from the house. He would soon be out of sight, and with an intense desire to stamp his image upon her mind just as he was now, the changed, repentant Arthur, Edith arose, and tottering to the window, looked after him, through blinding tears, as he passed slowly from her sight, and then crawling, rather than walking back to her bed, she wept herself to sleep.

It was a heavy, unnatural slumber, and when she awoke from it, the fever returned with redoubled violence, bringing her a second time so near the gates of death that Arthur St. Claire deferred his departure for several days, and Nina became again the nurse of the sick room. But all in vain were her soft caresses and words of love. Edith was unconscious of everything, and did not even know when Nina's farewell kiss was pressed upon her lips and Nina's gentle hands smoothed her hair for the last time. A vague remembrance she had of an angel flitting around the room, a bright-haired seraph, who held her up from sinking in the deep, dark river, pointing to the friendly shore where life and safety lay, and this was all she knew of a parting which had wrung tears from every one who witnessed it, for there was something wonderfully touching in the way the crazy Nina bade adieu to "Miggie," lamenting that she must leave her amid the cold northern hills, and bidding her come to the southland, where the magnolias were growing and flowers were blossoming all the day long. Seizing the scissors, which lay upon the stand, she severed one of her golden curls, and placing it on Edith's pillow, glided from the room, followed by the blessing of those who had learned to love the beautiful little girl as such as she deserved to be loved.

* * * * * *

One by one the grey December days went by, and Christmas fires were kindled on many a festal hearth. Then the New Year dawned upon the world, and still the thick, dark curtains shaded the windows of Edith's room. But there came a day at last, a pleasant January day, when the curtains were removed, the blinds thrown open, and the warm sunlight came in shining upon Edith, a convalescent. Very frail and beautiful she looked in her crimson dressing gown, and her little foot sat loosely in the satin slipper, Grace Atherton's Christmas gift. The rich lace frill encircling her throat was fastened with a locket pin of exquisitely wrought gold, in which was encased a curl of soft, yellow hair, Nina's hair, a part of the tress left on Edith's pillow. This was Richard's idea,--Richard's New Year's gift to his darling; but Richard was not there to share in the general joy.

Just across the hall, in a chamber darkened as hers had been, he was lying now, worn out with constant anxiety and watching. When Nina left, his prop was gone, and the fever which had lain in wait for him so long, kindled within his veins a fire like to that which had burned in Edith's, but his strong, muscular frame met it fiercely, and the danger had been comparatively slight.

All this Grace told to Edith on that morning when she was first suffered to sit up, and asked why Richard did not come to share her happiness, for in spite of one's mental state, the first feeling of returning health is one of joy. Edith felt it as such even though her heart was so sore that every beat was painful. She longed to speak of Grassy Spring, but would not trust herself until Victor, reading her feelings aright, said to her with an assumed indifference, "Mr. St. Claire's house is shut up, all but the kitchen and the negro apartments. They are there yet, doing nothing and having a good time generally."

"And I have had a letter from Arthur," chimed in Mrs. Atherton, while the eyes resting on Victor's face turned quickly to hers. "They reached Sunny Bank in safety, he and Nina, and Soph."

"And Nina," Edith asked faintly, "how is she?"

"Improving, Arthur thinks, though she misses you very much."

Edith drew a long, deep sigh, and when next she spoke, she said, "Take me to the window, please, I want to see the country."

In an instant, Victor, who knew well what she wanted, took her in his arms, and carrying her to the window, set her down in the chair which Grace brought for her; then, as if actuated by the same impulse, both left her and returned to the fire, while she looked across the snow-clad fields to where Grassy Spring reared its massive walls, now basking in the winter sun. It was a mournful pleasure to gaze at that lonely building, with its barred doors, its closed shutters, and the numerous other tokens it gave of being nearly deserted. There was no smoke curling from the chimneys, no friendly door opened wide, no sweet young face peering from the iron lattice of the Den, no Arthur, no Nina there. Nothing but piles of snow upon the roof, snow upon the window-sills, snow upon the doorsteps, snow upon the untrodden walk, snow on the leafless elms, standing there so bleak and brown. Snow everywhere, as cold, as desolate as Edith's heart, and she bade Victor take her back again to the warm grate where she might perhaps forget how gloomy and sad, and silent, was Grassy Spring.

"Did I say anything when I was delirious--anything I ought not to have said?" she suddenly asked of Grace; and Victor, as if she had questioned him, answered quickly,

"Nothing, nothing--all is safe."

Like a flash of lightning, Grace Atherton's eyes turned upon him, while he, guessing her suspicions, returned her glance with one as strangely inquisitive as her own.

"Mon Dieu! I verily believe she knows," he muttered, as he left the room, and repairing to his own, dived to the bottom of his trunk, to make sure that he still held in his possession the paper on which it had been "scratched out."

That night as Grace Atherton took her leave of Edith, she bent over the young girl, and whispered in her ear,

"I know it all. Arthur told me the night before he left. God pity you, Edith! God pity you!"

CHAPTER XXIV.
THE NINETEENTH BIRTH-DAY.

Edith was nineteen. She was no longer the childish, merry-hearted maiden formerly known as Edith Hastings. Her cruel disappointment had ripened her into a sober, quiet woman, whose songs were seldom heard in the halls of Collingwood, and whose bounding steps had changed into a slower, more measured tread.

Still, there was in her nature too much of life and vigor to be crushed out at once, and oftentimes it flashed up with something of its olden warmth, and the musical laugh fell again on Richard's listening ear. He knew she was changed, but he imputed it all to her long, fearful sickness; when the warm summer days came back, she would be as gay as ever, he thought, or if she did not he would in the autumn take her to FLORIDA, to visit Nina, for whom he fancied she might be pining. Once he said as much to her, but his blindness was a shield between them, and he did not see the sudden paling of her cheek and quivering of her lip.

Alas, for Richard, that he walked in so great a darkness. Hour by hour, day by day, had his love increased for the child of his adoption, until now she was a part of his very life, pervading every corner and crevice of his being. He only lived for her, and in his mighty love, he became selfishly indifferent to all else around him. Edith was all he cared for;--to have her with him;--to hear her voice,--to know that she was sitting near,--that by stretching forth his hand he could lay it on her head, or feel her beautiful cheeks,--this was his happiness by day, and when at night he parted unwillingly from her, there was still a satisfaction in knowing that he should meet her again on the morrow,--in thinking that she was not far away--that by stepping across the hall and knocking at her door he could hear her sweet voice saying to him,

"What is it, Richard?"

He liked to have her call him Richard, as she frequently did. It narrowed the wide gulf of twenty-one years between them, bringing him nearer to her, so near, in fact, that bridal veils and orange wreaths now formed a rare loveliness walked ever at his side; clothed in garments such as the mistress of Collingwood's half million ought to wear, and this maiden was Edith--the Edith who, on her nineteenth birth-day, sat in her own chamber devising a thousand different ways of commencing a conversation which she meant to have with her guardian, the subject of said conversation being no less a personage than Grace Atherton. Accidentally Edith had learned that not the Swedish baby's mother but Grace Elmendorff had been the lady who jilted Richard Harrington and that, repenting bitterly of her girlish coquetry, Mrs. Atherton would now gladly share the blind man's lot, and be to him what she had not been to her aged, gouty lord. Grace did not say all this to Edith, it is true, but the latter read as much in the trembling voice and tearful eyes with which Grace told the story of her early love, and to herself she said, "I will bring this matter about. Richard often talks of her to me, asking if she has faded, and why she does not come more frequently to Collingwood. I will speak to him at the very first opportunity, and will tell him of my mistake, and ask him who Eloise Temple's mother was, and why he was so much interested in her."

With this to engross her mind and keep it from dwelling too much upon the past, Edith became more like herself than she had been since that dreadful scene in the Deering woods. Even her long neglected piano was visited with something of her former interest, she practising the songs which she knew Grace could sing with her, and even venturing upon two or three duets, of which Grace played one part. It would be so nice, she thought, to have some female in the house besides old Mrs. Matson, and she pictured just how Grace would look in her white morning gowns, with her blue eyes and chestnut curls, presiding at the breakfast table and handling the silver coffee urn much more gracefully than she could do.

It was a pleasant picture of domestic bliss which Edith drew that April morning, and it brought a glow to her cheeks, whence the roses all had fled. Once, indeed, as she remembered what Arthur had said concerning Richard's probable intentions, and what she had herself more than half suspected, she shuddered with fear lest by pleading for Grace, she should bring a fresh trial to herself. But no, whatever

Richard might once have thought of her, his treatment now was so fatherly that she had nothing to fear, and with her mind thus at ease Edith waited rather impatiently until the pleasant April day drew to its close. Supper was over, the cloth removed, Victor gone to an Ethiopian concert, Mrs. Matson knitting in her room, Sarah, the waiting-maid, reading a yellow covered novel, and Richard sitting alone in his library.

Now was Edith's time if ever, and thrusting the worsted work she was crocheting into her pocket, she stepped to the library door and said pleasantly "You seem to be in a deep study. Possibly you don't want me now?"

"Yes, I do," he answered quickly. "I always want you."

"And can always do without me, too, I dare say," Edith rejoined playfully, as she took her seat upon a low ottoman, near him.

"No, I couldn't," and Richard sighed heavily. "If I had not you I should not care to live. I dreamed last night that you were dead, that you died while I was gone, and I dug you up with my own hands just to look upon your face again. I always see you in my sleep. I am not blind then, and when a face fairer, more beautiful than any of which the poets ever sang flits before me, I whisper to myself, 'that's Edith,--that's my daylight.'"

"Oh, mistaken man," Edith returned, laughingly, "how terribly you would be disappointed could you be suddenly restored to sight and behold the long, lank, bony creature *I* know as Edith Hastings-- low forehead, turned-up nose, coarse, black hair, all falling out, black eyes, yellowish black skin, not a particle of red in it--the fever took that away and has not brought it back. Positively, Richard, I'm growing horridly ugly. Even my hair, which I'll confess I did use to think was splendid, is as rough as a chestnut burr. Feel for yourself if you don't believe me," and she laid his hand upon her hair, which, though beautiful and abundant, still was quite uneven and had lost some of its former satin gloss.

Richard shook his head. Edith's description of her personal appearance made not a particle of difference with him. She might not, perhaps, have recovered her good looks, but she would in time. She was improving every day, and many pronounced her handsomer than before her sickness, for where there had been, perhaps, a superabundance of color and health there was now a pensive, subdued beauty, preferred by some to the more glowing, dashing style which had formerly distinguished Edith Hastings from every one else in Shannondale. Something like this he said to her, but Edith only laughed and continued her crocheting, wondering how she should manage to introduce Grace Atherton. It was already half-past eight, Victor might soon be home, and if she spoke to him that night she must begin at once. Clearing her throat and making a feint to cough, she plunged abruptly into the subject by saying, "Richard, why have you never married? Didn't you ever see anybody you loved well enough?"

Richard's heart gave one great throb and then grew still, for Edith had stumbled upon the very thing uppermost in his mind. What made her? Surely, there was a Providence in it. 'Twas an omen of good, boding success to his suit, and after a moment he replied,

"Strange that you and I should both be thinking of matrimony. Do you know that my dreaming you were dead is a sign that you will soon be married?"

"*I*, Mr. Harrington!" and Edith started quickly. "The sign is not true. I shall never marry, never. I shall live here always, if you'll let me, but I do want you to have a wife. You will be so much happier, I think. Shall I propose one for you?"

"Edith," Richard answered, "sit close to me while I tell you of one I once wished to make my wife."

Edith drew nearer to him, and he placed upon her head the hands which were cold and clammy as if their owner were nerving himself for some mighty effort.

"Edith, in my early manhood I loved a young girl, and I thought my affection returned, but a wealthier, older man came between us, and she chose his riches in preference to walking in my shadow, for such she termed my father."

"But she's repented, Mr. Harrington--she surely has," and Edith dropped her work in her earnestness to defend Grace Atherton. "She is sorry for what she made you suffer; she has loved you through all, and would be yours now if you wish it, I am sure. You DO wish it, Richard. You will forgive Grace Atherton," and in her excitement Edith knelt before him, pleading for her friend.

Even before he answered her she knew she pleaded in vain, but she was not prepared for what followed the silence Richard was first to break.

"Grace Atherton can never be to me more than what she is, a tried, respected friend. My boyish passion perished long ago, and into my later life another love has crept, compared with which my first was as the darkness to the full noonday. I did not think to talk of this to-night, but something compels me to do so--tells me the time has come, and Edith, you must hear me before you speak, but sit here where I can touch you, and when I'm through if what I've said meets with a responsive chord, lay your hand in mine, and I shall know the nature of your answer."

It was coming now--the scene which Arthur foresaw when, sitting in the Deering woods, with life and sense crushed out, he gave his Edith up to one more worthy than himself. It was the foreshadowing of the "SACRIFICE," the first step taken toward it, and as one who, seeing his destiny wrapping itself about him fold on fold, sits down stunned and powerless, so Edith sat just where he bade her sit, and listened to his story.

"Years ago, Edith, a solitary, wretched man I lived in my dark world alone, weary of life, weary of every thing, and in my weariness I was even beginning to question the justice of my Creator for having dealt so harshly with me, when one day a wee little singing bird, whose mother nest had been made desolate, fluttered down at my feet, tired like myself, and footsore even with the short distance it had come on life's rough journey. There was a note in the voice of this sinking bird which spoke to me of the past, and so my interest grew in the helpless thing until at last it came to nestle at my side, not timidly, for such was not its nature, but as if it had a right to be there--a right to be caressed and loved as I caressed and loved it, for I did learn to love it, Edith, so much, oh, so much, and the sound of its voice was sweeter to me than the music of the Swedish nightingale, who has filled the world with wonder.

"Years flew by, and what at first had been a tiny fledgling, became a very queen of birds, and the blind man's heart throbbed with pride when he heard people say of his darling that she was marvellously fair. He knew it was not for him to look upon her dark, rich, glowing beauty, but he stamped her features upon his mind in characters which could not be effaced, and always in his dreams her face sat on his pillow, watching while be slept, and when he woke bent over him, whispering, 'Poor blind man,' just as the young bird had whispered ere it's home was in his bosom.

"Edith, that face is always with me, and should it precede me to the better land, I shall surely know it from all the shining throng. I shall know my singing bird, which brought to our darkened household the glorious daylight, just as Arthur St. Claire said she would when he asked me to take her."

From the ottoman where Edith sat there came a low, choking sound, but it died away in her throat, and with her hands locked so firmly together that the taper nails made indentation in the tender flesh, she listened, while Richard continued:

"It is strange no one has robbed me of my gem. Perhaps they spared me in their pity for my misfortune. At all events, no one has come between us, not even Arthur St. Claire, who is every way a desirable match for her."

Again that choked, stifled moan, and a ring of blood told where the sharp nail had been, but Edith heeded nothing save Richard's voice, saying to her,

"You have heard of little streams trickling from the heart of some grim old mountain, growing in size and strength as they advanced, until at last they became a mighty river, whose course nothing could impede, Such, Edith, is my love for that singing bird. Little by little, inch by inch, it has grown in its intensity until there is not a pulsation of my being which does not bear with it thoughts of her. But my bird is young while I am old. Her mate should be one on whose head the summer dews are resting, one more like Arthur St Claire, and not an owl of forty years growth like me; but she has not chosen such an one, and hope has whispered to the tough old owl that his bright-eyed dove might be coaxed into his nest; might fold her wings there forever, nor seek to fly away. If this COULD be, Edith. Oh, if this could be, I'd guard that dove so tenderly that not a feather should be ruffled, and the winds of heaven should not blow too roughly on my darling. I'd line her cage all over with gold and precious stones, but the most costly gem of all should be the mighty unspeakable love I'd bear to her. Aye, that I do bear her now, Edith,--my daylight, my life. You surely comprehend me; tell me, then, can all this be? Give me the token I desire."

He stretched out his groping hand, which swayed back and forth in the empty air, but felt the clasp of no soft fingers clinging to it, and a wistful, troubled look settled upon the face of the blind man, just as a chill of fear was settling upon his heart.

"Edith, darling, where are you?" and his hand sought the ottoman where she had been, but where she was not now.

Noiselessly, as he talked, she had crept away to the lounge in the corner, where she crouched like a frightened deer, her flush creeping with nervous terror, and her eyes fastened upon the man who had repeated her name, asking where she was.

"Here, Richard," she answered at last, her eyelids involuntarily closing when she saw him rising, and knew he was coming toward her.

She had forgotten her promise to Arthur that she would not answer Richard "No," should he ask her to be his wife; that, like Nina's "scratching out," was null and void, and when he knelt beside her, she said half bitterly,

"It must not be; THE SINGING BIRD CANNOT MATE WITH THE OWL!"

Instantly there broke from the blind man's lips a cry of agony so pitiful, so reproachful in its tone, that Edith repented her insulting words, and winding her arms around his neck, entreated his forgiveness for having so cruelly mocked him..

"You called yourself so first," she sobbed, "or I should not have thought of it. Forgive me. Richard, I didn't mean it. I could not thus pain the noblest, truest friend I ever had. Forgive your singing bird. She surely did not mean it," and Edith pressed her burning cheeks against his own.

What was it she did not mean? That it could not be, or that he was an owl? He asked himself this question many times during the moment of silence which intervened; then as he felt her still clinging to him, his love for her rolled back upon him with overwhelming force, and kneeling before her as the slave to his master, he pleaded with her again to say IT COULD BE, the great happiness he had dared to hope for.

"Is there any other man whom my darling expects to marry?" he asked, and Edith was glad he put the question in this form, as without prevarication she could promptly answer,

"No, Richard, there is none."

"Then you may learn to love me," Richard said. "I can wait, I can wait; but must it be very long? The days will be so dreary, and I love you so much that I am lost if you refuse. Don't make my darkness darker, Edith."

He laid his head upon her lap, still kneeling before her, the iron-willed man kneeling to the weak young girl, whose hands were folded together like blocks of lead, and gave him back no answering caress, only the words,

"Richard, I can't. It's too sudden. I have thought of you always as my elder brother, Be my brother, Richard. Take me as your sister, won't you?"

"Oh, I want you for my wife," and his voice was full of pleading pathos. "I want you in my bosom, I need you there, darling. Need some one to comfort me. I've suffered so much, for your sake, too. Oh, Edith, my early manhood was wasted; I've reached the autumn time, and the gloom which wrapped me then in its black folds lies around me still, and will you refuse to throw over my pathway a single ray of sunlight? No, no, Edith, you won't, you can't. I've loved you too much. I've lost too much. I'm growing old--and--oh, Birdie, Birdie, I'M BLIND! I'M BLIND!"

She did not rightly interpret his suffering FOR HER SAKE. She thought he meant his present pain, and she sought to soothe him as best she could without raising hopes which never could be realized. He understood her at last; knew the heart he offered her was cast back upon him, and rising from his kneeling posture, he felt his way back to his chair, and burying his head upon a table standing near, sobbed as Edith had never heard man sob before, not even Arthur St. Claire, when in the Deering Woods he had rocked to and fro in his great agony. Sobs they were which seemed to rend his broad chest asunder, and Edith stopped her ears to shut out the dreadful sound.

But hark, what is it he is saying? Edith fain would know, and listening intently, she hears him unconsciously whispering to himself; "OH, EDITH, WAS IT FOR THIS THAT *I* SAVED YOU FROM THE RHINE, PERILING MY LIFE AND LOSING MY EYESIGHT? BETTER THAT YOU HAD DIED IN THE DEEP WATERS THAN THAT *I* SHOULD MEET THIS HOUR OF ANGUISH."

"Richard, Richard!" and Edith nearly screamed as she flew across the floor. Lifting up his head she pillowed it upon her bosom, and showering kisses upon his quivering lips, said to him, "Tell me-- tell me, am *I* that Swedish baby, *I* that Eloise Temple?"

He nodded in reply, and Edith continued: "the child for whose sake you were made blind! Why have you not told me before? I could not then have wounded you so cruelly. How can I show my gratitude? I am not worthy of you, Richard; not worthy to bear your name, much less to be your bride, but such as I am take me. I cannot longer refuse. Will you, Richard? May I be your wife?"

She knelt before HIM now; hers was the supplicating posture, and when he shook his head, she continued,

"You think it a sudden change, and so it is, but I mean it. I'm in earnest, I do love you, dearly, oh, so dearly, and by and by I shall love you a great deal more. Answer me--may I be your wife?"

It was a terrible temptation, and Richard Harrington reeled from side to side like a broken reed, while his lips vainly essayed to speak the words his generous nature bade them speak. He could not see the eagerness of the fair young face upturned to his--the clear, truthful light shining in Edith's beautiful dark eyes, telling better than words could tell that she was sincere in her desire to join her sweet spring life with his autumn days. He could not see this, else human flesh had proved too weak to say what he did say at last.

"No, my darling, I cannot accept a love born of gratitude and nothing more. You remember a former conversation concerning this Eloise when you told me you were glad you were not she, as in case you were you should feel compelled to be grateful, or something like that, where as you would rather render your services to me from love. Edith, that remark prevented me from telling you then that you were Eloise, the Swedish mother's baby."

Never before had the words "that Swedish mother" touched so tender a chord in Edith's heart as now, and forgetting every thing in her intense desire to know something of her own early history, she exclaimed, "You knew my mother, Richard. You have heard her voice, seen her face; now tell me of her, please. Where is she? And Marie, too, for there was a Marie. Let's forget all that's been said within the last half hour. Let's begin anew, making believe it's yesterday instead of now, and, when the story is ended, ask me again if the singing bird can mate with the eagle. The grand, royal eagle, Richard, is the best similitude for you," and forcing herself to sit upon his knee, she put her arms around his neck bidding him again tell her of her mother.

With the elastic buoyancy of youth Edith could easily shake off the gloom which for a few brief moments had shrouded her like a pall, but not so with Richard. "The singing-bird must not mate with the owl," rang continually in his ears. It was her real sentiment he knew, and his heart ached so hard as he thought how he had staked his all on her and lost it.

"Begin," she said, "Tell me where you first met my mother."

Richard heaved a sigh which smote heavily on Edith's ear, for she guessed of what he was thinking, and she longed to reassure him of her intention to be his sight hereafter, but he was about to speak and she remained silent.

"Your mother," he said "was a Swede by birth, and her marvellous beauty first attracted your father, whose years were double her own."

"I'm so glad," interrupted Edith, "As much as twenty-one years older, wasn't he?"

"More than that," answered Richard, a half pleased, half bitter smile playing over his dark face, "Forgive me, darling, but I'm afraid he was not as good a man as he should have been, or as kind to his young wife. When I first saw her she lived in a cottage alone, and he was gone. She missed him sadly, and her sweet voice seemed full of tears as she sang her girl baby to sleep. You have her voice, Edith, and its tones came back to me the first time I ever heard you speak. But I was telling of your father. He was dissipated, selfish and unprincipled,--affectionate and kind to Petrea one day, cold, hard and brutal the next. Still she loved him and clung to him, for he was the father of her child. You were a beautiful little creature, Edith, and I loved you so much that when I knew you had fallen from a bluff into the river, I unhesitatingly plunged after you."

"I remember it," cried Edith, "I certainly do, or else it was afterwards told to me so often that it seems a reality."

"The latter is probably the fact," returned Richard. "You were too young to retain any vivid recollections of that fall."

Still Edith persisted that she did remember the face of a little girl in the water as she looked over the rock, and of bending to touch the arm extended toward her. She remembered Bingen, too, with its purple grapes; else why had she been haunted all her life with vine-clad hills and plaintive airs.

"Your mother sang to you the airs, while your nurse, whose name I think was Marie, told you of the grapes growing on the hills," said Richard. "She was a faithful creature, greatly attached to your mother, but a bitter foe of your father. I was too much absorbed in the shadow stealing over me to pay much heed to my friends, and after they left Germany I lost sight of them entirely, nor dreamed that the little girl who came to me that October morning was my baby Eloise. Your voice always puzzled me, and something I overheard you saying to Grace one day about your mysterious hauntings of the past, together with an old song of Petrea's which you sang, gave me my first suspicion as to who you were, and decided me upon that trip to New York. Going first to the Asylum of which you were once an inmate, I managed after much diligent inquiry to procure the address of the woman who brought you there when you were about three years old. I had but little hope of finding her, but determining to persevere I sought out the humble cottage in the suburbs of the city. It was inhabited by an elderly woman who denied all knowledge of Edith Hastings until told that I was Richard Harrington. Then her manner changed at once, and to my delight I heard that she was Marie's sister. She owned the cottage, had lived there more than twenty years, and saw your mother die. Petrea, it seems, had left her husband, intending to return to Sweden, but sickness overtook her and she died in New York, committing you to the faithful Marie's care in preference to your father's. Such was her dread of him that she made Marie swear to keep your existence a secret from him, lest he should take you back to a place where she had been so wretched and where all the influences, she thought, were bad. She would rather you should be poor, she said, than to be brought up by him, and as a means of eluding discovery, she said you should not bear his name, and with her dying tears she baptised you Edith Hastings. After her decease Marie wrote to him that both of you were dead, and he came on at once, seemed very penitent and sorry when it was too late."

"Where was his home?" Edith asked eagerly; and Richard replied,

"That is one thing I neglected to enquire, but when I met him in Europe I had the impression that it was in one of the Western or South-western states."

"Is he still alive?" Edith asked again, a daughter's love slowly gathering in her heart in spite of the father's cruelty to the mother.

"No," returned Richard. "Marie, who kept sight of his movements, wrote to her sister some years since that he was dead, though when he died, or how, Mrs. Jamieson did not know. She, too, was ill when he came to her house, and consequently never saw him herself."

"And the Asylum--how came I there?" said Edith; and Richard replied,

"It seems your mother was an orphan, and had no near relatives to whom you could be sent, and as Marie was then too poor and dependent to support you she placed you in the Asylum as Edith Hastings, visiting you occasionally until she went back to France, her native country. Her intention was to return in a few months, but a violent attack of inflammatory rheumatism came upon her, depriving her of the use of her limbs, and confining her to her bed for years, and so prevented her from coming back. Mrs. Jamieson, however, kept her informed with regard to you, and told me that Marie was greatly when she heard you were with me, whom she supposed to be the same Richard Harrington who had saved your life, and of whom her mistress had often talked. Marie is better now, and when I saw her sister more than a year ago, she was hoping she might soon revisit America. I left directions for her to visit Collingwood, and for several months I looked for her a little, resolving if she came, to question her minutely concerning your father. He must have left a fortune, Edith, which by right is yours, if we can prove that you are his child, and with Marie's aid I hope to do this sometime. I have, however, almost given her up; but now that you know all I will go again to New York, and seek another interview with Mrs. Jamieson. Would it please you to have the little orphan, Edith Hastings, turn out to be an heiress?"

"Not for my own sake," returned Edith; "but if it would make you love me more, I should like it;" and she clung closer to him as he replied,

"Darling that could not be. I loved you with all the powers I had, even before I knew you were Petrea's child. Beautiful Petrea! I think you must be like her, Edith, except that you are taller. She was your father's second wife. This I knew in Germany, and also that there was a child of Mr. Temple's first marriage, a little girl, he said."

"A child--a little girl," and Edith started quickly, but the lightning flash which had once gleamed across her bewildered mind, when in the Den she stood gazing at the picture of Miggie Bernard, did not come back to her now, neither did she remember Arthur's story, so much like Richard's. She only thought that possibly there was somewhere in the world a dear, half-sister, whom she should love so much, could she only find her. Edith was a famous castle-builder, and forgetting that this half-sister, were she living, would be much older than herself, she thought of her only as a school-girl, whose home should be at Collingwood, and on whom MRS. RICHARD HARRINGTON would lavish so much affection, wasting on her the surplus love which, perhaps, could not be given to the father--husband. How then was her castle destroyed, when Richard said,

"She, too, is dead, so Mrs. Jamieson told me, and there is none of the family left save you."

"I wish I knew where mother was buried," Edith sighed, her tears falling to the memory of her girl mother, whose features it seamed to her she could recall, as well as a death-bed scene, when somebody with white lips and mournful black eyes clasped her in her arms and prayed that God would bless her, and enable her always to do right.

It might have been a mere fancy, but to Edith it was a reality, and she said within herself,

"Yes, darling mother, I will do right, and as I am sure yon would approve my giving myself to Richard, so I will be his wife."

One wild, longing, painful throb her heart gave to the past when she had hoped for other bridegroom than the middle-aged man on whose knee she sat, and then laying her hot face against his bearded cheek, she whispered,

"You've told the story, Richard. It does not need Marie to confirm it, though she, too, will come sometime to tell me who I am, but when she comes, I shan't be Edith Hastings, shall I. The initials won't be changed, though. They will be 'E.H.' still--Edith Harrington. It has not a bad sound, has it?"

"Don't, darling, please don't," and Richard's voice had in it a tone much like that which first rang through the room, when Edith said,

"It cannot be."

"Richard," and Edith took his cold face between her soft, warm hands, "Richard, won't you let the singing bird call you husband? If you don't, she will fly away and sing to some one else, who will prize her songs. I thought you loved me, Richard."

"Oh, Edith, my precious Edith! If I knew I could make the love grow where it is not growing--the right kind of love, I mean--I would not hesitate; but, darling, Richard Harrington would die a thousand deaths rather than take you to his bosom an unloving wife. Remember that, and do NOT mock me; do not deceive me. You think now in the first flush of your gratitude to me for having saved your life and in your pity for my blindness that you can do anything; but wait awhile--consider well--think how I shall be old while you still are young,--a tottering, gray-haired man, while your blood still retains the heat of youth. The Harringtons live long. I may see a hundred."

"And I shall then be seventy-nine; not so vast a difference," interrupted Edith.

"No, not a vast difference then," Richard rejoined, "but 'tis not then I dread. 'Tis now, the next twenty-five years, during which I shall be slowly decaying, while you will be ripening into a matured, motherly beauty, dearer to your husband than all your girlish loveliness. 'Tis then that I dread the contrast in you; not when both are old; and, Edith, remember this, you can never be old to me, inasmuch as I can never see you. I may feel that your smooth, velvety flesh is wrinkled, that your shining hair is thin, your soft round arms more sinewy and hard, but I cannot see it, and in my heart I shall cherish ever the image I first loved as Edith Hastings. You, on the contrary, will watch the work of death go on in me, will see my hair turn gray, my form begin to stoop, my hand to tremble, my eyes grow blear and watery, and when all has come to pass, won't you sicken of the shaky old man and sigh for a younger, more vigorous companion?"

"Not unless you show me such horrid pictures," Edith sobbed, impetuously, for in her heart of hearts she felt the truth of every word he uttered, and her whole soul revolted against the view presented to her of the coming time.

But she would conquer such feelings--she would be his wife, and drying her eyes she said, "I can give you my decision now as well as at any other time, but if you prefer it, I will wait four weeks and then bring you the same answer I make you now--I will be your wife."

"I dare not hope it," returned Richard, "You will change your mind, I fear, but, Edith, if you do not,--if you promise to be mine, don't forsake me afterwards, for I should surely die," and as if he already felt the agony it would cost him to give his darling up after he had once possessed her, he clasped his hands upon his heart, which throbbed so rapidly that Edith heard its muffled beat and saw its rise and fall. "I could not lose you and still live on without you, Edith," and he spoke impetuously, "You won't desert me, if you promise once."

"Never, never," she answered, and with a good night kiss upon his lips she went out from the presence of the man she already looked upon as her future husband, breathing freer when she stood within the hall where he was not, and freer still when in her own chamber there was a greater distance between them.

Alas, for Edith, and a thousand times alas, for poor, poor Richard!

CHAPTER XXV.
DESTINY.

Not for one moment did Edith waver in her purpose, and lest Richard should suspect what he could not see, she affected a gayety in his presence sadly at variance with her real feelings. Never had her merry laugh rang out so frequently before him--never had her wit been one half so sparkling, and when he passed his hands over her flushed cheek, feeling how hot it was, he said to himself, "The roses are coming back, she cannot be unhappy," and every line and lineament of the blind man's face glowed with the new-born joy springing up within his heart, and making the world around him one grand jubilee.

Victor was quick to note the change in his master, and without the least suspicion of the truth, he once asked Edith, "What made Mr. Harrington so young and almost boyish, acting as men were supposed to act when they were just engaged?"

"Victor," said Edith, after a moment's reflection, "can you keep a secret?"

"Certainly," he replied. "What is it, pray? Is Mr. Harrington matrimonially inclined?"

Edith's heart yearned for sympathy--for some one to sustain her-- to keep her from fainting by the wayside, and as she could not confide in Grace, Victor was her only remaining refuge. He had been the repository of all her childish secrets, entering into her feelings as readily and even more demonstratively than any female friend could have done. Richard would tell him, of course, as soon as it was settled, and as she knew now that it was settled, why not speak first and so save him the trouble. Thus deciding, she replied to his question,

"Yes, Richard is going to be married; but you must not let him know I told you, till the engagement is made public."

Victor started, but had no shadow of suspicion that the young girl before him was the bride elect. His master had once been foolish enough to think of her as such he believed, but that time was passed. Richard had grown more sensible, and Edith was the future wife of Arthur St. Claire. Nina would not live long, and after she was dead there would be no further hindrance to a match every way so suitable. This was Victor's theory, and never doubting that the same idea had a lodgment in the minds of both Arthur and Edith, he could not conceive it possible that the latter would deliberately give herself to Richard. Grace Atherton, on the contrary, would be glad to do it; she had been coaxing his master these forty years, and had succeeded in winning him at last. Victor did not fancy Grace; and when at last he spoke, it was to call both his master and Mrs. Atherton a pair of precious fools. Edith looked wonderingly at him as he raved on.

"I can't bear her, I never could, since I heard how she abused you. Why, I'd almost rather you'd be his wife than that gay widow."

"Suppose I marry him then in her stead," Edith said, laughingly. "I verily believe he'd exchange."

"Of course he would," Victor answered, bitterly. "The older a man grows, the younger the girl he selects, and it's a wonder he didn't ask you first."

"Supposing he had?" returned Edith, bending over a geranium to hide her agitation. "Supposing he had, and it was I instead of Grace to whom he is engaged."

"Preposterous!" Victor exclaimed. "You could not do such a thing in your right senses. Why, I'd rather see you dead than married to your father. I believe I'd forbid the banns myself," and Victor strode from the room, banging the door behind him, by way of impressing Edith still more forcibly with the nature of his opinion.

Edith was disappointed. She had expected sympathy at least from Victor, had surely thought he would he pleased to have her for his mistress, and his words, "I would rather see you dead," hurt her cruelly. Perhaps every body would say so. It was an unnatural match, this union of autumn and spring, but she must do something. Any thing was preferable to the aimless, listless life she was leading now. She could not be any more wretched than she was, and she might perhaps be happier when the worst was over and she knew for certain that she was Richard's wife. HIS WIFE! It made her faint and sick just to say those two words. What then would the reality be? She loved him dearly as a guardian, a brother, and she might in time love him as her husband. Such things had been. They could be again. Aye, more, they should he, and determining henceforth to keep her own counsel, and suffer Victor to believe it was Grace instead of herself, she ran into the garden, where she knew Richard was walking, and stealing to his side, caught his arm ere he was aware of her presence.

"Darling, is it you?" he asked, and his dark face became positively beautiful with the radiant love-light shining out all over it.

Every day the hope grew stronger that the cherished object of his life might be realized. Edith did not avoid him as he feared she would. On the contrary she rather sought his society than otherwise, never, however, speaking of the decision. It was a part of the agreement that they should not talk of it until the four weeks were gone, the weeks which to Richard dragged so slowly, while to Edith they flew on rapid wing; and with every rising sun, she felt an added pang as she thought how soon the twelfth of May would be there. It wanted but four days of it when she joined him in the garden, and for the first time since their conversation Richard alluded to it by asking playfully, "what day of the month it was?"

"The eighth;" and Edith's eyes closed tightly over the tears struggling to gain egress, then with a mighty effort she added, laughingly,

"When the day after to-morrow comes, it will be the tenth, then the eleventh, then the twelfth, and then, you know, I'm coming to you in the library. Send Victor off for that evening, can't you? He's sure to come in when I don't want him, if he's here," and this she said because she feared it would be harder to say yes if Victor's reproachful eyes should once look upon her, as they were sure to do, if he suspected her designs.

Richard could not understand why Victor must be sent away, but anything Edith asked was right, and he replied that Victor should not trouble them.

"There, he's coming now!" and Edith dropped the hand she held, as if fearful lest the Frenchman should suspect.

This was not the proper feeling, she knew, and returning to the house, she shut herself up in her room, crying bitterly because she could not make herself feel differently!

The twelfth came at last, not a balmy, pleasant day as May is wont to bring, but a rainy, dreary April day, when the gray clouds chased each other across the leaden sky, now showing a disposition to bring out patches of blue, and again growing black and heavy as the fitful showers came pattering down. Edith was sick. The strong tension of nerves she had endured for four long weeks was giving way. She could not keep up longer; and Richard breakfasted and dined without her, while with an aching head she listened to the rain beating against her windows, and watched the capricious clouds as they floated by. Many times she wished it all a dream from which she should awaken; and then, when she reflected that 'twas a fearful reality, she covered her head with the bed-clothes and prayed that she might die. But why pray for this? She need not be Richard's wife unless she chose--he had told her so repeatedly, and now she too said "I will not!" Strange she had not thus decided before and stranger still that she should be so happy now she had decided!

There was a knock at the door, and Grace Atherton asked to be admitted.

"Richard told me you were sick," she said, as she sat down by Edith's side; "and you do look ghostly white. What is the matter, pray?"

"One of my nervous headaches;" and Edith turned from the light so that her face should tell no tales of the conflict within.

"I received a letter from Arthur last night," Grace continued, "and thinking you might like to hear from Nina, I came round in the rain to tell you of her. Her health is somewhat improved, and she is now under the care of a West India physician, who holds out strong hopes that her mental derangement may in time be cured."

Edith was doubly glad now that she had turned her face away, for by so doing she hid the tears which dropped so fast upon her pillow.

"Did Arthur mention me?" she asked, and Grace knew then that she was crying.

Still it was better not to withhold the truth, and bending over her she answered,

"No, Edith, he did not. I believe he is really striving to do right."

"And he will live with Nina if she gets well?" came next from the depths of the pillows where Edith lay half smothered.

"Perhaps so. Would you not like to have him?" Grace asked.

"Ye-e-e-s. I sup-pose so. Oh, I don't know what I like. I don't know anything except that I wish I was dead," and the silent weeping became a passionate sobbing as Edith shrank further from Grace, plunging deeper and deeper among her pillows until she was nearly hidden from view.

Grace could not comfort her; there was no comfort as she saw, and as Edith refused to answer any of her questions upon indifferent topics, she ere long took her leave, and Edith was left alone. She had reversed her decision while Grace was sitting there, and the news from Florida was the immediate cause. She should marry Richard now, and her whole body shook with the violence of her emotions; but as the fiercest storm will in time expend its fury, so she grew still at last, though it was rather the stillness of despair than any healthful, quieting influence stealing over her. She hated herself because she could not feel an overwhelming joy at the prospect of Nina's recovery; hated Arthur because he had forgotten her; hated Grace for telling her so; hated Victor for saying he would rather see her dead than Richard's wife; hated Mrs. Matson for coming in to ask her how she was; hated her for staying there when she would rather be alone, and made faces at her from beneath the sheet; hated everybody but Richard, and in time she should hate him--at least, she hoped she should, for on the whole she was more comfortable when hating people than she had ever been when loving them. It had such a hardened effect upon her, this hatred of all mankind, such a don't care influence, that ahe rather enjoyed it than otherwise.

And this was the girl who, as that rainy, dismal day drew to its close and the sun went down in tears, dressed herself with a firm, unflinching hand, arranging her hair with more than usual care, giving it occasionally a sharp pull, as a kind of escape valve to her feelings and uttering an impatient exclamation whenever a pin proved obstinate and did not at once slip into its place. She was glad Richard was blind and could not see her swollen eyes, which, in spite of repeated bathings in ice-water and cologne would look red and heavy. Her voice, however, would betray her, and so she toned it down by warbling snatches of a love song learned ere she knew the meaning of love, save as it was connected with Richard. It was not Edith Hastings who left that pleasant chamber, moving with an unfaltering step down the winding stairs and across the marble hall, but a half-crazed, defiant woman going on to meet her DESTINY and biting her lip with vexation when she heard that Richard had company--college friends, who being in Shannondale on business had come up to see him.

This she learned from Victor, whom she met in the hall, and who added, that he never saw his master appear quite so dissatisfied as when told they were in the library, and would probably pass the night. Edith readily guessed the cause of his disquiet, and impatiently stamped her little foot upon the marble floor, for she knew their presence would necessarily defer the evil hour, and she could not live much longer in her present state of excitement.

"I was just coming to your room," said Victor, "to see if you were able to appear in the parlor. Three men who have not met in years are stupid company for each other; and then Mr. Harrington wants to show you off I dare say. Pity the widow wasn't here."

Victor spoke sarcastically, but Edith merely replied,

"Tell your master I will come in a few minutes."

Then, with a half feeling of relief, she ran back to her room, bathing her eyes afresh, and succeeding in removing the redness to such an extent, that by lamplight no one would suspect she had been crying. Her headache was gone, and with spirits somewhat elated, she started again for the parlor where she succeeded in entertaining Richard's guests entirely to his satisfaction.

It was growing late, and the clock was striking eleven when at last Richard summoned Victor, bidding him show the gentleman to their rooms. As they were leaving the parlor Edith came to Richard's side and in a whisper so low that no one heard her, save himself, said to him,

"Tell Victor he needn't come back."

He understood her meaning, and said to his valet,

"I shall not need your services to-night. You may retire as soon as you choose."

Something in his manner awakened Victor's suspicions, and his keen eyes flashed upon Edith, who, with a haughty toss of the head, turned away to avoid meeting it again.

The door was dosed at last; Victor was gone; their guests were gone, and she was alone with Richard, who seemed waiting for her to speak; but Edith could not. The breath she fancied would come so freely with Victor's presence removed, would scarcely come at all, and she felt the tears gathering like a flood every time she looked at the sightless man before her, and thought of what was to come. By a thousand little devices she strove to put it off, and remembering that the piano was open, she walked with a faltering step across the parlor, closed the instrument, smoothed the heavy cover, arranged the sheets of music, whirled the music stool as high as she could, turned it back as low as she could, sat down upon it, crushed with her fingers two great tears, which, with all her winking she could not keep in subjection, counted the flowers on the paper border and wondered how long she should probably live. Then, with a mighty effort she arose, and with a step which this time did not falter, went and stood before Richard, who was beginning to look troubled at her protracted silence. He knew she was near him now, he could hear her low breathing, and he waited anxiously for her to speak.

Edith's face was a study then. Almost every possible emotion was written upon it. Fear, anguish, disappointed hopes, cruel longings for the past, terrible shrinkings from the present, and still more terrible dread of the future. Then these passed away, and were succeeded by pity, sympathy, gratitude, and a strong desire to do right. The latter feelings conquered, and sitting down by Richard, she took his warm hand between her two cold ones, and said to him,

"'Tis the twelfth of May to-night, did you know it?"

Did he know it? He had thought of nothing else the livelong day, and when, early in the morning, he heard that she was sick, a sad foreboding had swept over him, lest what he coveted so much should yet be withheld. But she was there beside him. She had sought the opportunity and asked if he knew it was the twelfth, and, drawing her closer to him, he answered back: "Yes, darling; 'tis the day on which you were to bring me your decision. You have kept your word, birdie. You have brought it to me whether good or bad. Now tell me, is it the old blind man's wife, the future mistress of Collingwood, that I encircle with my arm?"

He bent down to listen for the reply, feeling her breath stir his hair, and hearing each heart-beat as it counted off the seconds. Then like a strain of music, sweet and rich, but oh, so touchingly sad, the words came floating in a whisper to his ear, "Yes, Richard, your future wife; but please, don't call yourself the old blind man. It makes you seem a hundred times my father. You are not old, Richard--no older than I feel!" and the newly betrothed laid her head on Richard's shoulder, sobbing passionately.

Did all girls behave like this? Richard wished he knew. Did sweet Lucy Collingwood, when she gave her young spring life to his father's brown October? Lucy had loved her husband, he knew, and there was quite as much difference between them as between himself and Edith. Possibly 'twas a maidenly weakness to cry, as Edith was doing. He would think so at all events. It were death to think otherwise, and caressing her with unwonted tenderness, he kissed her tears away, telling her how happy she had made him by promising to be his--how the darkness, the dreariness all was gone, and the world was so bright and fair. Then, as she continued weeping and he remembered what had heretofore passed between them, he said to her earnestly: "Edith, there is one thing I would know. Is it a divided love you bring me, or is it no love at all. I have a right to ask you this, my darling. Is it gratitude alone which prompted your decision? If it is, Edith, I would die rather than accept it. Don't deceive me, darling, I cannot see your face-- cannot read what's written there. Alas! alas! that I am blind to- night; but I'll trust you, birdie; I'll believe what you may tell me. Has an affection, different from a sister's, been born within the last four weeks? Speak! do you love me more than you did? Look into my eyes, dearest; you will not deal falsely with me then."

Like an erring, but penitent child, Edith crept into his lap, but did not look into the sightless eyes. She dared not, lest the gaze should wring from her quivering lips the wild words trembling there, "Forgive me, Richard, but I loved Arthur first." So she hid her face in his bosom, and said to him,

"I do not love you, Richard, as you do me. It came too sudden, and I had not thought about it. But I love you dearly, very dearly, and I want so much to be your wife. I shall rest so quietly when I have you to lean upon, you to care for. I am young for you, I know, but many such matches have proved happy, and ours assuredly will. You are so good, so noble, so unselfish, that I shall be happy with you. I shall be a naughty, wayward wife, I fear, but you can control me, and you must. We'll go to Europe sometime, Richard, and visit Bingen on the Rhine, where the little baby girl fell in the river, and the brave boy Richard jumped after her. Don't you wish you'd let me die? There would then have been no bad black-haired Edith lying in your lap, and torturing you with fears that she does not love you as she ought."

Edith's was an April temperament, and already the sun was shining through the cloud; the load at her heart was not so heavy, nor the future half so dark. Her decision was made, her destiny accepted, and henceforth she would abide by it nor venture to look back.

"Are you satisfied to take me on my terms?" she asked, as Richard did not immediately answer.

He would rather she had loved him more, but it was sudden, he knew, and she was young. He was terribly afraid, it is true, that gratitude alone had influenced her actions, but the germ of love was there, he believed; and by and by it would bear the rich, ripe fruit. He could wait for that; and he loved her so much, wanted her so much, needed her so much, that he would take her on any terms.

"Yes" he said at last, resting his chin upon her bowed head, "I am satisfied, and never since my rememberance, has there come to Richard Harrington a moment so fraught with bliss as this in which I hold you in my arms and know I hold my wife, my darling wife, sweetest name ever breathed by human tongue--and Edith, if you must sicken of me, do it now--to-night. Don't put it off, for every fleeting moment binds me to you with an added tie, which makes it harder to lose you."

"Richard," and, lifting up her head, Edith looked into the eyes she could not meet before, "I swear to you, solemnly, that never, by word or deed, will I seek to be released from our engagement, and if I am released, it will be because you give me up of your own free will. You will be the one to break it, not I."

"Then it will not be broken," came in a quick response from Richard, as he held closer to him one whom he now felt to be his forever.

The lamps upon the table, and the candles on the mantel flashed and smoked, and almost died away--the fire on the marble hearth gave one or two expiring gasps and then went out--the hands of the clock moved onward, pointing to long after midnight, and still Richard, loth to let his treasure go, kept her with him, talking to her of his great happiness, and asking if early June would be too soon for her to be his bride.

"Yes, yes, much too soon," cried Edith. "Give me the whole summer in which to be free. I've never been any where you know. I want to see the world. Let's go to Saratoga, and to all those places I've heard so much about. Then, in the autumn, we'll have a famous wedding at Collingwood, and I will settle down into the most demure, obedient of wives."

Were it not that the same roof sheltered them both, Richard would have acceded to this delay, but when he reflected that he should not be parted from Edith any more than if they were really married, he consented, stipulating that the wedding should take place on the anniversary of the day when she first came to him with flowers, and called him "poor blind man."

"You did not think you'd ever be the poor blind man's wife," he said, asking her, playfully, if she were not sorry even now.

"No," she answered. Nor was she. In fact, she scarcely felt at all. Her heart was palsied, and lay in her bosom like a block of stone--heavy, numb, and sluggish in its beat.

Of one thing, only, was she conscious, and that a sense of weariness--a strong desire to be alone, up stairs, where she was not obliged to answer questions, or listen to loving words, of which she was so unworthy. She was deceiving Richard, who, when his quick ear caught her smothered yawn, as the little clock struck one, bade her leave him, chiding himself for keeping her so long from the rest he knew she needed.

"For me, I shall never know fatigue or pain again," he said, as he led her to the door, "but my singing-bird is different--she must sleep. God bless you, darling. You have made the blind man very happy."

He kissed her forehead, her lips, her hands, and then released her, standing in the door and listening to her footsteps as they went up the winding stairs and out into the hall beyond--the dark, gloomy hall, where no light was, save a single ray, shining through the keyhole of Victor's door.

CHAPTER XXVI.
EDITH AND THE WORLD.

"Victor is faithful," Edith said, as she saw the light, and fancied that the Frenchman was still up, waiting to assist his master.

But not for Richard did Victor keep the watch that night. He would know how long that interview lasted below, and when it was ended he would know its result. What Victor designed he was pretty sure to accomplish, and when, by the voices in the lower hall, he knew that Edith was coming, he stole on tip-toe to the balustrade, and, leaning over, saw the parting at the parlor door, feeling intuitively that Edith's relations to Richard had changed since he last looked upon her. Never was servant more attached to his master than was Victor Dupres to his, and yet he was strongly unwilling that Edith's glorious beauty should be wasted thus.

"If she loved him," he said to himself, as, gliding back to his room, he cautiously shut the door, ere Edith reached the first landing. "If she loved him, I would not care. More unsuitable matches than this have ended happily--but she don't. Her whole life is bound with that of another, and she shrinks from Mr. Harrington as she was not wont to do. I saw it in her face, as she turned away from him. There'll be another grave in the Collingwood grounds--another name on the tall monument, 'Edith, wife of Richard Harrington, aged 20.'"

Victor wrote the words upon a slip of paper, reading them over until tears dimmed his vision, for, in fancy, the imaginative Frenchman assisted at Edith's obsequies, and even heard the grinding of the hearse wheels, once foretold by Nina. Several times he peered out into the silent hall, seeing the lamplight shining from the ventilator over Edith's door, and knowing by that token that she had not retired. What was she doing there so long? Victor fain would know, and as half-hour after half-hour went by, until it was almost four, he stepped boldly to the door and knocked. Long association with Victor had led Edith to treat him more as an equal than a servant; consequently he took liberties both with her and Richard, which no other of the household would dare to do, and now, as there came no response, he cautiously turned the knob and walked into the room where, in her crimson dressing-gown, her hair unbound and falling over her shoulders, Edith sat, her arms crossed upon the table, and her face upon her arms. She was not sleeping, for as the door creaked on its hinges, she looked up, half-pleased to meet only the good-humored face of Victor where she had feared to see that of Richard.

"Miss Edith, this is madness--this is folly," and Victor sat down before her. "I was a fool to think it was Mrs. Atherton."

"Victor Dupres, what do you mean? What do you know? Why are you here?" and Edith's eyes flashed with insulted pride; but Victor did not quail before them. Gazing steadily at her, he replied, "You are engaged to your guardian, and you do not love him."

"Victor Dupres, *I* DO!" and Edith struck her hand upon the table with a force which made the glass lamp rattle.

"Granted you do," returned Victor, "but how do you love him? As a brother, as a friend, as a father, if you will, but not as you should love your husband; not as you could love Arthur St. Claire, were he not bound by other ties,"

Across the table the blanched, frightened face of Edith looked, and the eyes which never before had been so black, scanned Victor keenly.

"What do you know of Arthur St. Claire's ties?" she asked at last, every word a labored breath.

Victor made no answer, but hurrying from the room, returned with the crumpled, soiled sheet of foolscap, which he placed before her, asking if she ever saw it before.

Edith's mind had been sadly confused when Nina read to her the SCRATCHING OUT, and she had forgotten it entirely, but it came back to her now, and catching up the papers, she recognized Richard's unmistakable hand-writing. He knew, then, of her love for Arthur--of the obstacle to that love--of the agony it cost her to give him up. He had deceived her--had won her under false pretenses, assuming that she loved no one. She did not think this of Richard, and in her eyes, usually so soft and mild, there was a black, hard, terrible expression, as she whispered hoarsely, "How came this in your possession?"

He told her how--thus exonerating Richard from blame, and the hard, angry look was drowned in tears as Edith wept aloud.

"Then he don't know it," she said at length, "Richard don't. I should hate him if he did and still wished me to be his wife."

"I can tell him," was Victor's dry response, and in an instant Edith was over where he sat.

"You cannot, you must not, you shall not. It will kill him if I desert him. He told me so, and I promised that I wouldn't-- promised solemnly. I would not harm a hair of Richard's head, and he so noble, so good, so helpless, with so few sources of enjoyment; but oh, Victor, I did love Arthur best--did love him so much," and in that wailing cry Edith's true sentiments spoke out. "I did love him so much--I love him so much now," and she kept whispering it to herself, while Victor sought in vain for some word of comfort, but could find none. Once he said to her, "Wait, and Nina may die," but Edith recoiled from him in horror.

"Never hint that Again," she almost screamed. "It's murder, foul murder. I would not have Nina die for the whole world--beautiful, loving Nina. I wouldn't have Arthur, if she did. I couldn't, for I am Richard's wife. I wish I'd told him early June instead of October. I'll tell him to-morrow and in four weeks more all the dreadful uncertainty will be ended. I ought to love him, Victor, he's done so much for me. I am that Swedish child he saved from the river Rhine, periling life and limb, losing his sight for me. He found it so that time he went with you to New York," and Edith's tears ceased as she repeated to Victor all she knew of her early history. "Shouldn't I marry him?" she asked, when the story was ended. "Ought I not to be his eyes? Help me, Victor. Don't make it so hard for me; I shall faint by the way if you do."

Victor conceded that she owed much to Richard, but nothing could make him think it right for her to marry him with her present feelings. It would be a greater wrong to him than to refuse him, but Edith did not think so.

"He'll never know what I feel," she said, and by and by I shall be better,--shall love him as he deserves. There are few Richards in the world, Victor."

"That is true," he replied, "but 'tis no reason why you must be sacrificed. Edith, the case is like this: I wish, and the world at large, if it could speak, would wish for Richard to marry you, but would not wish you to marry Richard."

"But I shall," interrupted Edith. "There is no possible chance of my not doing so, and Victor, you will help me.--You won't tell him of Arthur. You know how his unselfish heart would give me up if you did, and break while doing it. Promise, Victor."

"Tell me first what you meant by early June, and October," he said, and after Edith had explained, he continued, "Let the wedding be still appointed for October, and unless I see that it is absolutely killing you, I will not enlighten Mr. Harrington."

And this was all the promise Edith could extort from him.

"Unless he saw it was absolutely killing her, he would not enlighten Richard."

"He shall see that it will not kill me," she said to herself, "I will be gay whether I feel it or not. I will out-do myself, and if my broken heart should break again, no one shall be the wiser."

Thus deciding, she turned toward the window where the gray dawn was stealing in, and pointing to it, said:

"Look, the day is breaking; the longest night will have an end, so will this miserable pain at my heart. Daylight will surely come when I shall be happy with Richard. Don't tell him, Victor, don't; and now leave me, for my head is bursting with weariness."

He knew it was, by the expression of her face, which, in the dim lamp-light, looked ghastly and worn, and he was about to leave her, when she called him back, and asked how long he had lived with Mr. Harrington.

"Thirteen years," he replied. "He picked me up in Germany, just before he came home to America. He was not blind then."

"Then you never saw my mother?"

"Never."

"Nor Marie?"

"Never to my knowledge,"

"You were in Geneva with Richard, you say. Where were you, when-- when--"

Edith could not finish, but Victor understood what she would ask, and answered her,

"I must have been in Paris. I went home for a few months, ten years ago last fall, and did not return until just before we came to Collingwood. The housekeeper told me there had been a wedding at Lake View, our Geneva home, but I did not ask the particulars. There's a moral there, Edith; a warning to all foolish college boys, and girls, who don't half know their minds."

Edith was too intent upon her own matters to care for morals, and without replying directly, she said,

"Richard will tell you to-morrow or to-day, rather, of the engagement, and you'll be guarded, won't you?"

"I shall let him know I disapprove," returned Victor, "but I shan't say anything that sounds like Arthur St. Claire, not yet, at all events."

"And, Victor, in the course of the day, you'll make some errand to Brier Hill, and incidentally mention it to Mrs. Atherton. Richard won't tell her, I know, and I can't--I can't. Oh, I wish it were-- "

"The widow, instead of you," interrupted Victor, as he stood with the door knob in his hand. "That's what you mean, and I must say it shows a very proper frame of mind in a bride-elect."

Edith made a gesture for him to leave her, and with a low bow he withdrew, while Edith, alternately shivering with cold and flushed with fever, crept into bed, and fell away to sleep, forgetting, for the time, that there were in the world such things as broken hearts, unwilling brides, and blind husbands old enough to be her father.

* * * * * *

The breakfast dishes were cleared away, all but the exquisite little service brought for Edith's use when she was sick, and which now stood upon the sideboard waiting until her long morning slumber should end. Once Mrs. Matson had been to her bedside, hearing from her that her head was aching badly, and that she would sleep longer. This message was carried down to Richard, who entertained his guests as best he could, but did not urge them to make a longer stay.

They were gone now, and Richard was alone. It was a favorable opportunity for telling Victor of his engagement, and summoning the latter to his presence, he bade him sit down, himself hesitating, stammering and blushing like a woman, as he tried to speak of Edith. Victor might have helped him, but he would not, as he sat, rather enjoying his master's confusion, until the latter said, abruptly,

"Victor, how would you like to have a mistress here--a bona fide one, I mean, such as my wife would be?"

"That depends something upon who it was," Victor exclaimed, as if this were the first intimation he had received of it.

"What would you say to Edith?" Richard continued, and Victor replied with well-feigned surprise, "Miss Hastings! You would not ask that little girl to be your wife! Why you are twenty-five years her senior."

"No, no, Victor, only twenty-one," and Richard's voice trembled, for like Edith, he wished to be reassured and upheld even by his inferiors.

He knew Victor disapproved, that he considered it a great sacrifice on Edith's part, but for this he had no intention of giving her up. On the contrary it made him a very little vexed that his valet should presume to question his acts, and he said with more asperity of manner than was usual for him,

"You think it unsuitable, I perceive, and perhaps it is, but if we are satisfied, it is no one's else business, I think,"

"Certainly not," returned Victor, a meaning smile curling his lip, "if both are satisfied, I ought to be. When is the wedding?"

He asked this last with an appearance of interest, and Richard, ever ready to forgive and forget, told him all about it, who Edith was, and sundry other matters, to which Victor listened as attentively as if he had not heard the whole before. Like Edith, Richard was in the habit of talking to Victor more as if he were an equal than a servant and in speaking of his engagement, he said,

"I had many misgivings as to the propriety of asking Edith to be my wife--she is so young, so different from me, but my excuse is that I cannot live without her. She never loved another, and thus the chance is tenfold that she will yet be to me all that a younger, less dependent husband could desire."

Victor bit his lip, half resolved one moment to undeceive poor Richard, whom he pitied for his blind infatuation, but remembering his promise, he held his peace, until his master signified that the conference was ended, when he hastened to the barn, where he could give vent to his feeling in French, his adopted language being far too prosy to suit his excited mood. Suddenly Grace Atherton came into his mind, and Edith's request that he should tell her.

"Yes, I'll do it," he said, starting at once for Brier Hill "'Twill be a relief to let another know it, and then I want to see her squirm, when she hears all hope for herself is gone."

For once, however, Victor was mistaken. Gradually the hope that she could ever be aught to Richard was dying out of Grace's heart, and though, for an instant, she turned very white when, as if by accident, he told the news, it was more from surprise at Edith's conduct than from any new feeling that she had lost him. She was in the garden bending over a bed of daffodils, so he did not see her face, but he knew from her voice how astonished she was and rather wondered that she could question him so calmly as she did, asking if Edith were very happy, when the wedding was to be, and even wondering at Richard's willingness to wait so long.

"Women are queer any way," was Victor's mental comment, as, balked of his intention to see Grace Atherton squirm, he bade her good morning, and bowed himself from the garden, having first received her message that she would come up in the course of the day, and congratulate the newly betrothed.

Once alone, Grace's calmness all gave way; and though the intelligence did not affect her as it once would have done, the fibres of her heart quivered with pain, and a sense of dreariness stole over her, as, sitting down on the thick, trailing boughs of an evergreen, she covered her face with her hands, and wept as women always weep over a blighted hope. It was all in vain that her pet kitten came gamboling to her feet, rubbing against her dress, climbing upon her shoulder, and playfully touching, with her velvet paw, the chestnut curls which fell from beneath her bonnet. All in vain that the Newfoundland dog came to her side, licking her hands and gazing upon her with a wondering, human look of intelligent. Grace had no thought for Rover or for Kitty, and she wept on, sometimes for Arthur, sometimes for Edith, but oftener for the young girl who years ago refused the love offered her by Richard Harrington; and then she wondered if it were possible that Edith had so soon ceased to care for Arthur,

"I can tell from her manner," she thought; and with her mind thus brought to the call she would make at Collingwood, she dried her eyes, and speaking playfully to her dumb pets, returned to the house a sad, subdued woman, whose part in the drama of Richard Harrington was effectually played out.

That afternoon, about three o'clock, a carriage bearing Grace Atherton, wound slowly up the hill to Collingwood and when it reached the door a radiant, beautiful woman stepped out, her face all wreathed in smiles and her voice full of sweetness as she greeted Richard, who came forth to meet her.

"A pretty march you've stolen upon me," she began, in a light, bantering tone--"you and Edith--never asked my consent or said so much as 'by your leave' but no matter, I congratulate you all the same. I fancied it would end in this. Where is she--the bride- elect?"

Richard was stunned with such a volley of words from one whom he supposed ignorant of the matter, and observing his evident surprise Grace continued, "You wonder how I know, Victor told me this morning; he was too much delighted to keep it to himself. But say, where is Edith?"

"Here I am," and advancing from the parlor, where she had overheard the whole, Edith laughed a gay, musical laugh, as hollow and meaningless as Mrs. Atherton's forced levity.

Had she followed the bent of her inclinations she would not have left her pillow that day, but remembering Victor's words, "Unless I see it's killing you," she felt the necessity of exerting herself, of wearing the semblance of happiness at least, and about noon she had arisen and dressed herself with the utmost care, twining geranium leaves in her hair just as she used to do when going to see Arthur, and letting them droop from among her braids in the way he had told her was so becoming. Then, with flushed cheeks and bright, restless eyes, she went down to Richard, receiving his caresses and partially returning them when she fancied Victor was where he could see her,

"Women are queer," he said again to himself, as he saw Edith on Richard's knee, with her arm around his neck. "Their love is like a footprint on the seashore; the first big wave washes it away, and they are ready to make another. I reckon I shan't bother myself about her any more. If she loved Arthur as I thought she did, she couldn't hug another one so soon. It isn't nature--man nature, any way; but Edith's like a reed that bends. That character of Cooper's suits her exactly. I'll call her so to myself hereafter--Reed that bends," and Victor hurried off, delighted with his new name.

But if Victor was in a measure deceived by Edith's demeanor, Grace Atherton was not. Women distrust women sooner than men; can read each other better, detect the hidden motive sooner, and ere the two had been five minutes together, Grace had caught a glimpse of the troubled, angry current over which the upper waters rippled so smoothly that none save an accurate observer would have suspected the fierce whirlpool which lay just below the surface. Because, he thought, they would like it better, Richard left the two ladies alone at last and then turning suddenly upon Edith, Grace said,

"Tell me, Edith, is your heart in this or have you done it in a fit of desperation?"

"I have had a long time to think of it," Edith answered proudly. "It is no sudden act. Richard is too noble to accept it if it were. I have always loved him,--not exactly as I loved Arthur, it is true."

Here the whirlpool underneath threatened to betray itself, but with a mighty effort Edith kept it down, and the current was unruffled as she continued,

"Arthur is nearer my age--nearer my beau ideal, but I can't have him, and I'm not going to play the part of a love-lorn damsel for a married man. Tell him so when you write. Tell him I'm engaged to Richard just as he said I would be. Tell him I'm happy, too, for I know I'm doing right. It is not wicked to love Richard and it was wicked to love him."

It cost Edith more to say this than she supposed, and when she finished, the perspiration stood in drops beneath her hair and about her mouth.

"You are deceiving yourself," said Grace, who, without any selfish motive now, really pitied the hard, white-faced girl, so unlike the Edith of other days. "You are taking Richard from gratitude, nothing else. Victor told me of your parentage, but because he saved your life, you need not render yours as a return. Your heart is not in this marriage."

"Yes, it is--all the heart I have," Edith answered curtly. Then, as some emotion stronger than the others swept over her, she laid her head upon the sofa arm and sobbed, "You are all leagued against me, but I don't care. I shall do as I like, I have promised to marry Richard, and Edith Hastings never lied. She will keep her word," and in the eyes which she now lifted up, Grace saw the years glittering like diamonds.

Then a merry laugh burst from the lips of the wayward girl as she met Mrs.

Atherton's anxious glance, and running to the piano she dashed off most inspiriting waltz, playing so rapidly that the bright bloom came back, settling in a small round spot upon her cheek, and making her surpassingly beautiful even to Grace, whose great weakness was an unwillingness to admit that another's charms were superior to her own. When the waltz was ended Edith's mood had changed, and turning to Grace she nestled closely to her, and twining one of the silken curls around her fingers, said coaxingly,

"You think me a naughty child no doubt, but you do not understand me. I certainly do love Richard more than you suppose; and Grace, I want you to help me, to encourage me. Engaged girls always need it, I guess, and Victor is so mean, he says all sorts of hateful things about my marrying my father, and all that. Perhaps the village people will do so, too, and if they do, you'll stand up for me, won't you? You'll tell them how much I owe him--how much I love him, and, Grace," Edith's voice was very low now, and sad, "and when you write to Arthur don't repeat the hateful things I said before, but tell him I'm engaged; that I'm the Swedish baby; that I never shall forget him quite; and that I love Richard very much."

Oh, how soft and plaintive was the expression of the dark eyes now, as Edith ceased to speak, and pressed the hand which warmly pressed hers back, for Grace's womanly nature was aroused by this appeal, and she resolved to fulfill the trust reposed in her by Edith. Instead of hedging her way with obstacles she would help her, if possible; would encourage her to love the helpless blind man, whose step was heard In the hall. He was coming to rejoin them, and instantly into Edith's eyes there flashed a startled, shrinking look, such as the recreant slave may be supposed to wear when he hears his master's step. Grace knew the feeling which prompted that look full well. She had felt it many a time, in an intensified degree, stealing over her at the coming of one whose snowy looks and gouty limbs had mingled many a year with the dust of Shannondale, and on her lips the words were trembling, "This great sacrifice must not be," when Edith sprang up, and running out into the hall, met Richard as be came.

Leading him into the parlor, and seating him upon the sofa, she aat beside him, holding his hand in hers, as if she thus would defy her destiny, or, at the least, meet it bravely. Had Grace known of Victor's new name for Edith she too would have called her "Reed that bends," and as it was she thought her a most incomprehensible girl, whom no one could fathom, and not caring to tarry longer, soon took her leave, and the lovers were alone.

Arrived at home, Grace opened her writing desk and commenced a letter, which started next day for Florida, carrying to Arthur St. Claire news which made his brain reel and grow giddy with pain, while his probed heart throbbed, and quivered, and bled with a fresh agony, as on his knees by Nina's pillow he prayed, not that the cup of bitterness might pass from him--he was willing now to quaff that to its very dregs, but that Edith might be happy with the husband she had chosen, and that he, the desolate, weary Arthur might not faint beneath this added burden.

Five weeks went by--five weeks of busy talk among the villagers, some of whom approved of the engagement, while more disapproved. Where was that proud Southerner? they asked, referring to Arthur St. Claire. They thought him in love with Edith. Had he deserted her, and so in a fit of pique she had given herself to Richard? This was probably the fact, and the gossips, headed by Mrs. Eliakim Rogers, speculated upon it, while the days glided by, until the five weeks were gone, and Edith, sitting in Grace's boudoir, read, with eyes which had not wept since the day following her betrothal, the following extract from Arthur's letter to his cousin:

"Richard and Edith! Oh! Grace, Grace! I thought I had suffered all that mortal man could suffer, but when that fatal message came, I died a thousand deaths in one, enduring again the dreadful agony when in the Deering woods I gave my darling up. Oh, Edith, Edith, Edith, my soul goes after her even now with a quenchless, mighty love, and my poor, bruised, blistered heart throbs as if some great giant hand were pressing its festered wounds, until I faint with anguish and cry out, 'my punishment is greater than I can bear.'

"Still I would not have it otherwise, if I could. I deserve it all, aye, and more, too. Heaven bless them both, Richard and his beautiful singing bird. Tell her so, Grace. Tell her how I blessed her for cheering the blind man's darkness, but do not tell her how much it costs me to bid her, as I now do, farewell forever and ever, farewell."

It was strange that Grace should have shown this letter to Edith, but the latter coaxed so hard that she reluctantly consented, repenting of it however when she saw the effect it had on Edith. Gradually as she read, there crept over her a look which Grace had never seen before upon the face of any human being--a look as if the pent-up grief of years was concentrated in a single moment of anguish too acute to be described. There were livid spots upon her neck--livid spots upon her face, while the dry eyes seemed fading out, so dull, and dim, and colorless they looked, as Edith read the wailing cry with which Arthur St. Claire bade her his adieu.

For several minutes she sat perfectly motionless, save when the muscles of her mouth twitched convulsively, and when the hard, terrible look gave way--the spots began to fade--the color came back to her cheeks--the eyes resumed their wonted brilliancy--the fingers moved nervously, and Edith was herself. She had suffered all she could, and never again would her palsied heart know the same degree of pain which she experienced when reading Arthur's letter. It was over now--the worst of it. Arthur knew of her engagement--blessing her for it, and pitying he would not have it otherwise. The bitterness of death was past, and henceforth none save Grace and Victor suspected the worm which fed on Edith's very life, so light, so merry, so joyous she appeared; and Edith was happier than she had supposed it possible for her to be. The firm belief that she was doing right, was, of itself, a source of peace, and helped to sustain her fainting spirits, still there was about her a sensation of disquiet, a feeling that new scenes would do her good, and as the summer advanced, and the scorching July sun penetrated even to the cool shades of Collingwood, she coaxed Richard, Grace and Victor to go away. She did not care where, she said, "anything for a change; she was tired of seeing the same things continually. She never knew before how stupid Shannondale was. It must have changed within the last few months."

"I think it was you who have changed," said Grace, fancying that she could already foresee the restless, uneasy, and not altogether agreeable woman, which Edith, as Richard's wife, would assuredly become.

Possibly Richard, too, thought of this, for a sigh escaped him as he heard Edith find fault with her beautiful home.

Still he offered no remonstrance to going from home awhile, and two weeks more found them at the Catskill Mountain House, where at first not one of the assembled throng suspected that the beautiful young maiden who in the evening danced like a butterfly in their midst, and in the morning bounded up the rocky heights like some fearless, graceful chamois, was more than ward to the man who had the sympathy of all from the moment the whispered words went round, "He is blind."

Hour after hour would Edith sit with him upon the grass plat overlooking the deep ravine, and make him see with her eyes the gloriously magnificent view, than which there is surely none finer in all the world; then, when the looked toward the west, and the mountain shadow began to creep across the valley, the river, and the hills beyond, shrouding them in an early twilight, she would lead him away to some quiet sheltered spot, where unobserved, she could lavish upon him the little acts of love she knew he so much craved and which she would not give to him when curious eyes were looking on. It was a blissful paradise to Richard, and when in after years he looked back upon the past, he always recurred to those few weeks as the brightest spot in his whole life, blessing Edith for the happiness she gave him during that season of delicious quiet spent amid the wild scenery of the Catskill Mountains.

CHAPTER XXVII.
THE LAND OF FLOWERS.

It was the original plan for the party to remain two weeks or more at the Mountain House, and then go on to Saratoga, but so delighted were they with the place that they decided to tarry longer, and the last of August found them still inmates of the hotel, whose huge white walls, seen from the Hudson, stand out from the dark wooded landscape, like some mammoth snow bank, suggestive to the traveller of a quiet retreat and a cool shelter from the summer's fervid heat. Edith's health and spirits were visibly improved, and her musical laugh often rang through the house in tones so merry and gleeful that the most solemn of the guests felt their boyhood coming back to them as they heard the ringing laugh, and a softer light suffused their cold, stern eyes as they paused in the midst of some learned discussion to watch the frolicsome, graceful belle of the Mountain House--the bride elect of the blind man.

It was known to be so now. The secret was out--told by Victor, when closely questioned with regard to Edith's relationship to Mr. Harrington. It created much surprise and a world of gossip, but shielded Edith from attentions which might otherwise have been annoying, for more than Richard thought her the one of all others whose presence could make the sunshine of their life. But Edith was betrothed. The dun leaves of October would crown her a wife, and so one pleasant morning some half a score young men, each as like to the other as young men at fashionable places of resort are apt to be, kicked their patent leather boots against the pillars of the rear piazza, broke a part of the tenth commandment shockingly, muttered to themselves speeches anything but complimentary to Richard, and then, at the appearance of a plaid silk travelling dress and brown straw flat, rushed forward en masse, each contending frantically for the honor of assisting Miss Hastings to enter the omnibus, where Richard was already seated, and which was to convey a party to the glens of the Kauterskill Falls.

Edith had been there often. The weird wildness of the deep gorge suited her, and many an hour had she whiled away upon the broken rocks, watching the flecks of sunlight as they came struggling down through the overhanging trees, listening to the plaintive murmur of the stream, or gazing with delight upon the fringed, feathery falls which hung from the heights above like some long, white, gauzy ribbon. Richard, on the contrary, had never visited them before, and he only consented to do so now from a desire to gratify Edith, who acted as his escort in place of Victor. Holding fast to her hand he slowly descended the winding steps and circuitous paths, and then, with a sad feeling of helpless dependence, sat down upon the bank where Edith bade him sit, herself going off in girlish ecstasies as a thin spray fell upon her face and she saw above her a bright-hued rainbow, spanning the abyss.

"They are letting the water on," she cried, "Look, Richard! do look!" and she grasped his hand, while he said to her mournfully,

"Has Birdie forgotten that I am blind, and helpless, and old--that she must lead me as a child?"

There was a touching pathos in his voice which went straight to Edith's heart, and forgetting the rainbow, she eat down beside him, still keeping his hand in hers, and asked what was the matter? She knew he was unusually disturbed, for seldom had she seen upon his face a look of so great disquiet. Suddenly as she remembered his unwillingness to come there alone, it flashed upon her that it might arise from an aversion to seem so dependent upon a weak girl in the presence of curious strangers. With Victor he did not mind it, but with her it might be different, and she asked if it were not so.

"Hardly that, darling; hardly that;" and the sightless eyes drooped as if heavy with unshed tears. "Edith," and he pressed the warm hand he held, "ours will be an unnatural alliance. I needed only to mingle with the world to find it so. People wonder at your choice--wonder that one so young as you should choose a battered, blasted tree like me round which to twine the tendrils of your green, fresh life."

"What have you heard?" Edith asked, half bitterly, for since their engagement was known at the hotel, she had more than once suspected the truth of what he said to her. The world did not approve, but she would not tell Richard that she knew it, and she asked again what he had heard.

"The ear of the blind is quick," he replied; "and as I sat waiting in the stage this morning I heard myself denounced as a 'blind old Hunks,' a selfish dog, who had won the handsomest girl in the country. Then, as we were descending to this ravine you remember we stopped at the foot of some stairs while you removed a brier from your dress, and from a group near by I heard the whispered words, 'There they come--the old blind man, who bought his ward with money and gratitude. 'Twas a horrid sacrifice! Look how beautiful she is!' Darling, I liked to hear you praised, but did not like the rest. It makes me feel as if I were dragging you to the altar against your will. And what is worse than all, the verdict of the people here is the verdict of the world. Edith, you don't want me. You cannot wish to call one husband whose dependence upon you will always make you blush for your choice. It was gratitude alone which prompted your decision. Confess that it was, and I give you back your troth. You need not be the old blind man's wife."

For an instant Edith's heart leaped up, and the sun spots dancing on the leaves were brighter than she had ever seen them, but the feeling passed away, and laying both her hands reverently in Richard's, she said,

"I will be your wife. I care nothing for the world, and we won't mingle in it any more to cause remarks. We'll stay at Collingwood, where people know us best. Let's go home to-morrow. I'm tired of this hateful place. Will you go?"

Ere Richard could answer, Grace Atherton was heard exclaiming,

"Ah, here you are, I've hunted everywhere. Mr. Russell," and she turned to the dark man at her side, "this is Mr. Harrington--Miss Hastings--Mr. Russell, from Tallahassee." Edith did not at first think that Tallahassee was in Florida, not many miles from Sunnybank, and she bowed to the gentleman as to any stranger, while Grace, who had just arrived in another omnibus, explained to her that Mr. Russell was a slight acquaintance of Arthur's; that the latter being in town, and accidentally hearing that he was coming North, had intrusted him with some business matters, which would require his visiting Grassy Spring--had given him a letter of introduction to herself, said letter containing a note for Edith--that Mr. Russell had been to Shannondale, and ascertaining their whereabouts, had followed them, reaching the Mountain House in the morning stage.

"He can spend but one day here," she added, in conclusion, "and wishing him to see as much as possible of our northern grandeur I brought him at once to the Falls. Here is your note," and tossing it into Edith's lap she moved away.

A note from Arthur! How Edith trembled as she held it in her hand, and with a quick, furtive glance at sightless eyes beside her, she raised the dainty missive to her lips, feeling a reproachful pang as she reflected that she was breaking her vow to Richard. Why had Arthur written to her--she asked herself this question many times, while Richard, too, asked,

"What news from Florida?" ere she broke the seal and read, not words of changeless and dark despair, but words of entreaty that for the sake of Nina, sick, dying Nina, she would come at once to Florida, for so the crazy girl had willed it, pleading with them the live-long day to send for Miggie, precious Miggie, with the bright, black eyes, which looked her into subjection, and the soft hands which drove the ugly pain away.

"All the summer," Arthur wrote, "she has been failing. The heat seems to oppress her, and several times I've been on the point of returning with her to the North, thinking I made a mistake in bringing her here, but she refuses to leave Sunnybank. Old sights and familiar places have a soothing effect upon her, and she is more as she used to be before the great calamity fell upon her. Her disease is consumption, hereditary like her insanity, and as her physical powers diminish her mental faculties seem to increase. The past is not wholly a blank to her now; she remembers distinctly much that has gone by, but of nothing does she talk so constantly as of Miggie, asking every hour if I've sent for you-- how long before you'll come; and if you'll stay until she's dead. I think your coming will prolong her life; and you will never regret it, I am sure. Mr. Russell will be your escort, as he will return in three weeks."

To this note two postscripts were appended--the first in a girlish, uneven hand, was redolent of the boy Arthur's "Florida rose."

"Miggie, precious Miggie--come to Sunnybank; come to Nina. She is waiting for you. She wants you here--wants to lay her poor, empty head, where the bad pain used to be, on your soft, nice bosom--to shut her eyes and know it is your breath she feels--your sweet, fragrant breath, and not Arthur's, brim full of cigar smoke. Do come, Miggie, won't you? There's a heap of things I want to fix before I die, and I am dying, Miggie. I see it in my hands, so poor and thin, not one bit like they used to be, and I see it, too, in Arthur's actions. Dear Arthur boy! He is so good to me-- carries me every morning to the window, and holds me in his lap while I look out into the garden where we used to play, you and I. I think it was you, but my brain gets so twisted, and I know the real Miggie is out under the magnolias, for it says so on the stone, but I can't help thinking you are she. Arthur has a new name for me, a real nice name, too. He took it from a book, he says--about just such a wee little girl as I am. 'Child-wife,' that's what he calls me, and he strokes my hair so nice. I'm loving Arthur a heap, Miggie. It seems just as if he was my mother, and the name 'Child-wife' makes little bits of waves run all over me. He's a good boy, and God will pay him by and by for what he's been to me. Some folks here call me Mrs. St. Claire. Why do they? Sometimes I remember something about somebody somewhere, more than a hundred years ago, but just as I think I've got hold of it right, it goes away. I lose it entirely, and my head is so snarled up. Come and unsnarl it, wont you? Nina is sick, Nina is dying, Nina is crazy. You must come."

The second postscript showed a bolder, firmer hand, and Edith read,

"I, too, echo Nina's words, 'Come, Miggie, come.' Nina wants you, and I-- Heaven only knows how much I want you--but, Edith, were you in verity Richard's wife, you could not be more sacred to me than you are as his betrothed, and I promise solemnly that I will not seek to influence your decision. The time is surely coming when I shall be alone; no gentle Nina, sweet 'Child-wife' clinging to me. She will be gone, and her Arthur boy, as she calls me, free to love whomsoever he will. But this shall make no difference. I have given you to Richard. I will not wrong the blind man. Heaven bless you both and bring you to us."

The sun shone just as brightly in the summer sky--the Kauterskill fell as softly into the deep ravine--the shouts of the tourists were just us gay--the flecks of sunshine on the grass danced just as merrily, but Edith did not heed them. Her thoughts were riveted upon the lines she had read, and her heart throbbed with an unutterable desire to respond at once to that pleading call--to take to herself wings and fly away--away over mountain and valley, river and rill, to the fair land of flowers where Nina was, and where too was Arthur. As she read, she uttered no sound, but when at last Richard said to her,

"What is it, Birdie? Have you heard bad news?" her tears flowed at once, and leaning her head upon his shoulder, she answered,

"Nina is dying--dear little, bright-haired Nina. She has sent for me. She wants me to come so much. May I, Richard? May I go to Nina?"

"Read me the letter," was Richard's reply, his voice unusually low and sad.

Edith could not read the whole. Arthur's postscript must be omitted, as well as a portion of Nina's, but she did the best she could, breaking down entirely when she reached the point where Nina spoke of her Arthur boy's goodness in carrying her to the window.

Richard, too, was much affected, and his voice trembled as he said, "St. Claire is a noble fellow. I always felt strangely drawn toward him. Isn't there something between him and Nina--something more than mere guardianship?"

"They were engaged before she was crazy," returned Edith, while Richard sighed, "poor boy, poor boy! It must be worse than death. His darkness is greater than mine."

Then his thoughts came back to Edith's question, "May I go to Nina?" and his first feeling was that she might, even though her going would necessarily defer a day to which he was so continually looking forward, but when he remembered the danger to which she would be exposed from the intense heat at that season of the year, he shrank from it at once, mildly but firmly refusing to let her incur the fearful risk.

"Could I be assured that my bird would fly back to me again with its plumage all unruffled I would let her go," he said, "but the chances are against it. You would surely sicken and die, and I cannot let you go."

Edith offered no remonstrance, but her face was very white and her eyes strangely black as she said, "Let us go home, then; go to-morrow. This is no place for me, with Nina dying."

Nothing could please Richard more than to be back at Collingwood, and when Grace came to them he announced his intention of leaving on the morrow. Grace was willing, and Victor, when told of the decision, was wild with delight. Mr. Russell, too, decided to go with them to Shannondale, and when, next morning, the party came out to take the downward stage, they found him comfortably seated on the top, whither he had but little trouble in coaxing Grace, who expressed a wish to enjoy the mountain scenery as they descended.

"Will Miss Hastings come up, too?" he asked, but Edith declined and took her seat inside between Richard and Victor, the latter of whom had heard nothing of the letter; neither did Edith tell him until the next day when, arrived at Collingwood, they were alone for a moment in the library--then she explained to him that Nina was sick, possibly had sent for her.

"I thought things would work out after a time, though honestly I'd rather that little girl shouldn't die if it could be brought round any other way," was Victor's reply, which called a flush at once to Edith's cheek.

"Victor Dupres," said she, "never hint such a thing again. It is too late now; it cannot be--it shall not be; and if I go, Arthur has promised not to say one word which can influence me."

"If you go," repeated Victor, "Then you have some intention of going--I thought he had objected."

"So he has," returned Edith, the same look stealing into her eyes which came there at the Falls. "So he has, but if Nina lives till the middle of October I shall go. My mind is made up."

"Oh, consistency, thou art a jewel," muttered Victor, as hearing some one coming, he walked away. "Means to jump down the lion's throat, but does not expect to be swallowed! Splendid logic that!" and Victor shrugged his shoulders at what seemed so contradictory as Edith's talk and Edith's conduct.

As she had said, Edith meant to go, nay more, was determined to go, and when, on the third day after their return, Mr. Russell came for her final decision, she said to him, ere Richard had time to speak,

"I shall not go now; it is too early for that, but if Nina continues worse, I will come to her the latter part of October. I am writing so to her to-day."

Richard was confounded, and could only stammer out,

"Who is to be your escort?"

"You, Richard;" and Edith clasped his arm, thus reassuring him at once.

She had some thought, some consideration for him; she did not intend to desert him wholly, and he playfully tapped her chin, laughing to think how the little lady had boldly taken matters into her own hands, telling what should be with as much sang froid as if she were master instead of himself. And Richard rather liked the independent spirit of Edith, particularly when he found that he was not wholly left out of her calculations. And so he arranged with Mr. Russell, that if Nina were not better as the autumn advanced, Edith should perhaps go down to see her.

Arthur had made his marriage with Nina public as soon as he returned to Sunnybank, but as Mr. Russell's home was in Tallahassee, and he himself a quiet, taciturn man, he had not heard of it, and in speaking of Nina to Edith, he called her Miss Bernard, as usual, and thus Richard still remained in ignorance, never suspecting that golden haired Nina was the same young girl he had married years before.

Poor Richard, he was ignorant of many things and never dreamed how light and gay was Edith's heart at the prospect of going to Florida, even though she half expected that when she went it would be as his wife. But Richard determined it otherwise. It cost him a struggle so to do, but his iron will conquered every feeling, save those of his better judgment, and calling Edith to him one day two weeks after Mr. Russell's departure, he said,

"Birdie, I've come to the conclusion that a blind man like me will only be in your way, in case you go to Florida. I am not an interesting traveling companion. I require too much care, and I dread the curious gaze of strangers. It makes me very uncomfortable. So on the whole I'd rather stay at home and let Victor go in my stead. What does Birdie say?"

"She says you are the noblest, most unselfish man that ever lived," and Edith kissed his lips, chiding herself seriously for the spirit which whispered to her that she too would rather go without him. "I won't stay very long," she said. "Our wedding need not be deferred more than two months; say, till the first of January, at 7 o'clock, just as we before arranged it for October, only a more quiet affair, I shall then be your New Year's gift. Does that suit you, dearest?"

She did not often call him thus, and when she did she was sure of accomplishing her purpose. The strong man melted beneath a few words of love, becoming a very tool in the hands of a weak girl.

"Yes, darling," he replied, "that will do--but supposing we hear that Nina is better, or dead--what then?"

The mere possibility was terrible to Edith, but she answered calmly,

"Then we'll be married in October, just as first proposed;" and thus was the die cast, and a fresh link added to the chain of Edith's destiny. She was going to Florida; going to Arthur; and going alone, so far as Richard was concerned.

Spying Victor coming up the walk from the post-office, she ran out to meet him, telling him of the journey before him, and almost crying for joy when he placed in her hand a worn envelope bearing the post-mark of Tallahassee. It was from Arthur, and contained a few lines only, telling of Nina's increasing illness, and her restless, impatient desire for Miggie. In conclusion he wrote,

"We have had no fever this summer. You will be perfectly safe in coming any time after the middle of October. I shall welcome Mr. Harrington most cordially if he sees fit to accompany you."

Edith could read this to Richard, and she did, feeling a pang at the perfect faith with which he answered,

"Were it not for the tedious journey I believe I would go with you, but it's too much of an undertaking. I won't trammel you with so great a burden. I'd rather stay at home and anticipate my darling's return."

Then with the same forethought and careful consideration which marked all his actions, Richard consulted with her as to the beat time for her to start, fixing upon the 15th of October, and making all his arrangements subservient to this. He did not tell her how lonely he should be without her--how he should miss her merry laugh, which, strange to say, grew merrier each day; but he let her know in various ways how infinitely precious she was to him, and more than once Edith felt constrained to give up the journey, but the influences from Florida drew her strangely in that direction, and revolving to pay Richard for his self-denial by an increase of love when she should return, she busied herself with her preparations until the 15th of October came, and her trunks stood ready in the hall.

"If I could only read your letters myself, it would not seem one-half so bad," Richard said, when at the last moment, he held Edith's hand, "but there's a shadow over me this morning--a dark presentiment that in suffering you to leave me I am losing you forever."

Edith could not answer, she pitied him so much, and kissing his lips, she put from her neck his clinging arms, wiped his tears away, smoothed his ruffled hair, and then went out from his presence, leaving him there in his sorrow and blindness alone.

CHAPTER XXVIII.
SUNNYBANK.

Berry soon, Miss, an' we're thar. We turns the corner yonder, we drives 'cross the plain, down a hill, up anoder, an' then we's mighty nigh a mile from the spot."

Such was the answer made by Tom, the Bernard coachman to Edith's repeated inquiries, "Are we almost there."

For three successive days the Bernard carriage had been to Tallahassee in quest of the expected guest, whose coming was watched for so eagerly at Sunnybank, and who, as the bright October afternoon was drawing to its close, looked eagerly out at a huge old house which stood not very far distant with the setting sun shining on the roof and illuminating all the upper windows. A nearer approach showed it to be a large, square, wooden building, divided in the centre by a wide, airy hall, and surrounded on three sides by a verandah, the whole bearing a more modern look than most of the country houses in Florida, for Mr. Bernard had possessed considerable taste, and during his life had aimed at fitting up his residence somewhat after the northern fashion. To Edith there was something familiar about that old building, with its handsome grounds, and she said aloud,

"I've surely dreamed of Sunnybank."

"Berry likely, Miss," answered Tom, thinking the remark addressed to him, inasmuch as Edith's head protruded from the window. "Dreams is mighty onsartin. Git 'long, you Bill, none o'yer lazy carlicues, case don't yer mind thar's Mars'r Arthur on the v'randy, squinting to see if I's fotched 'em," and removing his old straw hat, Tom swung it three times around his head, that being the signal he was to give if Edith were in the carriage.

With an increased flush upon his brow, Arthur St. Claire hastened down, pausing at an inner room while he bent over and whispered to a young girl reclining on her pillow,

"Nina, darling, Miggie's come."

There was a low cry of unutterable delight, and Nina Bernard raised herself upon her elbow, looking wistfully toward the door through which Arthur had disappeared.

"Be quiet, la petite Nina," said a short, thick woman, who sat by the bed, apparently officiating in the capacity of nurse; then, as the carriage stopped at the gate, she glided to the window, muttering to herself, "Charmant charmant, magnifique," as she caught a full view of the eager, sparkling face, turned toward the young man hastening down the walk. Then, with that native politeness natural to her country, she moved away so as not to witness the interview.

"Arthur!"

"Edith!"

That was all they said, for Richard and Nina stood between them, a powerful preventive to the expression of the great joy throbbing in the heart of each, as hand grasped hand, and eye sought eye, fearfully, tremblingly, lest too much should be betrayed.

"Miggie, Miggie, be quick," came from the room where Nina was now standing up in bed, her white night dress hanging loosely about her forehead and neck.

It needed but this to break the spell which bound the two without, and dropping Edith's hand, Arthur conducted her to the house, meeting in the hall with Nina, who, in spite of Mrs. Lamotte had jumped from her bed and skipping across the floor, flung herself into Edith's arms, sobbing frantically,

"You did come, precious Miggie, to see sick Nina, didn't you, and you'll stay forever and ever, won't you, my own sweet Miggie, and Arthur's too? Oh, joy, joy, Nina's so happy to-night."

The voice grew very faint, the white lips ceased their pressure of kisses upon Edith's--the golden head began to droop, and Arthur took the fainting girl in his arms, carrying her back to her bed, where he laid her gently down, himself caring for her until she began to revive.

Meanwhile Edith was introduced to Mrs. Lamotte, a French woman, who once was Nina's nurse, and who had come to Sunnybank a few weeks before. Any one at all interested in Nina was sure of a place in Edith's affections, and she readily took Mrs. Lamotte's proffered hand, but she was not prepared for the peculiarly curious gaze fastened upon her, as Mrs. Lamotte waved off Teeny, the black girl, and taking her traveling bag and shawl, said to her,

"This way, s'il vous plait, Mademoiselle Marguerite. Pardonnez moi," she added quickly, as she met Edith's questioning glance, "Mademoiselle Miggie, as la petite Nina calls you."

Once in Edith's room, Mrs. Lamotte did not seem in haste to leave it, but continued talking in both English and French to Edith, who more than once, as the tones fell upon her ear, turned quickly to see if it were not some one she had met before.

"Je m'en irai," Mrs. Lamotte said at last, as she saw that her presence was annoying Edith; and as the latter offered no remonstrance, she left the room, and Edith was alone with her confused thoughts.

Where was she? What room was this, with the deep window seats, and that wide-mouthed fire-place? Who was this woman that puzzled her so? Edith kept asking herself these questions, but could find for them no satisfactory answer. Struggle as she might, she felt more like a child returned to its home than like a stranger in a strange land. Even the soft south wind, stealing through the open casement, and fanning her feverish cheek, had something familiar in its breath, as if it had stolen in upon her thus aforetime; and when across the fields, she heard the negroes' song as they came homeward from their toil, she laid her head upon the window sill, and wept for the something which swept over her, something so sweet, so sad, and yet so indescribable.

Fearing lest the Frenchwoman should return, she made a hasty toilet, and then stole down to Nina, who, wholly exhausted with the violence of her emotions at meeting Edith, lay perfectly still upon her pillow, scarcely whiter than her own childish face, round which a ray of the setting sun was shining, encircling it with a halo of glorious beauty, and making her look like an angel of purity and love. She did not attempt to speak as Edith came in, but her eyes smiled a welcome, and her thin, wasted fingers pointed to where Edith was to sit upon the bed beside her. Arthur sat on the other side, holding one of Nina's hands, and the other was given to Edith, who pressed it to her lips, while her tears dropped upon it like rain. The sight of them disturbed the sick girl, and shaking her wealth of curls which, since Edith saw them, had grown thick and long, she whispered,

"Don't, Miggie; tears are not for Nina; she's so glad, for she is almost home. She'll go down to the river brink with your arms and Arthur boy's around her. Precious Miggie, nice Arthur. Nina is happy to-night."

Such were the disjointed sentences she kept whispering, while her eyes turned from Edith to Arthur and from Arthur back to Edith, resting longer there, and the expression of the face told of the unutterable joy within. Softly the twilight shadows stole into the room, and the servants glided in and out, casting furtive and wondering glances at Edith, who saw nothing save the clear blue eyes shining upon her, even through the gathering darkness, and telling her of the love which could not be expressed.

As it grew darker Nina drew the two hands she clasped together-- Arthur's and Edith's--laid them one above the other upon her bosom, pressed her own upon them, and when, at last, the candles were brought in and placed upon the table, Edith saw that the weary lids had closed and Nina was asleep. Every effort, however, which she made to disengage her hand from its rather embarrassing position, threatened to arouse the sleeper, and for nearly half an hour she sat there with her hand beneath Arthur's, but she dared not look at him, and with her face turned away, she answered his questions concerning Shannondale and its inhabitants.

After a time Mrs. Lamotte came in and asked if mademoiselle would like to retire. Edith would far rather have gone to her room alone, but Mrs. Lamotte seemed bent upon hovering near her, and as there was no alternative she followed her up the stairs and into the chamber, where she had lain aside her things. To her great relief her companion did not stay longer than necessary, and ere the entire household was still, Edith was dreaming of Collingwood and Richard.

The next morning was bright, balmy, and beautiful, and at an early hour Edith arose and went down to Nina, who heard her step in the hall, and called to her to come.

"Darling Miggie, I dreamed you were gone," she said, "and, I cried so hard that it woke Arthur up. He sleeps here every night, on that wide lounge," and she pointed toward a corner, "I've grown so silly that I won't let any body else take care of me but Arthur boy--he does it so nice and lifts me so carefully. Hasn't he grown pale and thin?"

Edith hardly knew, for she had not ventured to look fully at him, but she assumed that he had, and Nina continued: "He's a darling boy, and Nina loves him now."

"How is your head this morning," Edith asked, and Nina replied, "It's better. It keeps growing better, some days it's clear as a bell, but I don't like it so well, for I know then that you ain't Miggie,--not the real Miggie who was sent home in mother's coffin. We have a new burying ground, one father selected long ago, the sweetest spot you ever saw, and they are moving the bodies there now. They are going to take up my last mother, and the little bit of Miggie to-day, and Marie is so flurried."

Arthur's step was now heard in the hall, and this it was which so excited Edith that she failed to catch the word Marie, or to understand that it was Mrs. Lamotte who was worried about the removal of the bodies. In a moment Arthur appeared, bringing a delicate bouquet for Nina, and a world of sunshine to Edith. He was changed, Edith saw as she looked at him now, and yet she liked his face better than before. He seemed to her like one over whom the fire had passed, purifying as it burned, and leaving a better metal than it had found. He was wholly self-possessed this morning, greeting her as if the scene in the Deering woods had never been enacted, and she could hardly believe that they were the same, the Arthur of one year ago, and the Arthur of to-day; the quiet, elegant young man, who, with more than womanly tenderness, pushed Nina's curls back under her lace cap, kissed her forehead, and then asked Edith if she did not look like a little nun with her hair so plain.

Nina liked to be caressed, and she smiled upon him a smile so full of trusting faith and love, that Edith's eyes filled with tears, and her rebellious heart went out toward Arthur as it had never done before, inasmuch as she felt that he was now far more worthy of her.

Very rapidly the morning passed away, and it was after three o'clock P.M., when, as Arthur sat with Edith upon the cool piazza, one of the negroes came running up, the perspiration starting from every pore, and himself almost frantic with excitement.

"What is it, Caesar?" Arthur asked. "What has happened to you?"

"Nothing to me, Mars'r," returned the negro; "but sumfin mighty curis happen over dar," and he pointed in the direction where his comrades were busy removing the family dead to a spot selected by Mr. Bernard years before as one more suitable than the present location. "You see, we was histin' de box of the young Miss and de chile, when Bill let go his holt, and I kinder let my hands slip off, when, Lor' bless you, the box busted open, an' we seen the coffin spang in the face. Says Bill, says he--he's allus a reasonin', you know--an', says he, 'that's a mighty narrer coffin for two;' and wid that, Mr. Berry, the overseer, Miss," turning to Edith, "He walked up, and findin' de screws rattlin' and loose, just turned back de top piece, an', as true as Caesar's standin' here, there wasn't no chile thar; nothin' 'tall but the Miss, an' she didn't look no how; never should have guessed them heap of bones had ever been Miss Petry."

Edith started from her chair and was about to speak when a hand was laid upon her wrist, and turning, she saw Mrs. Lamotte standing behind her, and apparently more excited than herself.

"Come with me," she said, leading the unresisting Edith away, and leaving Arthur to follow Caesar.

Of all the household at Sunnybank no one had been so much interested in the removal of the bodies as Mrs. Lamotte, and yet her interest was all centered upon the grave of Miggie Bernard's mother. When that was disturbed, she was watching from her window, and when the accident occurred which revealed the fraud of years, she hurried down and, with a cat-like tread, glided behind Edith's chair where she stood while Caesar told his story.

It would be impossible to describe Edith's feeling as she followed the strange woman up to her own room, sitting down just where Mrs. Lamotte bade her sit, and watching nervously the restless rolling of the eyes, which had no terror for her now, particularly after their owner said to her in French,

"Do you know me, Edith Hastings, Eloise Temple, Marguerite Bernard? Have we never met before?"

Like the rushing of some mighty, pent up flood the past swept over her then, almost bearing her senses down with the headlong tide; link after link was joined, until the chain of evidence was complete, and with a scream of joy Edith went forward to the arms unfolded to receive her.

"Marie, Marie!" she cried, "How is it? When was it? Where was it? Am I anybody or not, tell me?"

Then question followed question go rapidly that Marie, with all her voluble French and broken English, was hardly able to keep up. But the whole was told at last; everything was clear to Edith as the daylight, and tottering to the bed, she asked to be alone, while she wept and prayed over this great joy, which had come so suddenly upon her.

"Nina, Nina. I thank thee, oh, my Father, for sweet, precious Nina."

That was all she could say, as with her face in the pillows, she lay until the sun went down, and night fell a second time on Sunnybank.

"No one shall tell her but myself," she thought as she descended to Nina's room, where Arthur was telling of the discovery they had made--a discovery for which he could not account, and about which the negroes, congregated together in knots, were talking, each offering his or her own theory with regard to the matter, and never once thinking to question Mrs. Lamotte, who, they knew, had been with Mrs. Bernard when she died.

"Oh, Miggie!" Nina cried. "HAVE you heard? do you know? Little Miggie isn't there where we thought she was. She's gone. Nobody's there but my other mother."

"Yes, I know," Edith answered, and laying her hand on Arthur's she said, "Please, Mr. St Claire, go away awhile. I must see Nina alone. Don't let anybody disturb us, will you? Go to Mrs. Lamotte. Ask her what I mean. She can tell you. She told me."

Thus importuned, Arthur left the room, and Edith was alone with Nina.

CHAPTER XXIX.
THE SISTERS.

Oh, how Edith yearned to take that sweet young creature to her bosom, and concentrate in one wild, passionate hug the love of so many wasted years; but Nina must not be unduly startled if she would make her comprehend what she had to tell, and conquering her own agitation with a wondrous effort she sat down upon the bed, and said,

"How is my darling? Is her head all in a twist?"

Nina smiled, a rational, knowing smile, and answered,

"There wasn't the least bit of a twist in it till Arthur told me about that in the graveyard, and then it began to thump so loud, but with you sitting here, I'm better. You do me so much good, Miggie. Your eyes keep me quiet. Where do you suppose she is--the other Miggie; and how did she get out of the coffin?"

"Nina," said Edith, "can you understand me if I tell you a story about a little girl who resembled your sister Miggie?"

Nina liked stories and though she would rather have talked of the real Miggie, she expressed a willingness to listen, and by the dim candle light Edith saw that the blue eyes, fixed so intently upon her, still retained the comparatively rational expression she had observed when she first came in. Moving a little nearer to her, she began,

"A great many years ago, nearly eighteen, we will say, a beautiful little girl, eight years old, I guess, with curls like yours, waited one night in just such a house as this, for her father, who had been long in Europe, and who was to bring her a new mother, and a dear baby sister, two years old or thereabouts."

"Didn't I wear my blue dress, trimmed with white?" Nina asked suddenly, her mind seeming to have followed Edith's, and grasped the meaning of what she heard.

"I dare say you did," Edith answered; "at all events this little girl was very beautiful as she waited in the twilight for the travellers."

"Call the little girl Nina, please, I'll get at it better then," was the next interruption; and with a smile, Edith said,

"Nina, then, waited till they came--her father, her new mother Petrea, and--"

"Beautiful Petrea," Nina exclaimed, "la belle Petrea, black hair like yours, Miggie, and voice like the soft notes of the piano. She taught me a heap of tunes which I never have forgotten, but tell me more of the black-eyed baby, Nina's precious sister. I did hug and squeeze her so--'la jolie enfant,' Marie called her."

Nina seemed to have taken the story away from Edith, who, when she ceased speaking, again went on:

"Eloise Marguerite was the baby sister's name; Eloise, for a proud aunt, who, after they came home, would not suffer them to call her so, and she was known as Marguerite, which Nina shortened into Miggie, Nina darling," and Edith spoke sadly now. "Was your father always kind to Petrea?"

There was a look in Nina's face like a scared bird, and raising her hands to her head, she said,

"Go away, old buzzing. Let Nina think what it was they used to do- -pa and grandma and aunt Eloise. I know now; grandma and auntie were proud of the Bernard blood, they said, and they called Petrea vulgar, and baby sister a brat; and pa--oh, Miggie, I reckon he was naughty to the new mother. He had a buzz in his head most every night, not like mine, but a buzz that he got at the dinner and the side-board, where they kept the bottles, and he struck her, I saw him, and Marie, she was here, too, she stepped between them, and called him a drunken, deceitful beast, and a heap more in French. Then one morning when he was gone to New Orleans, and would come home pretty soon, mother and Marie and Miggie went a visiting to Tallahassee, or somewhere, and they never came back again, though pa went after them as soon as he got home. Why didn't they, Miggie?"

"Petrea was very unhappy here," Edith answered. "Mr. Bernard abused her, as did his haughty mother, and once when he was gone Petrea said she would go to Tallahassee to see a lady who had visited her at Sunnybank. So she went with Marie, and Miggie, then three years old, but did not stop in Tallahassee. They ran away to New York, where Marie's sister lived. Here Petrea was taken sick and died, making Marie promise that Miggie should never go back to her bad father and his proud family. And Marie, who hated them bitterly, all but Nina, kept her word. She wrote to Sunnybank that both were dead, and the letter was forwarded by your grandmother to Mr. Bernard, who had gone after his wife, but who lay drunk many days at a hotel. The letter sobered him, and as it contained Marie's address, he found her at last, crying bitterly for little Miggie, up stairs asleep, but he thought her in the coffin with her mother. Marie said so and he believed her, bringing the bodies back to Sunnybank, and burying them beneath the magnolias."

"And built a great marble there with both their names cut on it," chimed in Nina, fearful lest any part of the story should be omitted.

"Yes," returned Edith, "he raised a costly monument to their memory; but don't you wish to know what became of Miggie?"

"Yes, yes, oh, yes, go on," was Nina's answer; and Edith continued,

"Marie was too poor to take care of Miggie, and she put her in the Asylum."

"The Asylum!" Nina fairly screamed. "Nina's baby sister in the nasty old Asylum. No, no, it ain't. I won't, I shan't listen to the naughty story," and the excited girl covered her head with a pillow.

But Edith removed it gently, and with a few loving words quieted the little lady, who said again, "Go on."

"It was the Orphan Asylum, where Nina's sister was put, but they didn't call her Miggie. Her dying mother gave her another name lest the father should some time find her, and there in that great noisy city Miggie lived five or six long years, gradually forgetting everything in the past, everything but Marie's name and the airs her mother used to sing. Miggie had a taste for music, and she retained the plaintive strains sung to her as lullabys."

"I know them, too," Nina said, beginning to hum one, while Edith continued,

"After a time Marie went back to France. She did not mean to stay long, but she was attacked with a lingering, painful sickness, and could not return to Miggie, whom a beautiful lady took at last as her waiting-maid. Then Arthur came--Arthur, a boy--and she saw Nina's picture."

"The one in the locket! Nina asked, and Edith answered, "Yes, 'twas in a locket, and it puzzled Miggie till she spoke the name, but thought it was Arthur who told her."

"Wait, wait," cried Nina, suddenly striking her forehead a heavy blow; "I'm getting all mixed up, and something flashes across my brain like lightning. I reckon it's a streak of sense. It feels like it."

Nina was right. It was "a streak of sense," and when Edith again resumed her story the crazy girl was very calm and quiet.

"After a time this Miggie went to live with a blind man--with Richard," and Edith's hands closed tightly around the snowy fingers, which crept so quickly toward her. "She grew to be a woman. She met this golden-haired Nina, but did not know her, though Nina called her Miggie always, because she looked like Petrea, and the sound to Miggie was very sweet, like music heard long ago. They loved each other dearly, and to Miggie there was nothing in the whole world so beautiful, so precious, as poor little crazy Nina, Arthur's Nina, Dr. Griswold's Nina, 'Snow-Drop,' Richard called her. You remember Richard, darling?"

"Yes, yes, I remember everything," and Nina's chest began to heave, her chin to quiver, her white lips, too, but still she shed no tear, and the dry, blue eyes seemed piercing Edith's very soul as the latter continued, rapidly, "Nina came home to Florida; she sent for Miggie, and Miggie came, finding Marie who told her all-- told her where the baby was--and the real Miggie fell on her face, thanking the good Father for giving her the sweetest, dearest sister a mortal ever had. Do you understand me, darling? Do you know now who I am--know who Miggie is?"

Edith's voice began to falter, and when she had finished she sat gazing at the fairy form, which trembled and writhed a moment as if in fearful convulsions, then the struggling ceased, the features became composed, and raising herself in bed Nina crept closer and closer to Edith, her lips quivering as if she fain would speak but had not the power. Slowly the little hands were raised and met together around Edith's neck; nearer and nearer the white face came to the dark glowing one, until breath met breath, lip met lip, golden tresses mixed with raven braids, and with a cry which made the very rafters ring and went echoing far out into the darkness, Nina said, "You are--that--that--ba-baby--the one we thought was dead. You are my--my--Nina's--oh, Miggie, say it for me or Nina'll choke to death. She can't think what the right word is--the word that means MIGGIE," and poor exhausted Nina fell back upon the pillow, while Edith, bending over her, whispered in her ear, "Miggie means SISTER, darling; your SISTER; do you hear?"

"Yes, yes," and again the wild, glad cry went ringing through the house, as Nina threw herself a second time on Edith's bosom. "Sister, sister, Nina's sister. Nina's little Miggie once, great, tall Miggie now,--mine, my own--nobody's sister but mine. Does Arthur know, Ho, Arthur! come quick! He is coming, don't you hear him. Arthur, Arthur, Miggie is mine. My precious sister," and Nina Bernard fell back fainting just as Arthur appeared in the room, and just as from the yard without there went up from the congregated blacks, who together with their master and Victor, had listened to Marie's story, a deafening shout, a loud huzza for "Miggie Bernard," come back to Sunnybank, and back to those who generously admitted her claim, and would ere long acknowledge her as their mistress.

The few particulars which Edith had omitted in her story to Nina may, perhaps, be better told now than at any other time. Mr. Bernard, while in Paris, had been implicated in some disgraceful affair which rendered him liable to arrest, and taking the name of Temple, by way of avoiding suspicion, he fled to Germany, where he met and married the beautiful Swedish Petrea, who, being young and weary of a governess's life, was the more easily charmed with his wealth and rather gentlemanly address. Because it suited his peculiar nature to do so, he kept his real name from her until they reached New York, when, fearful of meeting with some of his acquaintances there, he confessed the fraud, laughing at it as a good joke, and pronounced Petrea over nice for saying he had done wrong.

The year which followed their arrival at Sunnybank was a year of wretchedness and pining home-sickness on the part of both mistress and maid, until at last the former, with her love for her husband changed to hate, determined to leave him; and in his absence, planned the visit to Tallahassee, going instead to New York, where she died at the house of Mrs. Jamieson, Marie's sister. Even to the last, the dread of her hated husband prevailed, and she made Marie swear that her child should not go back to him.

"She will be happier to be poor," she said, "and I would rather far that not a cent of the Bernard property should ever come into her possession than that she should return to Sunnybank; but sometime, Marie, when she is older, you may tell her my sad story, and if he has become a better man, tell her who she is, and of the bright-haired Nina. They will love each other, I am sure, for Nina possesses nothing in common with her father, and lest she should think ill of me for having married him, tell her how young, how inexperienced I was, and how he deceived me, withholding even his real name."

This was the point on which Petrea dwelt the most, shrinking, with a kind of pride, from having it generally known, and persisting in calling herself Temple to Mrs. Jamieson, who supposed this to be her real name, inasmuch as Marie had called her so on the occasion of her first visit after landing in New York the year previous, and before the deception had been confessed.

"Don't undeceive her," Petrea said to Marie, who did her mistress's bidding; and as Mrs. Jamieson was sick when Mr. Bernard came, she did not see him, and was thus effectually kept in ignorance that Edith's real name was Marguerite Bernard, else she had divulged it to Richard, when in after years he came inquiring for her parentage.

The rest the reader knows, except indeed, how Marie came to Sunnybank a second time, and why she had so long neglected Edith. She was with her mistress in Germany when Richard saved the child from drowning. She never forgot him, and when from her sister she learned that Edith was with him, she felt that interference on her part was unnecessary. So even after recovering from her illness she deferred returning to America, marrying, at last, and living in an humble way in Paris, where she more than once saw Mr. Bernard in the streets, when he was there with Nina. So many years had elapsed since his first visit that he had no fears of arrest, and openly appeared in public, recognised by none save Marie, who never could forget him. Her husband's sudden death determined her upon coming to America and looking up her child. The vessel in which she sailed was bound for New Orleans, and, with a desire to visit Sunnybank once more, she first wended her way thither, expecting to find it inhabited by strangers; for, from an American paper, which accidentally fell into her hands, she had heard of Mr. Bernard's decease, and later still had heard from one who was Nina's waiting maid while in Paris, that she, too, was dead. How this information was obtained she did not know, but believing it to be authentic, she supposed strangers, of course, were now the tenants of Sunnybank; and anticipated much pleasure in restoring to the so-called Edith Hastings her rightful heritage. Great then was her surprise to find Nina living, and when she heard that Edith was soon expected in Florida, she determined to await her coming.

This was the story she told to Edith and also to the negroes, many of whom remembered their unfortunate young mistress and her beautiful baby Miggie still; but for the missing body they might have doubted Marie's word, but that was proof conclusive, and their loud hurrahs for Miss Miggie Bernard were repeated until Nina came back to consciousness, smiling as she heard the cry and remembered what it meant.

"Go to them--let them see you, darling," she said; and, with Arthur as her escort, Edith went out into the midst of the sable group, who crowded around her, with blessings, prayers, tears and howlings indescribable, while many a hard, black hand grasped hers, as negro after negro called her "mistress," adding some word of praise, which showed how proud they were of this beautiful, queenly scion of the Bernard stock, which they had feared would perish with Nina. Now they would be kept together--they would not be scattered to the four winds, and one old negro fell on his knees, kissing Edith's dress, and crying,

"Cato bresses yon for lettin' his bones rot on de ole plantation."

Edith was perplexed, for to her the discovery had only brought sweet images of sistership with Nina. Money and lands formed no part of her thoughts, and turning to Arthur she asked what it all meant.

Arthur did not reply at once, for he knew he held that which would effectually take away all right from Edith. After Nina, he was Mr. Bernard's chosen heir, but not for an instant did he waver in the course he should pursue, and when the interview was ended with the negroes, and Edith was again with Nina, he excused himself for a moment, but soon returned, bearing in his hand Mr. Bernard's will, which he bade Edith read.

And she did read it, feeling intuitively as if her father from the grave were speaking to her, the injured Petrea's child, and virtually casting her aside.

The tears gathered slowly in her eyes, dropping one by one upon the paper, which without a word she handed back to Arthur.

"What is it, Arthur boy?" Nina asked. "What is it that makes Miggie cry?"

Arthur doubted whether either of the girls would understand him if he entered into an explanation involving many technical terms, but he would do the best he could, and sitting down by Nina, he held her upon his bosom, while he said, "Does my little girl remember the time when I met her in Boston, years ago, and Charlie Hudson brought me papers from her father?"

"Yes," answered Nina; "there was one that had in it something about straight jackets, and when I read it, I hit my head against the bureau. It's never been quite right since. Is this the letter that made Miggie cry?"

"No," returned Arthur. "This is your father's will, made when he thought there was no Miggie. In it, I am, his heir after you, and Miggie hasn't a cent."

"You may have mine, Miggie. Nina'll give you hers, she will," and the little maiden made a movement toward Edith, while Arthur continued,

"Yon can't, darling. It's mine after you;" and this he said, not to inflict fresh pain on Edith, but to try Nina, and hear what she would say.

There was a perplexed, troubled look in her eyes, and then, drawing his head close to her, she whispered,

"Couldn't you scratch it out, just as Richard did, only he didn't. That's a good boy. He will, Miggie," and she nodded toward Edith, while Arthur rejoined,

"Would it please my child-wife very much to have me scratch it out?"

He had never called her thus before Edith until now, and he stole a glance at her to witness the effect. For an instant she was white as marble; then the hot blood seemed bursting from the small round spot where it had settled in her cheeks, and involuntarily she extended her hand toward him in token of her approval. She could not have reassured him better than by this simple act, and still retaining her hand, he went on,

"When I came to Florida, after Mr. Bernard's death, my first step was to have the will proved, and consequently this sheet is now of very little consequence; but as you both will, undoubtedly, breathe more freely if every vestige of this writing is removed. I will destroy it at once, and, as soon as possible, take the legal steps for reinstating Edith."

Then releasing Edith's hand, Arthur took the candle from the stand, and said to Nina,

"Have you strength to hold it?"

"Yes, yes," she cried, grasping it eagerly, while, with a hand far steadier than hers, Arthur held the parchment in the flame, watching as the scorched, brown flakes dropped upon the floor, nor sending a single regret after the immense fortune he was giving up.

It was done at last. The will lay crisped and blackened upon the carpet; Edith, in her own estimation was reinstated in her rights, and then, as if demanding something for the sacrifice, Arthur turned playfully to her, and winding his arm around her said,

"Kiss me once as a sister, for such you are, and once for giving you back your inheritance."

The kisses Arthur craved were given, and need we say returned! Alas, those kisses! How they burned on Edith's lips, making her so happy--and how they blistered on Arthur's heart, making him doubt the propriety of having given or received them. His was the braver spirit now. He had buffeted the billow with a mightier struggle than Edith had ever known. Around his head a blacker, fiercer storm had blown than any she had ever felt, and from out that tumultuous sea of despair he had come a firmer, a better man, with strength to bear the burden imposed upon him. Were it not so he would never have sent for Edith Hastings--never have perilled his soul by putting himself a second time under her daily influence. But he felt that there was that within him which would make him choose the right, make him cling to Nina, and so he wrote to Edith, meeting her when she came as friend meets friend, and continually thanking Heaven which enabled him to hide from everyone the festered wound, which at the sound of her familiar voice smarted and burned, and throbbed until his soul was sick and faint with pain.

The discovery of Edith's parentage filled him with joy--joy for Nina, and joy because an opportunity was thus afforded him of doing an act unselfish to the last degree, for never for a single moment did the thought force itself upon him that possibly Edith might yet be his, and so the property come back to him again. He had given her up, surrendered her entirely, and Richard's interests were as safe with him as his gold and silver could have been. Much he wished he knew exactly the nature of her feelings toward her betrothed, but he would not so much as question Victor, who, while noticing his calmness and self-possession, marvelled greatly, wondering the while if it were possible that Arthur's love were really all bestowed on Nina. It would seem so, from the constancy with which he hung over her pillow, doing for her the thousand tender offices, which none but a devoted husband could do, never complaining, never tiring even when she taxed his good nature to its utmost limit, growing sometimes so unreasonable and peevish that even Edith wondered at his forbearance.

It was a whim of Edith's not to write to Richard of her newly-found relationship. She would rather tell it to him herself, she said, and in her first letter, she merely mentioned the incidents of her journey, saying she reached Sunnybank in safety, that Nina was no better, that Mr. St. Claire was very kind, and Victor very homesick, while she should enjoy herself quite well, were it not that she knew he was so lonely without her. And this was the letter for which Richard waited so anxiously, feeling when it came almost as if he had not had any, and still exonerating his singing bird from blame, by saying that she could not write lovingly to him so long us she knew that Mrs. Matson must be the interpreter between them.

It was an odd-looking missive which he sent back and Edith's heart ached to its very core as she saw the uneven handwriting, which went up and down, the lines running into and over each other, now diagonally, now at right angles, and again darting off in an opposite direction as he held his pencil a moment in his fingers and then began again. Still she managed to decipher it, and did not lose a single word of the message intended for Nina.

"Tell little Snowdrop the blind man sends her his blessing and his love, thinking of her often as he sits here alone these gloomy autumn nights, no Edith, no Nina, nothing but lonesome darkness. Tell her that he prays she may get well again, or if she does not, that she may be one of the bright angels which make the fields of Jordan so beautiful and fair"

This letter Edith took to Nina one day, when Arthur and Victor had gone to Tallahassee, and Mrs. Lamotte was too busy with her own matters to interrupt them. Nina had not heard of the engagement, for Arthur could not tell her, and Edith shrank from the task as from something disagreeable. Still she had a strong desire for Nina to know how irrevocably she was bound to another, hoping thus to prevent the unpleasant allusions frequently made to herself and Arthur. The excitement of finding a sister in Miggie, had in a measure overturned Nina's reason again, and for many days after the disclosure she was more than usually wild, talking at random of the most absurd things, but never for a moment losing sight of the fact that Edith was her sister. This seemed to be the one single clear point from which her confused ideas radiated, and the love she bore her sister was strong enough to clear away the tangled web of thought and bring her at last to a calmer, more natural state of mind. There were hours in which no one would suspect her of insanity, save that as she talked childish, and even meaningless expressions were mingled with what she said, showing that the woof of her intellect was defective still, and in such a condition as this Edith found her that day when, with Richard's letter in her hand, she seated herself upon the foot of the bed and said, "I heard from Richard last night. You remember him, darling?"

"Yes, he made me Arthur's wife; but I wish he hadn't for then you would not look so white and sorry."

"Never mind that," returned Edith, "but listen to the message he sent his little Snowdrop," and she read what Richard had written to Nina.

"I wish I could be one of those bright angels," Nina said, mournfully, when Edith finished reading; "but, Miggie, Nina's so bad. I can think about it this morning, for the buzzing in my head is very faint, and I don't get things much twisted, I reckon. I've been bad to Arthur a heap of times, and he was never anything but kind to me. I never saw a frown on his face or heard an impatient word, only that sorry look, and that voice so sad."

"Don't, Nina, don't.

"Even Dr. Griswold was not patient as Arthur. He was quicker like, and his face would grow so red. He used to shake me hard, and once he raised his hand, but Arthur caught it quick and said 'No, Griswold, not that--not strike Nina,' and I was tearing Arthur's hair out by handfuls, too. That's when I bit him. I told you once."

"Yes, I know," Edith replied; "but I wish to talk of something besides Arthur, now. Are you sure you can understand me?"

"Yes, it only buzzed like a honey-bee, right in here," and Nina touched the top of her head, while Edith continued.

"Did Arthur ever tell you who it was that fell into the Rhine?"

"Yes, Mrs. Atherton wrote, and I cried so hard, but he did not say your name was Eloise, or I should have guessed you were Miggie, crazy as I am."

"Possibly Grace did not so write to him," returned Edith; "but let me tell you of Edith Hastings as she used to be when a child;" and with the blue eyes of Nina fixed upon her, Edith narrated that portion of her history already known to the reader, dwelling long upon Richard's goodness, and thus seeking to prepare her sister for the last, the most important part of all.

"After Arthur deceived me so," she said," I thought my heart would never cease to ache, and it never has."

"But it will--it will," cried Nina, raising herself in bed. "When I'm gone, it will all come right. I pray so every day, though it's hard to do it sometimes now I know you are my sister. It would be so nice to live with you and Arthur, and I love you so much. You can't begin to know," and the impulsive girl fell forward on Edith's bosom sobbing impetuously, "I love you so much, so much, that it makes it harder to die; but I must, and when the little snow-birds come back to the rose bushes beneath the windows of Grassy Spring a great ways off, the hands that used to feed them with crumbs will be laid away where they'll never tear Arthur boy's hair any more. Oh, I wish they never had--I wish they never had," and sob after sob shook Nina's delicate frame as she gave vent to her sorrow for the trial she had been to Arthur. Edith attempted to comfort her by saying, "He has surely forgiven you, darling; and Nina, please don't talk so much of dying, Arthur and I both hope you will live yet many years."

"Yes, Arthur does," Nina rejoined quickly, "him praying so one night when he thought I was asleep--I make believe half of the time, so as to hear what he says when he kneels down over in that corner; and once, Miggie, a great while ago, it was nothing but one dreadful groan, except when he said, 'God help me in this my darkest hour, and give me strength to drink this cup.' But there wasn't any cup there for I peaked, thinking maybe he'd go some of my nasty medicine, and it wasn't dark, either for there were two candles on the mantel and they shone on Arthur's face, which looked to me as if it were a thousand years old. Then he whispered, 'Edith, Edith,' and the sound was so like a wail that I felt my blood growing cold. Didn't you hear him, Miggie, way off to the north; didn't you hear him call? God did, and helped him, I reckon, for he got up and came and bent over me, kissing me so much, and whispering, 'My wife, my Nina.' It was sweet to be so kissed, and I fell away to sleep; but Arthur must have knelt beside me the livelong night, for every time I moved I felt his hand clasp mine. The next day he told me that Richard saved you from the river, and his lips quivered as if he feared you were really lost."

Alas! Nina had come nearer the truth than she supposed, and Edith involuntarily echoed her oft-repeated words, "Poor Arthur," for she knew now what had preceded that cry of more than mortal anguish which Arthur sent to Grace after hearing first of the engagement.

"Nina" she said, after a moment's silence, "before that time of which you speak, there came a night of grief to me--a night when I wished that I might die, because Richard asked me to be his wife-- me, who looked upon him as my father rather than a husband. I can't tell you what he said to me, but it was very touching, very sad, and my heart ached so much for the poor blind man."

"But you didn't tell him yes," interrupted Nina. "You couldn't. You didn't love him. It's wicked to act a lie Miggie--as wicked as 'tis to tell one. Say you told him no; it chokes me just to think of it."

"Nina," and Edith's voice was low and earnest in its tone, "I thought about it four whole weeks and at last I went to Richard and said, 'I will be your wife.' I have never taken it back, I am engaged to him, and I shall keep my word. Were it not that you sent for me I should have been his bride ere this. I shall be his bride on New Year's night."

Edith spoke rapidly, as if anxious to have the task completed, and when at last it was done, she felt that her strength was leaving her, so great had been the effort with which she told her story to Nina. Gradually as she talked Nina had crept away from her, and sitting upright in bed, stared at her fixedly, her face for once putting on the mature dignity of her years, and seeming older than Edith's. Then the clear-minded, rational Nina spoke out, "Miggie Bernard, were you ten thousand times engaged to Richard, it shall not be. You must not stain your soul with a perjured vow, and you would, were this sacrifice to be. Your lips would say 'I love,' but your heart would belie the words, and God's curse will rest upon you if you do Richard this cruel wrong. He does not deserve that you should deal so treacherously with him, and Miggie, I would far rather you were lying in the grave-yard over yonder, than to do this great wickedness. You must not, you shall not," and in the eyes of violet blue there was an expression beneath which the stronger eyes of black quailed as they had done once before, when delirium had set its mark upon them.

It was in vain that Edith persisted in saying she did, or at least should love Richard as he deserved. Nina was not to be convinced, and at last, in self-defence, Edith broke out bitterly against Arthur as the immediate cause of her sufferings. Had he not been faithless to his marriage vow, and might she not keep hers quite as well as he kept his.

Nina was very white, and the swollen veins stood out full upon her forehead as she lay panting on her pillow, but the eyes never for an instant left Edith's, as she replied, "Arthur was in fault, Miggie, greatly in fault, but there was much to excuse his error. He was so young; not as old as you, Miggie, and Sarah Warren urged us on. I knew afterward why she did it, too. She is dead now, and I would not speak against her were it not necessary, but, Miggie, she wanted Dr. Griswold, and she fancied he liked me, so she would remove me from her path; and she did. She worked upon my love of the romantic, and Arthur's impulsive nature, until she persuaded us to run away. While we were on the road, Arthur whispered to me, 'Let's go back,' but I said, 'No,' while Sarah, who overheard him, sneered at him as cowardly, and we went on. Then father took me off to Paris, and I dared not tell him, he was so dreadful when he was angry; and then I loved Charlie Hudson, and loved him the more because I knew I musn't."

The mature expression was passing rapidly from Nina's face, and the child-like one returning in its stead as she continued,

"I couldn't bear to think of Arthur, and before I came home I determined never to live with him as his wife. I didn't know then about this buzzing in my head, and the first thing I did when alone with him at the Revere House was to go down on my knees and beg of him not to make me keep my vow. I told him I loved Charlie best, and he talked so good to me--said maybe I'd get over it, and all that. Then he read pa's letter, which told what I would some time be, and he didn't ask me after that to live with him, but when he came from Florida and found me so dreadful, he put his arms around me, loving-like, and cried, while I raved like a fury and snapped at him like a dog. You see the buzzing was like a great noisy factory then, and Nina didn't know what she was doing, she hated him so, and the more he tried to please her the more she hated him. Then, when I came to my senses enough to think I did not want our marriage known, I made him promise not to tell, in Florida or anywhere, so he didn't, and the weary years wore on with people thinking I was his ward. Dr. Griswold was always kind and good, but not quite as patient and woman-like as Arthur. It seemed as if he had a different feeling toward me, and required more of me, for he was not as gentle when I tore as Arthur was. I was terribly afraid of him, though, and after a while he did me good. The buzzing wasn't bigger than a mill-wheel, and it creaked just as a big wheel does when there is no water to carry it. It was crying that I wanted. I had not wept in three years, but the sight of you touched a spring somewhere and the waters poured like a flood, turning the wheel without that grating noise that used to drive me mad, and after that I never tore but once. He didn't tell you, because I asked him not, but I scratched him, struck Phillis, burned up his best coat, broke the mirror, and oh, you don't know how I did cut up! Then the pain went away and has never come back like that. Sometimes I can see that it was wrong for him to love you and then again I can't, but if it was he has repented so bitterly of it since. He would not do it now. He needn't have told you, either, for everybody was dead, and it never would have come back to me if he hadn't said it in the Deering Woods. Don't you see?"

"Yes, I see," cried Edith, her tears dropping fast into her lap, "I see that I tempted him to sin. Oh, Arthur, I am most to blame-- most to blame."

"And you will give up Richard, won't you?" Nina said. "Arthur is just as good, just as noble, just as true, and better too, it may be, for he has passed through a fiercer fire than Richard ever did. Will you give up Richard?"

"I can't," and Edith shook her head. "The chords by which he holds me are like bands of steel, and cannot be sundered. I promised solemnly that by no word or deed would I seek to break our engagement, and I dare not. I should not be happy if I did."

And this was all Nina could wring from her, although she labored for many hours, sometimes rationally, sometimes otherwise, but always with an earnest simplicity which showed how pure were her motives, and how great her love for Edith.

CHAPTER XXX.
ARTHUR AND NINA.

It was rather late in the evening when Arthur returned, looking more than usually pale and weary, and still there was about him an air of playful pleasantry, such as there used to be, when Edith first knew him. During the long ride to Tallahassee, Victor, either from accident or design, touched upon the expected marriage of his master, and although Arthur would not ask a single question, he was a deeply-interested auditor, and listened intently, while Victor told him much which had transpired between himself and Edith, saying that unless some influence stronger than any he or Grace could exert were thrown around her, she would keep her vow to Richard, even though she died in keeping it.

"Girls like Edith Hastings do not die easily," was Arthur's only comment, and Victor half wished he had kept his own counsel and never attempted to meddle in a love affair.

But if Arthur said nothing, he thought the more, and the warfare within was not the less severe, because his face was so unruffled and his manner so composed. Thought, intense and almost bewildering, was busy at work, and ere the day was done, he had resolved that he would help Edith if all else forsook her. He would not throw one single obstacle across her pathway. He would make the sacrifice easier for her, even if to do it, he suffered her to think that his own love had waned. Nothing could more effectually cure her, and believing that she might be happy with Richard if she did not love another, he determined to measure every word and act so as to impress her with the conviction that though she was dear to him as a sister and friend, he had struggled with his affection for her and overcome it. It would be a living death to do this, he knew--to act so contrary to what he felt, but it was meet that he should suffer, and when at last he was left alone--when both were lost to him forever--Edith and his child-wife Nina, he would go away across the sea, and lose, if possible, in foreign lands, all rememberance of the past. And this it was that made him seem so cheerful when he came in that night, calling Edith "little sister," winding his arm around Nina, kissing her white face, asking if she had missed him any, if she were glad to have him back, and how she and Miggie had busied themselves during the day.

"We talked of you, Arthur, and of Richard," Nina said. "Miggie has promised to many him! Did you know it?"

"Yes, I know it," was Arthur's reply; "and there is no person in the world to whom I would sooner give her than to Richard, for I know he will leave nothing undone to make her happy."

There was no tremor in Arthur's voice, and Nina little guessed how much it cost him thus to speak, with Edith sitting near. Looking up into his face with a startled, perplexed expression, she said, "I did not expect this, Arthur boy. I thought you loved Miggie."

"Nina, please don't," and Edith spoke entreatingly, but Nina answered pettishly, "I ain't going to please, for everything has got upside down. It's all going wrong, and it won't make a speck of difference, as I see, whether I die or not."

"I think I'd try to live then," Arthur said, laughingly, while Edith hailed the appearance of Marie as something which would put a restraint upon Nina.

It had been arranged that Edith should take Arthur's place in the sick room that night, but Nina suddenly changed her mind, insisting that Arthur should sleep there as usual.

"There's a heap of things I must tell you," she whispered to him; "and my head is clearer when it's darker and the candles are on the stand."

So Edith retired to her own room, and after a time Arthur was alone with Nina. He was very tired, but at her request he sat down beside her, where she could look into his face and see, as she said, if he answered her for true. At first it was of herself she spoke--herself, as she used to be.

"I remember so well," she said "when you called me your Florida rose, and asked for one of my curls. That was long ago, and there have been years of darkness since, but the clouds are breaking now--daylight is coming up, or rather Nina is going out, into the daylight, where there is no more buzzing, no more headache. Will

I be crazy in Heaven, think?"

"No, darling, no," and Arthur changed his seat from the chair to the bed, where he could be nearer to the little girl, who continued,

"I've thought these many weeks how good you've been to me--how happy you have made my last days, while I have been so bad to you, but you musn't remember it against me, Arthur boy, when I'm dead and there isn't any naughty Nina anywhere, neither at the Asylum, nor Grassy Spring, nor here in bed, nothing but a teenty grave, out in the yard, with the flowers growing on it, I say you must not remember the wicked things I've done, for it wasn't the Nina who talks to you now. It was the buzzing Nina who tore your hair, and scratched your face, and bit your arm. Oh, Arthur, Nina's so sorry now; but you musn't lay it up against me."

"No, my darling, God forbid that I, who have wronged you so terribly, should remember aught against you," and Arthur kissed the slender hands which had done him so much mischief.

They were harmless now, those little waxen hands, and they caressed Arthur's face and hair as Nina went on.

"Arthur boy, there's one question I must ask you, now there's nobody to hear, and you will tell me truly. Do you love me any-- love me differently from what you did when I was in the Asylum, and if the buzzing all was gone, and never could come back, would you really make me your wife just as other husbands do--would you let me sit upon your knee, and not wish it was some one else, and in the night when you woke up and felt me close to you would you be glad thinking it was Nina? And when you had been on a great long journey, and were coming home, would the smoke from the chimney look handsomer to you because you knew it was Nina waiting for you by the hearth-stone, and keeping up the fire? Don't tell me a falsehood, for I'll forgive you, if you answer no."

"Yes, Nina, yes. I would gladly take you as my wife if it could be. My broken lily is very precious to me now, far more so than she used to be. The right love for her began to grow the moment I confessed she was my wife, and when she's gone, Arthur will be so lonely."

"Will you, Arthur boy? Will you, as true as you live and breathe, miss poor, buzzing Nina? Oh, I'm so glad, so glad," and the great tears dimmed the brightness of the blue eyes, which looked up so confidingly at Arthur. "I, too, have loved you a heap; not exactly as I loved Charlie Hudson, I reckon, but the knowing you are my husband, makes Nina feel kind of nice, and I want you to love me some--miss me some--mourn for me some, and then, Arthur, Nina wants you to marry Miggie. There is no buzzing; no twist in her head. It will rest as quietly on your bosom where mine has never lain, not as hers will, I mean, and you both will be so happy at last--happy in knowing that Nina has gone out into the eternal daylight, where she would rather be. You'll do it, Arthur; she must not marry Richard, and you must speak to her quick, before she goes home, so as to stop it, for New Year's is the time. Will you, Arthur?"

There was an instant of silence in the room--Nina waiting for Arthur to speak, and Arthur mustering all his strength to answer her as he felt he must.

"My darling," laying his face down upon her neck among her yellow curls, "I shall never call another by the dear name I call you now, my wife."

"Oh, Arthur," and Nina's cheeks flushed with indignant surprise, that he, too, should prove refractory. Everything indeed, was getting upside down. "Why not?" she asked. "Don't you love Miggie?"

"Yes, very, very dearly! but it is too much to hope that she will ever be mine. I do not deserve it. You ask me my forgiveness, Nina. Alas! alas! I have tenfold more need of yours. It did not matter that we both wearied of our marriage vows, made when we were children--did not matter that you are crazy--I had no right to love another.

"But you have paid for it all a thousand times!" interrupted Nina. "You are a better Arthur than you were before, and Nina never could see the wrong in your preferring beautiful, sensible Miggie, to crazy, scratching, biting, teasing Nina, even if Richard had said over a few words, of which neither of us understood the meaning, or what it involved, this taking for better or worse. It surely cannot be wrong to marry Miggie when I'm gone, and you will, Arthur, you will!"

"No, Nina, no! I should be adding sin to sin did I seek to change her decision, and so wrong the noble Richard. His is the first, best claim. I will not interfere. Miggie must keep her word uninfluenced by me. I shall no raise my voice against it."

"Oh, Arthur, Arthur!" Nina cried, clasping her hands together; "Miggie does not love him, and you surely know the misery of a marriage without love. It must not be! It shall no be! you can save Miggie, and you must!"

Every word was fainter than the preceding, and, when the last was uttered, Nina's head dropped from Arthur's shoulder to the pillow, and he saw a pinkish stream issuing from her lips. A small blood vessel had been ruptured, and Arthur, who knew the danger, laid his hand upon her mouth as he saw her about to speak, bidding her be quiet if she would not die at once.

Death, however long and even anxiously expected is unwelcome at the last, and Nina shrank from its near approach, laying very still, while Arthur summoned aid. Only once she spoke, and then she whispered, "Miggie," thus intimating that she would have her called. In much alarm Edith came, trembling when she saw the fearful change which had passed over Nina, whose blue eyes followed her movements intently, turning often from her to Arthur as If they fain would utter what was in her mind. But not then was Nina St. Claire to die. Many days and nights were yet appointed her, and Arthur and Edith watched her with the tenderest care; only these two, for so Nina would have it. Holding their hands in hers she would gaze from one to the other with a wistful, pleading look, which, far better than words, told what she would say, were It permitted her to speak, but in the deep brown eyes of Arthur, she read always the same answer, while Edith's would often fill with tears as she glanced timidly at the apparently cold, silent man, who, she verily believed, had ceased to love her.

But Nina knew better. Clouded as was her reason, she penetrated the mask he wore, and saw where the turbulent waters surged around him, while with an iron will and a brave heart he contended with the angry waves, and so outrode the storm. And as she watched them day after day, the purpose grew strong within her that if it were possible the marriage of Edith and Richard should be prevented, and as soon as she was able to talk she broached the subject to them both.

"Stay, Miggie," she said to Edith, who was stealing from the room. "Hear me this once. You are together now, you and Arthur."

"Nina," said the latter, pitying Edith's agitation, "You will spare us both much pain if you never allude again to what under other circumstances might have been."

"But I must," cried Nina. "Oh, Arthur, why won't you go to Richard and tell him all about it?"

"Because it would be wrong," was Arthur's answer, and then Nina turned to

Edith, "Why won't you, Miggie?"

"Because I have solemnly promised that I would not," was her reply.

And Nina rejoined, "Then I shall write. He loved little Snow Drop. He'll heed what she says when she speaks from the grave. I'll send him a letter."

"Who'll take it or read it to him if you do?" Arthur asked, and the troubled eyes of blue turned anxiously to Edith.

"Miggie, sister, won't you?"

Edith shook her head, not very decidedly, it is true, still it was a negative shake, and Nina said, "Arthur boy, will you?"

"No, Nina, no."

Hia answer was determined, and poor, discouraged Nina sobbed aloud, "Who will, who will?"

In the adjoining room there was a rustling sound--a coming footstep, and Victor Dupres appeared in the door. He had been an unwilling hearer of that conversation, and when Nina cried "who will?" he started up, and coming into the room as if by accident, advanced to the bedside and asked in his accustomed friendly way, "How is Nina to-night?" Then bending over her so that no one should hear, he whispered softly, "Don't tell them, but I'll read that letter to Richard!"

Nina understood him and held his hand a moment while she looked the thanks she dared not speak.

"Nina must not talk any more" Arthur said, as Victor walked away, "she is wearing out too fast," and with motherly tenderness he smoothed her tumbled pillow--pushed back behind her ears the tangled curls--kissed her forehead, and then went out into the deepening night, whose cool damp air was soothing to his burning brow, and whose sheltering mantle would tell no tales of his white face or of the cry which came heaving up from where the turbulent waters lay, "if it be possible let this temptation pass from me, or give me strength to resist it."

His prayer was heard--the turmoil ceased at last--the waters all were stilled, and Arthur went back to Nina, a calm, quiet man, ready and willing to meet whatever the future might bring.

CHAPTER XXXI.
LAST DAYS.

"Aunt Hannah will stay with me to-night," Nina said to Arthur the next day, referring to an old negress who had taken cure of her when a child; and Arthur yielded to her request the more willingly, because of his own weariness.

Accordingly old Hannah was installed watcher in the sick room, receiving orders that her patient should not on any account be permitted to talk more than was absolutely necessary. Nina heard this injunction of Arthur and a smile of cunning flitted across her face as she thought how she would turn it to her own advantage in case Hannah refused to comply with her request, which she made as soon as they were left alone.

Hannah must first prop her up in bed, she said, and then give her her port-folio, paper, pen and ink. As she expected, the negress objected at once, bidding her be still, but Nina declared her intention of talking as fast and as loudly as she could, until her wish was gratified. Then Hannah threatened calling Arthur, thereupon the willful little lady rejoined, "I'll scream like murder, if you do, and burst every single blood-vessel I've got, so bring me the paper, please, or shall I got it myself," and she made a motion as if the would leap upon the floor, while poor old Hannah, regretting the task she had undertaken, was compelled to submit and bring the writing materials as desired.

"Now you go to sleep," Nina said coaxingly, and as old Hannah found but little difficulty in obeying the command, Nina was left to herself while she wrote that long, long message, a portion of which we give below.

"DEAR MR. RICHARD:

"Poor blind man! Nina is so sorry for you to-night, because she knows that what she has to tell you will crush the strong life all out of your big heart, and leave it as cold and dead as she will be when Victor reads this to you. There won't be any Nina then, for Miggie and Arthur, and a heap more, will have gone with their way out where both my mothers are lying, and Miggie'll cry, I reckon when she hears the gravel stones ruttling down just over my head, but I shall know they cannot hit me, for the coffin-lid will be between, and Nina'll lie so still. No more pain; no more buzzing; no more headache; no more darkness; won't it be grand, the rest I'm going to. I shan't be crazy in Heaven. Arthur says so; and he knows.

"Poor Arthur! It is of him and Miggie I am writing to you, if I ever can get to them; and Richard; when you hear this read, Nina'll be there with you; but you can't see her, because you're blind, and you couldn't see if you weren't, but she'll be there just the same. She'll sit upon your knee, and wind her arms around your neck, so as to comfort you when the great cry comes in, the crash like the breaking up of the winter ice on the northern ponds, and when you feel yourself all crushed like they are in the spring, listen and you'll hear her whispering, 'Poor Richard, Nina pities you so much! She'll kiss your tears away, too, though maybe you won't feel her. And, Richard, you'll do right, won't you. You'll give Miggie up. You'll let Arthur have her, and so bring back the sunshine to her face. She's so pale now and sorry, and the darkness lies thickly around her.

"There are three kinds of darkness, Richard. One like mine, when the brain has a buzz in the middle, and everything is topsy-turvy. One, like yours, when the world is all shut out with its beauty and its flowers; and then there's another, a blacker darkness when the buzz is in the heart, making it wild with pain. Such, Richard is the darkness, which lies like a pall around our beautiful sister Miggie, and it will deepen and deepen unless you do what Nina asks you to do, and what Miggie never will, because she promised that she wouldn't-----"

Then followed the entire story of the marriage performed by Richard, of the grief which followed, of Arthur's gradually growing love of Edith, of the scene of the Deering Woods, of the incidents connected with Edith's sickness, her anguish at parting with Arthur, her love for him still, her struggles to do right, and her determination to keep her engagement even though she died in doing it.

All this was told in Nina's own peculiar style; and then came her closing appeal that Richard himself should break the bonds and set poor Miggie free.

"... It will be dreadful at first, I know, and may be all three of the darknesses will close around you for a time,--darkness of the heart, darkness of the brain, and darkness of the eyes, but it will clear away and the daylight will break, in which you will be happier than in calling Miggie your wife, and knowing how she shrinks from you, suffering your caresses only because she knows she must, but feeling so sick at her stomach all the time, and wishing you wouldn't touch her. I know just how it feels, for when Arthur kissed me, or took my hand, or even came in my sight, before the buzz got into my head, it made me so cold and faint and ugly, the way the Yankees mean, knowing he was my husband when I wanted Charlie Hudson. Don't subject Miggie to this horrid fate. Be generous and give her up to Arthur. He may not deserve her more than you, but she loves him the best and that makes a heap of difference.

"It's Nina who asks it, Richard; dead Nina not a living one. She is sitting on your knee; her arms are round your neck; her face against yours and you must not tell her no, or she'll cling to you day and night, night and day; when you are in company and when you are alone. When it is dark and lonely and all but you asleep, she'll sit upon your pillow and whisper continually, 'Give Miggie up; give Miggie up,' or if you don't, and Miggie's there beside you, Nina'll stand between you; a mighty, though invisible shield, and you'll feel it's but a mockery, the calling her your wife when her love is given to another.

"Good bye, now, Richard, good bye. My brain begins to buzz, my hand to tremble. The lines all run together, and I am most as blind as you. God bless you, Mr. Richard; bless you any way, but a heap more if you give Miggie up. May be He'll give you back your sight to pay for Miggie. I should rather have it than a wife who did not love me; and I'll tease Him till He'll let me bring it to you some day.

"Good bye, again, good bye.
"NINA ARTHUR BERNARD."

The night was nearly worn away ere the letter was finished; and Nina's eyes flashed with unwonted fire as laughing aloud at the Arthur added to her name, she laid it away beneath her pillow and then tried herself to sleep. But this last was impossible, and when the morning broke she was so much worse that the old nurse trembled lest her master should censure her severely for having yielded to her young mistress's whim. Mild and gentle as he seemed, Arthur could, if necessary, be very stern, and knowing this, old Hannah concluded at last that if Nina did not betray herself she would not, and when Arthur came, expressing his surprise at the change, and asking for its cause, she told glibly "how restless and onquiet Miss Nina done been flirtin' round till the blood all got in her head and she was dreadful."

"You should have called me," Arthur said, sitting down by Nina, whose feverish hands he clasped, while he asked, "Is my little girl's head very bad this morning?"

Nina merely nodded, for she really was too weak to talk, and Arthur watched her uneasily, wondering why it was that her eyes were fixed so constantly upon the door, as if expecting some one. When breakfast was announced she insisted that both he and Edith should leave her, and, the moment they were gone, she asked for Victor, who came at once, half guessing why he was sent for.

"Under my pillow," she whispered, as he bent over her, and in an instant the letter, of whose existence neither Arthur nor Edith suspected, was safe in Victor's pocket.

Nina had accomplished her object, and she became unusually quiet. Richard would get the letter--Richard would do right, she knew, and the conviction brought to her a deep peace, which nothing ever after disturbed. She did not speak of him again, and her last days were thus pleasanter to Edith, who, from the sweet companionship held with her gentle sister, learned in part what Nina Bernard was, ere the darkness of which she had written to Richard crept into her brain. Fair and beautiful as the white pond lily, she faded rapidly, until Arthur carried her no longer to the window, holding her in his arms while she looked out upon the yard and garden where she used to play--but she lay all day upon her bed holding Edith's hands, and talking to her of that past still so dim and vague to the latter. Marie, too, often joined them, repeating to Edith many incidents of interest connected with both her parents, but speaking most of the queenly Petrea, whom Edith so strongly resembled. Nina, too, remembered her well, and Edith was never weary of hearing her tell of the "beautiful new mamma," who kissed her so tenderly that night when she first came home, calling her la petite enfant, and placing in her arms a darling little sister, with eyes just like the stars!

Very precious to Edith was the memory of those days, when she watched the dying Nina, who, as death drew near, clung closer and closer to her sister, refusing to let her go.

"I want you with me," she said, one afternoon, when the late autumn rain was beating against the window-pane, and the clouds hung leaden and dull in the Southern sky. "I want you and Arthur, both, to lead me down to the very edge of the river, and not let go my hands until the big waves wash me away, for Nina's a wee bit of a girl, and she'll be afraid to launch out alone upon the rushing stream. I wish you'd go too, Miggie,--go over Jordan with me. Why does God make me go alone?"

"You will not go alone, my darling!" and Edith's voice was choked with tears as she told the listening Nina of one whose arm would surely hold her up, so that the waters should not overflow.

"It's the Saviour you mean," and Nina spoke reverently. "I loved Him years ago before the buzzing came, but I've been so bad since then, that I'm afraid that He'll cast me off. Will He, think? When I tell him I am little Nina Bernard come from Sunnybank, will He say, 'Go 'way old crazy Nina, that tore poor Arthur boy's hair?'"

"No, no, oh, no," and Edith sobbed impetuously as she essayed to comfort the bewildered girl, whose mind grasped but faintly the realities of eternity.

"And you'll stand on the bank till I am clear across," she said, when Edith had ceased speaking, "You and Arthur stand where I can see you if I should look back. And, Miggie, I have a presentiment that Nina'll go to-night, but I don't want any body here except you and Arthur. I remember when grandma died the negroes howled so dismally, and they didn't love her one bit either. They used to make mouths at her, and hide her teeth. But they do love me, and their screeches will get my head all in a twist. I'd rather they wouldn't know till morning; then when they ask for me Arthur'll tell them sorry like that Nina's dead; Nina's gone into the daylight, and left a world of love to them who have been so kind to her. Don't let them crowd up around me, or make too much ado. It isn't worth the while, for I'm of no account, and you'll be good to them Miggie--good to the poor ignorant blacks. They are your's after me, and I love them a heap. Don't let them be sold, will you?"

Here Nina paused, too much exhausted to talk longer, and when about dark Arthur came in, he found her asleep with Edith at her side, while upon her face and about her nose there was a sharp, pitched look he had never seen before. Intuitively, however, he knew that look was the harbinger of death, and when Edith told him what Nina had said, he felt that ere the morning came his broken lily would be gone.

Slowly the evening wore on, and one by one the family retired, leaving Arthur and Edith alone with the pale sleeper whose slumbers ended not until near the midnight hour; silently, sadly, Arthur and Edith watched her, she on one side, he upon the other, neither speaking for the sorrow which lay so heavy at their hearts, She was very beautiful as she lay there so motionless, and Arthur felt his heart clinging more and more to his fair, childish wife, while his conscience smote him cruelly for any wrong he might have done to her. She was going from him now so fast, and as the clock struck twelve the soft blue eyes unclosed and smiled up in his face with an expression which, better than words could do, told that she bore no malice toward him, nothing but trusting faith and confiding love. He had been kind to her, most kind, and she told him so again, for she seemed to know how dear to him such testimonial would be when she was gone.

"The clouds are weeping for Nina," she said, as she heard the rain still beating against the window. "Will it make the river deeper, think? I hear its roar in the distance. It's just beginning to heave in sight, and I dread it so much. 'Twill be lonesome crossing this dismal, rainy night. Oh, Arthur--boy, Arthur--boy, let me stay with you. Can't you keep me? Can't you hide me somewhere? you, Miggie? I won't be in the way. It's so icy, and the river is so deep. Save me, do!" and she stretched out her hands to Arthur as if imploring him to hold her back from the rushing stream bearing down so fast upon her.

Forcing down his own great grief, Arthur took her in his arms and hugging her fondly to him, sought to comfort her by whispering of the blessed Saviour who would carry her in His bosom beyond the swelling flood, and Nina, as she listened, grew calm and still, while something like the glory of the better land shone upon her face as she repeated after him, "There'll be no night, no darkness there, no headache, no pain,--nor buzzing either?" she suddenly asked. "Say, will there be any buzzing brains in Heaven?"

Arthur shook his head, and she continued, "That will be so nice, and Dr. Griswold will be so glad when he knows Nina is not crazy. He's gone before, I reckon, to take care of me,--gone where there's nothing but daylight, glorious, grand; kiss me again, Arthur boy. 'Tis sweet to die upon your bosom with Miggie standing near, and when you both are happy in each other's love, don't quite forget little Nina,--Nina out under the flowers, will you? She's done a heap of naughtiness, I know; but she's sorry, Arthur, she is so sorry that she ever bit your arm or tore your hair! Poor hair! Pretty brown hair! Bad Nina made the white threads come," and her childish hands caressed the thick brown locks mingling with her sunny curls, as Arthur bent over her, answering only with his tears, which fell in torrents.

"Don't, darling, don't," he said, at last. "The bad has all been on my side, and I would that you should once more say I am forgiven."

Nina gazed wonderingly at him a moment, then made a motion that he should lay her back upon the pillow.

"Now put your head down here, right on my neck--so."

He complied with her request, and placing both her bands upon the bowed head of the young man, Nina whispered,

"May the Good Shepherd, whose lamb Nina hopes to be, keep my Arthur boy, and bless him a hundred fold for all he's been to me, and if he has wronged me, which I don't believe, but if he has, will God please forgive him as fully, as freely as Nina does--the best Arthur boy that ever lived. I'll tell God all about it, and how I pestered you, and how good you were, my Arthur boy--Nina's Arthur first and Miggie's after me. Now put your arms around me again," she said, as she finished the blessing which brought such peace to Arthur. "Put them around me tight, for the river is almost here. Don't you hear its splashing? Miggie, Miggie," she cried, shivering as with an ague chill, "hold my hand with all your might, but don't let me pull you in. I'm going down the bank. My feet are in the water, and it's so freezing cold. I'm sinking, too, and the big waves roll over me. Oh, Arthur, you said it would not hurt," and the dim eyes flashed upon the weeping man a most reproachful glance, as if he had deceived her, while the feet were drawn shudderingly up, as if they had, indeed, touched the chill tide of death, and shrank affrighted from it. Edith could only sob wildly, as she grasped the clammy hand stretched toward her, but Arthur, more composed, whispered to the dying girl,

"Yea, though I walk through the valley of the shadow of death, I will fear no evil, for thou, Lord, art with me; thy staff and thy rod, they comfort me."

"Look away to the shore," he continued, as Nina ceased to struggle, and lay still on his bosom. "Look away to the glorious city--my darling is almost there."

"Yes, yes, I do, I am," came faintly up, and then with a glad cry of joy, which rang in their ears for many a day and night, Nina said,

"You may lay me down, my Arthur boy, and take your arm away. There's a stronger one than yours around me now. The arm that Miggie told me of, and it will not let me down. I'm going over so easy, easy, in a cradle-like, and Dr. Griswold's there waiting for clipped-winged birdie. He looks so glad, so happy. It is very nice to die; but stand upon the bank, Arthur and Miggie. Wait till I'm across."

They thought she had left them, when softly, sweetly, as if it were a note of heavenly music sent back to them from the other world, there floated on the air the words,

"Climb up the bank, I'm most across. I do not see you now. MOTHER- -and Miggie's mother--and Dr. Griswold have waded out to meet me. The darkness is passed, the daylight has dawned; Miggie precious, and darling Arthur boy, good-bye, for Nina's gone, good-bye."

The white lips never moved again, the waxen hands lay lifelessly in Arthur's, the damp, bright hair lay half-uncurled upon the pillow, the blue eyes were closed, the aching head was still, the "twisted brain" had ceased to "buzz," the Darkness for her was over, and Nina had gone out into the Daylight.

CHAPTER XXXII.
PARTING WITH THE DEAD, AND PARTING WITH THE LIVING.

Softly the morning broke and the raindrops glittered like diamonds in the rising sun, whose rays fell mockingly upon desolate Sunnybank, where the howling of the blacks mingled with the sobs of those more nearly bereaved. Very troublesome had the beautiful departed been in life; none knew how troublesome one-half so well as Arthur, and yet of all the weeping band who gathered around her bed, none mourned her more truly than did he who had been her husband in name for eleven years. Eleven years! How short they seemed, looked back upon, and how much sorrow they had brought him. But this was all forgotten, and in his heart there was naught save tender love for the little maiden now forever at rest.

All the day he sat by her, and both Edith and Victor felt that it was not the mere semblance of grief he wore, while others of the household, who knew nothing of his past in connection with Edith, said to each other, "It is strange he should love her so well when she was so much care to him."

They did not know it was this very care for her; this bearing with her which made her so dear to him, and as the mother longs for and wishes back the unfortunate but beloved child which made her life so wearisome so Arthur mourned and wept for Nina, thanking God one moment that her poor, pain-worn head was at rest, and again murmuring to himself, "I would that I had her back again."

He scarcely spoke to Edith, although he knew whenever her footsteps crossed the threshold of the darkened room; knew when she bent over Nina; heard the kisses she pressed on the cold lips; and even watched until it was dry the tear she once left on Nina's cheek, but he held no communication with her, and she was left to battle with her grief alone. Once, indeed, she went to him and asked what Nina should be buried in, and this for a time roused him from his apathetic grief.

"Nina must be buried in white," he said; "she looked the best in that; and, Edith, I would have her curls cut off, all but those that shade her face. You have arranged them every day. Will you do so once more if I will hold her up?"

Edith would rather the task had devolved upon some one else, but she offered no objection, though her tears fell like rain when she brought the curling-stick and brush and began to separate the tangled locks, while Arthur encircled the rigid form with his arm, as carefully as if she still were living, watching her with apparent interest as she twined about her fingers the golden hair. But when, at last, she held the scissors which were to sever those bright tresses, his fortitude all gave way, for he remembered another time when he had held poor Nina, not as he held her now, but with a stronger, firmer grasp, while, by rougher hands than Edith's, those locks were shorn away. Groan after groan came from his broad chest, and his tears moistened the long ringlets he so lovingly caressed.

"You may cut them now," he said at last, holding his breath as if the sharp steel were cutting into his heart's core, as, one by one, the yellowish curls were severed, and dropped, some into Edith's lap, while others, lodging upon his fingers, curled about them with a seemingly human touch, making him moan bitterly, as he pressed them to his lips, and then shook them gently off.

Nina's hair, like her sister's, had been her crowning glory--so thick, so wavy, so luxuriant it was; and when the task was done, and the tresses divided, five heavy curls were Arthur's and five more were Edith's.

"Where shall I put yours?" Edith asked, and for a moment Arthur did not answer.

In a rosewood box, into which he had not looked for years, there was a mass of longer, paler, more uneven curls than these, but Arthur would not distress Edith by telling her about them, and he replied, at last, "I will put them away, myself." Then taking them from her and going to his own private chamber, he opened the box and dropped them in, weeping when he saw how strongly they contrasted with the other faded crazy curls, as he called them.

In a plain white muslin, which had been made for Nina at Grassy Spring, they arrayed her for the coffin, the soft, rich lace encircling her throat and falling about her slender arms folded so meekly together. Flowers were twined about her head--flowers were on her pillow--flowers in her hands--flowers upon her bosom-- flowers of purest white, and meet emblems of the sweet young girl, whose features, to the last, retained the same childlike, peaceful expression which had settled upon them when she called back to Arthur, "Climb up the bank. I'm most across."

The day of her burial was balmy and warm, and the southern wind blew softly across the fields as the weeping band followed the lost one across the threshold and laid her away where the flowers of spring would blossom above her little grave. Very lonely and desolate seemed the house when the funeral train returned to it, and the lamentations of the blacks broke out afresh as they began to realize that their young mistress was really gone, and henceforth another must fill her place. Would it be Arthur or would it be the queenly Edith, whose regal beauty had captivated all their hearts? Assembled in the kitchen they discussed this question, giving to neither the preference, for though they had tried Arthur and found him a kind and humane master, they felt that after Nina, Edith had the right. Then, as other than blacks will do, they speculated upon the future, wondering why both Arthur and Edith could not rule jointly over them; they would like that vastly, and had nearly decided that it would be, when Victor, who was with them, tore down their castle by telling them that Edith was already engaged to some one else. This changed the channel of conversation, and Victor left them wondering still what the future would bring.

Slowly the evening passed, in kitchen and in parlor and only those who have felt it can tell the unspeakable loneliness of that first evening after the burial of the dead. Several times Arthur started as if he would go to the bed standing empty in the corner, while Edith, too, fancied that she heard the name "Miggie," spoken as only Nina could speak it. Then came a feeling of desolation as the thought was forced upon them, "She is gone;" and as the days went on till three suns had risen on her grave, the loneliness increased until Edith could bear it no longer, and to Victor she said, "We will go back to Richard, who is waiting so anxiously for us."

Everything which Arthur could do he did to reinstate Edith in her rights. Not one dollar of the Bernard estate had he ever spent for himself and very little for Nina, preferring to care for her out of his own resources and thus the property had increased so rapidly that Edith was richer than her wildest hopes. But not one feather did this weigh with her, and on the day when matters were arranged, she refused to do or say anything about it, persisting so obstinately in her refusal, that the servants whispered slily to each other, "That's a heap of old marster's grit thar."

For a time Arthur coaxed and reasoned with her; then finding that this did not avail, he changed the mode of treatment, and, placing a chair by his own, said to her commandingly, "Edith, sit here!" and she sat there, for there was that in Arthur's sternness which always enforced obedience.

"It cannot be more unpleasant for you than for me, but it is necessary," he said to her, in a low tone, as she sank into her seat, and ashamed of her willfulness, Edith whispered back, "I am sorry I behaved so like a child. Forgive me won't you?"

Still it grated harshly, this being compelled to listen while the lawyer, summoned by Arthur, talked to her of lands and mortgages, of bank stock, and, lastly, of the negroes. Would she have them sold, or what? Then Edith roused from her apathy. Nina had entrusted them to her, and she would care for them. They should not be sold, and so she said; they should still live at Sunnybank, having free papers made out in case of accident to herself, or, if they preferred, they should go with her at once to Collingwood, and Sunnybank to be sold.

"Oh, Heavens!" exclaimed Victor, who had stationed himself behind Edith. "Forty niggers at Collingwood! Mr. Harrington never would stand that. Leave them here."

Arthur smiled at the Frenchman's evident distress, while Edith made a gesture that Victor should be still, and then continued, "It may be better to leave them here for a time at least, and Mr. Harrington shall decide upon their future home."

She said this naturally, and as a matter of course, but her heart leaped to her throat when she saw the pallor which for an instant overspread Arthur's face at her allusion to one who would soon have the right to rule her and hers.

"Is Mr. Harrington your guardian, Miss Bernard?" the lawyer asked, and ere Edith could reply, Arthur answered for her, "He is to be her husband."

The lawyer bowed and went on with his writing, all unconscious of the wounds his question had tore open, leaving them to bleed afresh as both Arthur and Edith assumed a mask of studied indifference, never looking at or addressing each other again while that painful interview lasted. It was over at length, and the lawyer gone. Matters were adjusted as well they could be at present. The negroes were to remain at Sunnybank under charge of an overseer as usual, while Arthur was to stay there, too, until he decided upon his future course. This was his own proposition, and Edith acceded to it joyfully. There were no sweet home associations, connected in her mind with Sunnybank, it is true, for she was too young when she left it to retain more than a dim, shadowy remembrance of a few scenes and places; but it had been Nina's home; there she was born, there she had lived, there she had died, and Edith felt that it would not be one half so dreary looked back upon, if Arthur would stay there always.

"Why can't you?" she asked of him when in the evening she sat with him in the rather gloomy parlor. "I'll make you my agent in general, giving you permission to do whatever you please, or would you rather live at Grassy Spring?"

"Anywhere but there," was Arthur's quick response, "I shall sell Grassy Spring and go abroad. I shall be happier so. I have never known the comfort of a home for any length of time, and it does not matter where I am. My mother, as Grace may have told you, was a gay, fashionable woman, and after the period of mourning had expired, I only remember her resplendent in satin and diamonds, kissing me goodnight ere her departure for some grand party. Then, when I was eight years old, she, too, died, leaving me to the care of a guardian. Thus, you see, I have no pleasant memories of a home, and the cafes of Paris will suit me as well as anything, perhaps. Once I hoped for something better, but that is over now, Nina is dead, while you, on whom, as my wife's sister, I have some claim, will soon be gone from here and I shall be alone. I shall sell Grassy Spring,--shall place the negroes there in your keeping, and then next spring leave the country, never to return, it may be."

He ceased speaking, and there was a silence in the room which Edith could not break. Arthur had told her frankly of his intended future, but she could not speak of hers--could not tell him that Collingwood's doors were ever open to him--that she would be his sister in very deed--that Richard would welcome him as a brother for her sake, and that the time might come when they could be happy thus. All this passed through her mind, but not a word of it escaped her lips, lest by doing so she would betray her real feelings. Arthur did not seem to her now as he had done a few days previous; their relations to each other had changed, and were there no Richard, it would not be wicked to love him now. Nina was gone; the past was more than atoned for; the marble, at first unsightly to some degree, had been hewn and polished, and though the blows had each struck deep, they wrought in Arthur St. Claire a perfect work. Ennobled, subdued, and purified, he was every way desirable, both as brother, friend, and husband, but he was not for her, and the consciousness that it was so, palsied her powers of speech.

Wishing to say something to break the awkward silence, Arthur asked at last, if it were true, as Victor had said, that she intended starting for Collingwood the day after to-morrow, and then she burst into tears, but made him no reply, only passionate sobs which smote cruelly upon his heart, for well he guessed their meaning. He could read Edith Hastings aright--could fathom her utmost thoughts, find he knew how she shrank from the future dreading a return to Collingwood, and what awaited her there. He knew, too, that but a few words from himself were needed to keep her at Sunnybank with him forever. Others might be powerless to influence her decision, but he was not; he could change her whole future life by whispering in her ear, "Stay with me, Edith; don't go back," but the Arthur of to-day was stronger than the Arthur of one year ago, and though the temptation was a terrible one, he met it bravely, and would not deal thus treacherously with Richard, who had so generously trusted her with him. Edith must keep her vow, and when at last he spoke, it was to say something of the journey, as if that had all the time been uppermost in his mind.

"He does not love me any more, and I don't care," was Edith's mental comment, as she soon after left him and hurried to her room, where she wept herself to sleep, never suspecting how long and dreary was that night to the young man whose eyelids never for a moment closed, and who, as the day was breaking, stole out to Nina's grave, finding there a peace which kept his soul from fainting.

At the breakfast table he was the same easy, elegant, attentive host he always was in his own house, conversing pleasantly upon indifferent topics, but he could not look at her now, on this her last day with him; could not endure to hear her voice, and he avoided her presence, seeing as little of her as possible, and retiring unusually early, even though he read in her speaking eyes a wish that he would tarry longer.

The next morning, however, he knew the instant she was astir, listening eagerly to the sound of her footsteps as she made her hasty toilet, and watching her from his window as she went to Nina's grave, sobbing out her sad farewell to the loved dead. He saw her, too, as she came back to the house, and then with a beating heart went down to meet her.

The breakfast was scarcely touched, and the moment it was over Edith hurried to her chamber, for it was nearly time to go. The trunks were brought down-- Edith's and Marie's--for the latter was to live henceforth with her young mistress; the servants had crowded to the door, bidding their mistress good bye, and then it was Arthur's turn. Oh, who shall tell of the tempest which raged within as he held for a moment her soft, white hand in his and looked into the face which, ere he saw it again, might lose its girlish charm for him, inasmuch as a husband's kisses would have been showered upon it. Many times he attempted to speak, but could not, and pressing his lips to hers, he hastened away, going straight to Nina's grave which had become to him of late a Bethel.

Scarcely was he gone, when Tom, the driver, announced that something was the matter with the harness, and by this delay, Edith gained a few moments, which she resolved to spend with Nina. She did not know that Arthur, too, was there, until she came close upon him as he bent over the little mound. He heard her step, and turning toward her, and, half bitterly, "Edith, why will you tempt me so?"

"Oh, Arthur, don't," and with a piteous cry Edith sank at his feet, and laying her face on Nina's grave, sobbed out, "I did not know that you were here, but I am so glad that you are, for I cannot be without your blessing, you must tell me I am doing right, or I shall surely die. The world is so dark--so dark."

Arthur had been tempted before--sorely, terribly tempted--but never like this, and recoiling a pace or two, he stood with the dead Nina between himself and she weeping heavily, while the wild thought swept over him, "Is it right that I should fiend her away? " but over her an instant, and stretching his hand across the grave, he laid it on the head of the kneeling girl, giving her the blessing she so much craved, and then bidding her leave him.

"They are calling to you," he added, as he heard Victor's voice in the distance, and struggling to her feet, Edith started to go, but forgetting all sense of propriety in that dreadful parting, she turned to him again and said,

"I am going, Arthur, but I must ask one question. It will make my future brighter if I know you love me still, be it ever so little. Do you, Arthur, and when you know I am Richard's wife will you think of me sometimes, and pity me, too? I shall need it so much!"

Arthur had not expected this, and he reeled as if smitten with a heavy blow. Leaning for support against Petrea's monument, whence Miggie's name had been effaced, he gasped:

"God help me, Edith! You should have spared me this. Do I love you? Oh Edith, alas, alas! Here with Nina, whom, Heaven is my witness, I did love truly at the last--here with her, I say, lying dead between us, I swear to you that never was maiden loved as I this moment love you; but I cannot make you mine. I dare not prove thus treacherous to Richard, who trusted you with me, and, Edith, you can be happy with him, and you will. You must forget that I ever crossed your path, thinking of me only as one who was your sister's husband. And God will give you strength to do this if you ask it of him aright I shall not forgot you, Edith. That cannot be. Across the sea, wherever I may be, I shall remember you, enshrining your memory in my heart, together with Nina, whom I so much wish I had loved earlier, and so have saved us both from pain. And now go--go back to Collingwood, and keep your vow to Richard. He is one of God's noblest works, an almost perfect man. You will learn to love him. You will be happy. Do not write to me till it is over, then send your cards, and I shall know 'tis done. Farewell, my sister--farewell forever."

Without a word of reply Edith moved away, nor cast a backward glance at the faint, sick man, who leaned his burning forehead against the gleaming marble; while drop after drop of perspiration fell upon the ground, but brought him no relief. He heard the carriage wheels as they rolled from the door, and the sound seemed grinding his life to atoms, for by that token he knew that Edith was gone--that to him there was nothing left save the little mound at his feet and the memory of his broken lily who slept beneath it. How he wanted her now--wanted his childish Nina--his fair girl-wife, to comfort him. But it could not be, Nina was dead--her sweet, bird-like voice was hushed; it would never meet his listening ear again, and for him there was nothing left, save the wailing wind to whisper sadly to him as she was wont to do, "Poor Arthur boy, poor Arthur boy."

CHAPTER XXXIII.
HOME.

Oh, what a change it was from sunny Florida to England, just how both Edith and Victor shivered, arrived at the last stage of their journey, they looked out upon the snow-clad hills and leafless trees which fitted out by bare and brown against the winter sky. West Shannondale! the brakeman shouted, and Edith drew her furs around her, for in a few moments more their own station would be reached.

"The river is frozen; it must be very cold," said Victor, pointing to the blue-black stream; skimmered over with a thin coat of ice.

"Yes, very, very cold," and Edith felt the meaning of the word in more senses than one.

Why wasn't she glad to be home again? Why did her thoughts cling so to distant Sunnybank, or her heart die within her as waymark after waymark told her Collingwood was near? Alas! she was not a loving, eager bride elect, returning to the arms of her beloved, but a shrinking, hopeless, desolate woman, going back to meet the destiny she dared not avoid. The change was all in herself, for the day was no colder, the clouds no greyer, the setting sun no paler than New England wintry days and clouds and suns are wont to be. Collingwood was just the same, and its massive walls rose as proudly amid the dark evergreens around it as they had done in times gone by, when to the little orphan it seemed a second Paradise. Away to the right lay Grassy Spring, the twilight shadows gathering around it, piles of snow resting on its roof, and a thin wreath of smoke curling from a single chimney in the rear.

All this Edith saw as in the village omnibus she was driven toward home, Richard was not expecting them until the morrow, and thus no new fires were kindled, no welcoming lights hung out, and the house was unusually gloomy and dark. During Edith's absence Richard had staid mostly in the library, and there he was sitting now, with his hands folded together in that peculiarly helpless way which characterized all his motions. He heard the sound of wheels, the banging of trunks, and then his ear caught a footstep it knew full well, a slow, shuffling tread, but Edith's still, and out into the silent hall he groped his way, watching there until she came.

How he hugged her to his bosom--never heeding that she gave him back but one answering kiss, a cold, a frozen thing, which would not thaw even after it touched his lips, so full of life and warmth. Poor, deluded man! he fancied that the tears he felt upon his face were tears of joy at being home again; but alas! alas! they were tears wrung out by a feeling of dreary home-sickness--a longing to be somewhere else--to have some other one than Richard chafing her cold hands and calling her pet names. He looked older, too, than he used to do, and Edith thought of what he once had said about her seeing the work of decay go on in him while she yet was young and vigorous. Still her voice was natural as she answered his many questions and greeted Mrs. Matson who came in to see her as soon as she heard of her arrival.

"In mourning!" the latter exclaimed as with womanly curiosity she inspected Edith's dress.

Richard started, and putting his hand to Edith's neck, felt that her collar was of crape, and a shadow passed over his face. He liked to think of her as a bright plumaged bird, not as sombre- hued and wearing the habiliments which come only from some grave.

"Was it necessary that my darling should carry her love for a stranger quite so far as this?" he asked. "Need you have dressed in black?"

Without meaning it, his tone implied reproach, and it cut Edith cruelly, making her wish that she had told him all, when she wrote that she was coming home.

"Oh, Richard," she cried, "don't chide me for these outward tokens of sorrow. Nina, dear, darling Nina, was my sister--my fathers child. Temple was only a name he assumed to avoid arrest, so it all got wrong. Everything is wrong," and Edith sobbed impetuously, while Richard essayed to comfort her.

The dress of black was not displeasing to him now, and he passed his hands caressingly over its heavy folds as if to ask forgiveness for having said aught against it.

Gradually Edith grew calm, and after she had met the servants, and the supper she could not taste was over, she repeated to Richard the story she had heard from Marie, who had stopped for a time in New York to visit her sister.

A long time they sat together that night, while Richard told her how lonely he had been without her, and asked her many questions of Nina's last days.

"Did she send no message to me?" he said. "She used to like me, I fancied."

Edith did not know how terrible a message Nina had sent to him, and she replied, "She talked of you a great deal, but I do not remember any particular word. I told her I was to be your wife." and Edith's voice trembled, for this was but a prelude to what she meant to say ere she bade him good night. She should breathe so much more freely if she knew her bridal was not so near, and her sister's death was surely a sufficient reason for deferring it.

Summoning all her courage, she arose, and sitting on Richard's knee, buttoned and unbuttoned his coat in a kind of abstracted manner, while she asked if it might be so. "I know I promised for New Year's night," she said, "but little Nina died so recently and I loved her so much, May it be put off, Richard--put over until June?"

Edith had not thought of this in Florida, but here at home, it came to her like succor to the drowning, and she anxiously awaited Richard's answer.

A frown for an instant darkened his fine features, for he did not like this second deferring the day, but he was too unselfish to oppose it, and he answered,

"Yes, darling, if you will have it so. It may be better to wait at least six months, shall it be in June, the fifteenth say?"

Edith was satisfied with this, and when they parted her heart was lighted of a heavy load, for six months seemed to her a great, great while.

The next day when Grace came up to call on Edith, and was told of the change, she shrugged her shoulders, for she knew that by this delay Richard stood far less chance of ever calling Edith his wife. But she merely said it was well, congratulating Edith upon her good fortune in being an heiress, and asking many questions about Arthur and Nina, both, and at last taking her leave without a hint as to her suspicions of the future. To Edith the idea had never occurred. She should marry Richard of course, and nothing could happen to defer the day a third time. So she said at least to Victor, when she told him of the arrangement, and with a very expressive whistle, Victor, too, shrugged his shoulders, thinking, that possibly he need not read Nina's letter after all. He would rather not if it could be avoided, for he knew how keen the pang it would indict upon his noble master, and he would not add one unnecessary drop to the cup of sorrow he saw preparing for poor Richard.

After a few days of listless languor and pining home-sickness, Edith settled into her olden routine of reading, talking and singing to Richard, who thought himself happy even though she did not caress him as often as she used to do, and was sometimes impatient and even ill-natured towards him.

"She mourns so much for Nina," was the excuse which Richard wrote down in his heart for all her sins, either of omission or commission; and in a measure he was right.

Edith did mourn for sweet little Nina, but mourned not half so much for her as for the hopes forever fled--for Arthur, at whose silence she greatly marvelled, thinking that she would write to him as to her brother, and then shrinking from the task because she knew not what to say.

Spite of her feelings the six months she had thought so long were passing far too rapidly to suit her. Time lingers for no one, and January glided into February, February into March, whose melting snows and wailing winds gave place at last to April, and then again the people of Shannondale begun to talk of "that wedding," fixed for the 15th of June. Marie had become domesticated at Collingwood, but the negroes, who now called Edith mistress, still remained at Grassy Spring, waiting until Arthur should come, or some message be received from him. It was four months now since Edith left Sunnybank, and in all that time no tiding had come to her from Arthur. Grace's letters were unanswered, and Grace herself was beginning to feel alarmed, when one afternoon, Victor called Edith to an upper balcony and pointing in the direction of Grassy Spring, bade her look where the graceful columns of smoke were rising from all its chimneys, while its windows were opened wide, and the servants hurried in and out, seemingly big with some important event.

"Saddle Bedouin," said Edith, more excited than she had deemed it possible for her to be. "Mr. St. Claire must be expected, I am going down to see."

Victor obeyed, and without a word to Richard, Edith was soon galloping off toward Grassy Spring, where she found Grace hurriedly giving orders to the delighted blacks, who tumbled over each other in their zeal to have everything in readiness for "Marster Arthur." He was coming that night, so Grace had told them, she having received a telegram that morning from New York, together with a letter.

"He started North the first of Feb." she said to Edith, "taking Richmond on the way, and has been detained there ever since by sickness. He is very feeble yet, but is anxious to see us all. He has received no letters from me, it seems, and thinks you are married."

Edith turned very white for a moment, and then there burned upon her cheek a round, red spot, induced by the feeling that the believing she was married had been the immediate cause of Arthur's illness. Edith was no longer the pale, listless woman who moved so like a breathing statue around Collingwood, but a flushed, excited creature, flitting from room to room, and entering heart and soul into Grace's plans for having everything about the house as cheerful and homelike as possible for the invalid. She should stay to welcome him, too, she said, bidding one of the negroes put Bedouin in the stable and then go up to Collingwood to tell Richard where she was.

Arthur was indeed coming to Grassy Spring, brought thither by the knowing that something must be done with the place ere he went to Europe as he intended doing, and by the feverish desire to see Edith once more even though she were the wife of Richard, as he supposed her to be. Grace's first letter had been lost, and as he had been some weeks on the way he knew nothing of matters at Collingwood, though occasionally there crept into his heart a throb of hope that possibly for Nina's sake the marriage had been deferred and Edith might be Edith Hastings still. It was very sad coming back to the spot so fraught with memories of Nina, and this it was in part which made him look so pale and haggard when at last he stood within the hall and was met by Grace, who uttered an exclamation of surprise at seeing him so changed.

"I am very tired," he said, with the tone and air of an invalid, "Let me rest in the library awhile, before I see the negroes. Their noise will disturb me," and he walked into the very room where Edith stood waiting for him.

She had intended to meet him as a brother, the husband of her sister, but the sight of his white, suffering face swept her calmness all away, and with a burst of tears she cried, "Oh, Arthur, Arthur, I did not think you had been so sick. Why did you not let us know; I would have come to you," and she brought herself the arm-chair which he took, smiling faintly upon her and saying,

"It was bad business being sick at a hotel, and I did sometimes wish you were there, but of course I could not expect you to leave your husband. How is he?"

Edith could hear the beating of her heart and feel the blood tingling her cheeks as she replied, "You mean Richard, but he is not my husband. He--"

Quickly, eagerly Arthur looked up, the expression of his face speaking volumes of joy, surprise, and even hope, but all this faded away, leaving him paler, sicker-looking than before, as Edith continued,

"The marriage was a second time deferred on account of Nina's death. It will take place in June."

Grace had left the room and an awkward silence ensued during which Arthur looked absently into the fire, while Edith gazed out upon the darkening sky, wondering if life would always be as hard to bear as now, and half wishing that Arthur St. Claire had staid at Sunnybank until the worst was over.

There was a sound of wheels outside, and Edith heard Richard as he passed into the hall. He had received her message, and thinking it proper for him to welcome Mr. St. Claire, he had come to Grassy Spring to do so, as well as to escort Edith home. Richard could not see how much Arthur was changed, but his quick ear detected the weak, tremulous tones of the voice, which tried to greet him steadily, and so the conversation turned first upon Arthur's recent illness, and then upon Nina, until at last, as Richard rose to leave, he laid his arm across Edith's shoulder and said playfully, "You know of course, that what you predicted, when years ago you asked me to take a certain little girl, is coming true. Edith has promised to be my wife. You will surely remain at Grassy Spring through the summer, and so be present at our wedding on the 15th of June. I invite you now."

"Thank you," was all Arthur could say, as with his accustomed politeness he arose to bid his guests good night; but his lip quivered as he said it, and his eye never for a moment rested upon Edith, who led Richard in silence to the carriage, feeling that all she loved in the wide world was left there in the little library where the light was shining, and where, although she did not know it, Grace was ministering to the half fainting Arthur.

The sight of Edith and Richard had effected him more than he supposed it would, but the worst was over now, and as he daily grew stronger in the bracing northern air he felt more and more competent to meet what lay before him.

CHAPTER XXXIV.
NINA'S LETTER.

After a week or two had passed, Arthur went occasionally to Collingwood, where Richard greeted him most cordially, urging him to come more frequently and wondering why he always seemed in so much haste to get away. On the occasion of these visits Edith usually kept out of the way, avoiding him so studiously that Richard began to fear she might perhaps dislike him, and he resolved to ask her the first good opportunity. But Edith avoided him, too, never coming now to sit with him alone; somebody must always be present when she was with him, else had her bursting heart betrayed the secret telling so fearfully upon her. Oh, how hateful to her were the preparations for her bridal, which had commenced on a most magnificent scale, for Richard, after waiting so long, would have a grand wedding, and that all who chose might witness the ceremony, it was to be performed in the church, from which the guests would accompany him back to Collingwood.

All Shannondale was interested, and the most extravagant stories were set afloat, not only concerning the trouseau of the bride, but the bride herself. What ailed her? What made her so cold, so white, so proudly reserved, so like a walking ghost? She, who had been so full of vigorous life, so merry, so light-hearted. Could it be the mourning for sweet little Nina, or was it--?

And here the knot of gossippers, at the corner of the streets, or in the stores, or in the parlors at home, would draw more closely together as they whispered,

"Does she love Richard Harrington as she ought? Is not her heart given rather to the younger, handsomer St. Claire?"

How they pitied her if it were so, and how curiously they watched her whenever she appeared in their midst, remarking every action, and construing it according to their convictions.

Victor, too, was on the alert, and fully aware of the public feeling. Day after day he watched his young mistress, following her when she left the house alone, and seeing her more than once when in the Deering woods she laid her face in the springing grass and prayed that she might die. But for her promise, sworn to Richard, she would have gone to him, and kneeling at his feet begged him to release her from her vow, and so spare her the dreadful trial from which she shrank more and more as she saw it fast approaching.

Edith was almost crazy, and Arthur, whenever he chanced to meet her, marvelled at the change since he saw her last. Once he, too, thought of appealing to Richard to save her from so sad a fate as that of an unloving wife, but he would not interfere, lest by so doing he should err again, and so in dreary despair, which each day grew blacker and more hopeless, Edith was left alone, until Victor roused in her behalf, and without allowing himself time to reflect, sought his master's presence, bearing with him Nina's letter, and the soiled sheet on which Richard had unwittingly scratched out Arthur's marriage.

It was a warm, balmy afternoon, and through the open windows of the library, the south wind came stealing in, laden with the perfume of the pink-tinted apple blossoms, and speaking to the blind man of the long ago, when it was his to see the budding beauties now shut out from his sight. The hum of the honey-bee was heard, and the air was rife with the sweet sounds of later spring. On the branch of a tree without, a robin was trilling a song. It had sung there all the morning, and now it had come back again, singing a second time to Richard, who thought of the soft nest up in the old maple, and likened that robin and its mate to himself and Edith, his own singing-bird.

But why linger so long over that May-day which Richard remembered through many, many future years, growing faint and sick as often as the spring brought back the apple-blossom perfume or the song of mated robins. It is, alas, that we shrink as Victor did from the task imposed, that, like him, we dread the blow which will strike at the root of Richard's very life, and we approach tearfully, pityingly, half remorsefully, as we stand sometimes by a sunken grave, doubting whether our conduct to the dead were always right and just. So Victor felt, as he drew near to Richard; and sitting down beside him said,

"Can I talk with you awhile about Miss Hastings?" Richard started. Victor had come to tell him she was sick, and he asked if it were not so.

"Something has ailed her of late," he said.

"She is greatly changed since Nina's death. She mourns much for her sister."

"Yes," returned Victor, "she loved Nina dearly, but it is more than this which ails her. God forbid that I should unnecessarily wound you, Mr. Harrington, but I think it right for you to know."

The dark face, shaded with the long beard, was very white now, and the sightless eyes had in them a look of terror as Richard asked,

"What is it, Victor? Tell me."

"Come to the sofa first," Victor rejoined, feeling intuitively that he was safer there than in that high arm-chair, and with unusual tenderness he led his master to the spot, then sitting down beside him, he continued, "Do you remember Nina once made you write something upon a sheet of paper, and that you bade me ascertain what it was?"

"Yes, I remember," answered Richard, "you told me you had not read it, and imputing it to some crazy fancy of no importance, I gave it no more thought. What of it, Victor?"

"I had not read it then," answered Victor, "but I have done so since, I have it in my possession--here in my hand. Would you like to hear it?"

Richard nodded, and Victor read aloud: "I, the blind man, Richard Harrington, do hereby solemnly swear that the marriage of Arthur St. Claire and Nina Bernard, performed by me and at my house, is null and void,"

"What! Read it again! It cannot be that I heard aright," and Richard listened while Victor repeated the lines. "Arthur and Nina! Was she the young girl wife, he, the boy husband, who came to me that night?" Richard exclaimed. "Why have I never known of this before? Why did Edith keep it from me? Say, Victor," and again Richard listened, this time, oh, how eagerly, while Victor told him what he knew of that fatal marriage, kept so long a secret, and as he listened, the beaded drops stood thickly upon his forehead and gathered around his ashen lips, for Victor purposely let fall a note of warning which shot through the quivering nerves of the blind man like a barbed burning arrow, wringing from him the piteous cry,

"Oh, Victor, Victor, does she--does Edith love Arthur? Has she loved him all the time? Is it this which makes her voice so sad, her step so slow? Speak--better that I know it now than after 'tis too late. What other paper is it you are unfolding?"

"'Tis a letter from Nina to you. Can you hear it now?"

"Yes, but tell me first all you know. Don't withhold a single thing. I would hear the whole."

So Victor told him what he knew up to the time of their going to Florida; and then, opening Nina's letter, he began to read, pausing, occasionally, to ask if he should stop.

"No, no; go on!" Richard whispered, hoarsely, his head dropping lower and lower, until the face was hidden from view and the chin rested upon the chest, which heaved with every labored breath.

Once at the words, "When you hear this Nina'll be there with you. She'll sit upon your knee and wind her arms around your neck"--he started, and seemed to be thrusting something from his lap-- something which made him shiver. Was it Nina? He thought so, and strove to push her off but when Victor read, "She will comfort you when the great cry comes in--the crash like the breaking up of the ice in the Northern ponds," he ceased to struggle, and Victor involuntarily stopped when he saw the long arms twine themselves as it were around an invisible form. Then he commenced again: "And when you feel yourself broken up like they are in the spring, listen and you'll hear me whispering, 'Poor Richard! I pity you so much, and I'll kiss your tears away.'"

Did he hear her? hear Nina whispering comfort to his poor bruised heart? We cannot tell. We only know he bent his ear lower, as if to catch the faintest breath; but alas! there were no tears to kiss away. The blind eyes could not weep--they were too hot, too dry for that--and blood-red rings of fire danced before them as they did when Nina came to him with the startling news that Miggie was dead in the Deering woods.

Victor was reading now about these woods and the scene enacted there, and Richard understood it all, even to the reason why Edith had persisted in being his wife. The deepest waters run silently, it is said, and so, perhaps, the strongest heart when crushed to atoms lies still as death, and gives outwardly no token of its anguish. True it is that Richard neither moaned, nor moved, nor spoke; only the head drooped lower, while the arms clung tightly to the fancied form he held, as if between himself and Nina, wherever she was that dreary day, there was a connecting link of sympathy which pervaded his whole being, and so prevented him from dying outright as he wished he could.

It was finished at last, Nina's letter--and it seemed to Richard as if the three kinds of darkness, of which she told him, had indeed settled down upon him, so confused was his brain, so crushed his heart, and so doubly black his blindness. He looked to Victor like some great oak, scathed and blasted with one fell blow, and he was trembling for the result, when the lips moved and he caught the words, "Leave me little Snow Drop. Go back to Heaven, whence you came. The blind man will do right."

Slowly then the arms unclosed, and as if imbued with sight, the red eyes followed something to the open window and out into the bright sunshine beyond; then they turned to Victor, and a smile broke over the stormy features as Richard whispered:

"Nina's gone! Now take me to my room."

Across the threshold Victor led the half-fainting man, meeting with no one until his master's chamber was reached, when Edith came through the hall, and, glancing in, saw the white face on the pillow, where Victor had laid his master down, Richard heard her step, and said, faintly, "Keep her off; I cannot bear it yet!" But even while he spoke Edith was there beside him, asking, in much alarm, what was the matter. She did not observe how Richard shuddered at the sound of her voice; she only thought that he was very ill, and, with every womanly, tender feeling aroused, she bent over him and pressed upon his lips a kiss which burned him like a coal of fire. She must not kiss him now, and, putting up his hands with the feebleness of a little child, he cried piteously,

"Don't Edith, don't! Please leave me for a time. I'd rather be alone!"

She obeyed him then, and went slowly out, wondering what it was which had so affected him as to make even her presence undesirable.

Meantime, with hand pressed over his aching eyes, to shut out, if possible, the rings of fire still dancing before them, Richard Harrington thought of all that was past and of what was yet to come.

"How can I lose her now," he moaned, "Why didn't she tell me at the first? It would not then have been half so bad. Oh, Edith, my lost Edith. You have not been all guiltless in this matter. The bird I took to my bosom has struck me at last with its talons, and struck so deep. Oh, how it aches, how it aches, and still I love her just the same; aye, love her more, now that I know she must not be mine. Edith, oh, my Edith!"

Then Richard's thoughts turned upon Arthur. He must talk with him, and he could not meet him there at Collingwood. There were too many curious eyes to see, too many ears to listen. At Grassy Spring they would be more retired, and thither he would go, that very night. He never should sleep again until he heard from Arthur's own lips a confirmation of the cruel story. He could not ask Edith. Her voice would stir his heart-strings with a keener, deeper agony than he was enduring now. But to Arthur he could speak openly, and then too--Richard was loth to confess it, even to himself, but it was, never the less, true--Arthur, though a man, was gentler than Edith. He would be more careful, more tender, and while Edith might confirm the whole with one of her wild, impulsive outbursts, Arthur would reach the same point gradually and less painfully.

"Order the carriage, Victor," he said, as it was growing dark in the room. "I am going to Grassy Spring,"

It was in vain that Victor attempted to persuade him to wait until the morrow. Richard was determined, and when Edith came from her scarcely tasted supper, she saw the carriage as it passed through the Collingwood grounds on its way to Grassy Spring, but little dreamed of what would be ere its occupant returned to them again.

CHAPTER XXXV.
THE FIERY TEST.

Arthur was not at home. From the first he had intended making Edith a bridal present--a life-sized portrait of Nina, which he knew she would value more than gifts of gold and silver. He had in his possession a daguerreotype taken when she was just eighteen, and sent to him by her father among other things, of which Charlie Hudson was the bearer. From this he would have a picture painted, employing the best artist in Boston, and it was upon this business that he left Grassy Spring the previous day, saying he should probably be home upon the next evening's train.

Just before Richard arrived at Grassy Spring, however, a telegram had been received to the effect that Arthur was detained and would not return until midnight. This Phillis repeated to Richard, who for an instant stood thinking, and then said to Victor, "I shall stay. I cannot go back to Collingwood till I have talked with Arthur. But you may go, I would rather be left alone, and, Victor, you will undoubtedly think it a foolish fancy, but I must sleep in Nina's room. There will be something soothing to me in a place so hallowed by her former presence. Ask old Phillis if I may. Tell her it is a whim, if you like, but get her consent at all hazards."

Phillis' consent was easily won, and after Victor was gone, Richard sat alone in the parlor until nearly eleven, when, feeling weary, he consented to retire, and Ike led him up the two flights of stairs into the Den, where he had never been before.

"I do not need your services," he said to the negro, who departed, having first lighted the gas and turned it on to its fullest extent out of compliment to the blind man.

Gas was a luxury not quite two years old in Shannondale, and had been put in Arthur's house just before he left for Florida. Collingwood being further from the village could not boast of it yet and consequently Richard was not as much accustomed to it as he would otherwise have been. On this occasion he did not know that it was lighted until, as he stood by the dressing bureau, he felt the hot air in his face. Thinking to extinguish the light by turning the arm of the fixture just as he remembered having done some years before, he pushed it back within an inch of the heavy damask curtain which now shaded the window, and too much absorbed in his own painful reflections to think of ascertaining whether the light was out or not, he groped his way to the single bed, and threw himself upon it, giving way to a paroxysm of grief.

It was strange that one in his frame of mind should sleep, but nature was at last exhausted, and yielding to the influence of the peculiar atmosphere slowly pervading the room, he fell away into a kind of lethargic slumber, while the work of destruction his own hand had prepared, went silently on around him. First the crimson curtain turned a yellowish hue, than the scorched threads dropped apart and the flame crept into the inner lining of cotton, running swiftly through it until the whole was in a blaze, and the wood- work of the window, charred and blackened, and bore the deadly element still onward, but away from the unconscious Richard, leaving that portion of the room unscathed, and for the present safe. Along the cornice under the lathing, beneath the eaves they crept--those little fiery tongues-- lapping at each other in wanton, playfulness, and whispering to the dry old shingles on the roof above of the mischief they meant to do.

Half an hour went by, and from the three towers of Shannondale the deep toned bells rang out the watchword of alarm, which the awakened inhabitants caught up, echoing it from lip to lip until every street resounded with the fearful cry, "Fire, fire, Grassy Spring is all on fire."

Then the two engines were brought, from their shelter, and went rattling through the town and out into the country, a quarter of a mile away, to where the little forked tongues had grown to a mammoth size, darting their vicious heads from beneath the rafters, reaching down to touch the heated panes, hissing defiance at the people below, and rolling over the doomed building until billow of flame leaped billow, both licking up in their mad chase the streams of water poured continually upon them.

Away to the eastward the night express came thundering on, and one of its passengers, looking from his window, saw the lurid blaze, just as once before he had seen the bonfire crazy Nina kindled, and as he watched, a horrible fear grow strong within him, manifesting itself at last in the wild outcry, "'Tis Grassy Spring, 'tis Grassy Spring."

Long before the train reached the depot, Arthur St. Claire, had jumped from the rear car, and was flying across the meadow toward his burning home, knowing ere he reached it that all was lost. Timbers were falling, glass was melting, windows were blazing, while at every step the sparks and cinders whirled in showers around his head.

And where all this time was Richard? Victor was asking that question--Victor, just arrived, and followed by the whole household of Collingwood. They were the last to waken, and they came with headlong haste; but Victor's longer strides outran them all, and when Arthur appeared, he was asking frantically for his master. The negroes in their fright had forgotten him entirely, and the first words which greeted Arthur were, "Mr. Harrington is in the building!"

"Where? where?" he shrieked, darting away, and dragging Victor with him.

"In Nina's room. He would sleep there," Victor answered, and with another cry of horror, Arthur sprang to the rear of the building, discovering that the stairs leading to the Den were comparatively unharmed as yet.

"Who will save him?" he screamed, and he turned toward Victor, who intuitively drew back from incurring the great peril.

There was no one to volunteer, and Arthur said,

"I will do it myself."

Instantly a hundred voices were raised against it. It were worse than madness, they said. The fire must have caught in the vicinity of that room, and Richard was assuredly dead.

"He may not be, and if he is not, I will save him or perish too," was Arthur's heroic reply, as he sprang up the long winding stairs, near which the flames were roaring like some long pent up volcano.

He reached the door of the Den. It was bolted, but with superhuman strength he shook it down, staggering backward as the dense cloud of yellowish smoke rolled over and around him, warning him not to advance. But Arthur heeded no warning then. By the light which illumined the entire front of the house, he saw that two sides of the room were not yet touched; the bed in the recess was unharmed, but Richard was not there, and a terrible fear crept over Arthur lest he had perished in his attempt to escape. Suddenly he remembered Nina's cell, and groping his way through fire and smoke, he opened the oaken door, involuntarily breathing a prayer of thanksgiving when he saw the tall form stretched upon the empty bedstead. He had probably mistaken the way out, and by entering here, had prolonged his life, for save through the glass ventilator the smoke could not find entrance to that spot. Arthur knew that he was living, for the lips moved once and whispered, "Edith," causing Arthur's brain to reel, and the cold sweat to start from every pore as he thought for what and for whom he was saving his rival. Surely in that terrible hour, in Nina's cell, with death staring him in the face on every side, Arthur St. Claire atoned for all the past, and by his noble unselfishness proved how true and brave he was.

Snatching from the nail the heavy sack, he wound it round Richard's head to shield him from the flames, then recollecting that on the bed without there was a thick rose blanket, he wrapped that too around him, and bending himself with might and main, bore him in his arms across the heated floor and out into the narrow hall, growing sick and faint when he saw the wall of fire now rolling steadily up the stairway.

"Oh, must I die!" he groaned, as he leaned panting against the wall, listening to the roar without, which sounded in his ear like demons yelling over their prey.

Life looked very fair to the young man then; even life without Edith was preferable far to a death like this. He was too young to die and the heart which had said in its bitterness, "there is nothing worth living for," clung tenaciously to a world which seemed so fast receding from view.

By leaving Richard there, by stripping him of his covering, and folding it about himself, he could assuredly leap down those stairs, and though he reached the bottom a scarred, disfigured thing, life would be in him yet; but Arthur did not waver, Richard should share his fate, be it for weal or woe, and with a prayer for help, he turned aside into a little room from which a few wide steps led up into the cupola. Heaven surely saved this way for him, for the fire was not there yet, and he passed in safety to the roof, where he stood, many dizzy feet from the shouting multitude, who, hoping he might take advantage of it, were watching for him to appear, greeting him with many a loud huzza, and bidding him take courage. The engines had been brought to bear on this part of the building, subduing the fire to such an extent that it was barely possible for him to reach the northern extremity, where, by jumping upon a flat, lower roof, whose surface was tin, and then walking a beam over a sea of hissing flame, he could reach the ladder hoisted against the wall. All this they made him understand, and with but little hope of his success they watched him breathlessly as he trod the black, steaming shingles, which crisped the soles of his boots, and penetrated even to his flesh. He has passed that point in safety, he leaps upon the wing, staggering, aye, falling with his burden, and when he struggles to his feet, the red blaze, wheeling in circles around him, shows where the blood is flowing from a wound upon the forehead. The batteries of the engine are directed toward him now, and they saturate his clothes with water, for the most fearful, most dangerous part is yet to come, the treading that single beam. Will he do it? Can he do it? Untrammeled he might, but with that heavy form he hugs so carefully to him, never! So the crowd decide, and they shout to him, "Leave him; he is dead. Save yourself, young man;" but the brave Arthur answers, "No," and half wishes he were blind, so as to shut out the seething vortex into which one misstep would plunge him. And while he stood there thus, amid the roaring of the flames, and the din of the multitude, there floated up to him a girlish voice,

"Shut your eyes, Arthur, make believe you are blind, and maybe you can walk the beam."

It was Edith. He saw her where she stood, apart from all the rest, her long black hair unbound just as she sprang from her pillow, her arms outstretched toward him, and the sight nerved him to the trial. He looked at her once more, it might be for the last time, but he would carry the remembrance of that clear face even to eternity, and with a longing, wistful glance he closed his eyes and prepared to do her bidding. Then it seemed to him that another presence than Edith's was around him, another voice than hers was whispering words of courage, Nina, who went before, guiding his footsteps, and lightening his load, screening him from the scorching heat and buoying him up, while he walked the blackened beam, which shook and bent at every tread, and at last fell with a crash, but not until the ladder was reached, and a dozen friendly arms were outstretched for Richard, and for him, too, for sight and strength had failed him when they were no longer needed. With countless blessings on the noble young man, they laid him on the grass at Edith's side, wounded, burned, smoke-stained, and totally unconscious.

It was well for Richard that the entire household of Collingwood were there to care for him, for Edith's thoughts were all bestowed on Arthur. She hardly looked at Richard, but kneeling down by Arthur, kissed, and pitied, and wept over his poor, raw, bleeding hands, wiped the blood from the wound on the forehead, thinking even then how it would be concealed by the brown hair--the hair all singed and matted, showing how fiercely he had battled for his life. Many gathered around her as she sat there with his head pillowed on her lap, and from the anguish written on her face learned what it was about which the curious villagers had so long been pondering.

"He must go home with me," Grace Atherton said, "My carriage will soon be here."

This reminded Edith that she too must act, and beckoning to Victor, she bade him hasten to Collingwood and see that his masters room was made comfortable.

This was the first token she had given that she knew of Richard's presence near her. She had heard them say that he still lived; that not a hair of his head was singed or a thread of his night garments harmed, and for this she was glad, but nothing could have tempted her to leave Arthur, and she sat by him until the arrival of the carriages which were to convey the still unconscious men to their respective homes.

At Collingwood, however, her whole attention was given to Richard, who, as he began to realise what was passing around him, seemed so much disturbed at having her near him that Victor whispered to her, "Hadn't you better go out? I think your presence excites him."

Edith had fancied so too, and wondering much why it should, she left him and going to her own room, sat down by the window, gazing sadly across the fields, to where Grassy Spring lay in the morning sunshine a blackened, mouldering ruin.

CHAPTER XXXVI.
THE SACRIFICE.

For a few days Edith hoped that the fire might defer her marriage a little longer but almost the first thing which Richard addressed directly to her was, "Let the preparations go on as usual; there need be no delay."

So the dressmakers were recalled and bridal finery tossed about until the whole was finished and the last sewing woman departed, taking with her, as her predecessors had done, a large budget of items touching the cool indifference of the bride elect and the icy reserve of the bridegroom, who was greatly changed, they said. It is true he was kind and considerate, as of old, and his voice, whenever he spoke to Edith, was plaintively sad and touching, but he preferred to be much alone, spending his time in his chamber, into which few save his valet was admitted. And thus no one suspected the mighty conflict he was waging with himself, one moment crying out, "I cannot give her up," and again moaning piteously, "I must, I must."

The first meeting between himself and Arthur after the fire had been a most affecting one, Richard sobbing like a child, kissing the hands wounded so cruelly for him, and whispering amid his sobs, "You saved my life at the peril of your own, and I shall never forget it. God help me to do right."

Many times after this he rode down to Brier Hill whither Edith had frequently preceded him; but Richard never uttered a word of reproach when near the window he heard a rustling sound and knew who was sitting there. Neither would he ask a single question when soft footsteps glided past him and out into the hall, but he always heard them until they died away, and he knew those little feet were treading the verge of the grave he had dug within his heart. It was not yet filled up--that grave--but his mighty love for Edith may coffined there, and he only waited for the needful strength to bury it forever by verbally giving her up.

And while he waited the May-days glided by, and where the apple blossoms once had been, the green hard fruit was swelling now, the lilacs, purple and limp, had dropped from the tree, the hyacinths and daffodils were gone, and June with her sunny skies and wealth of roses, queened it over Collingwood. It lacked but a week now of the day appointed for the wedding, and Edith wished the time would hasten, for anything was preferable to the numb, apathetic feeling which lay around her heart. She had no hope that she should not be Richard's wife, and she wondered much at his manner, trying more than once to coax him from his strange mood by playful words, and even by caresses, which won from him no response--only once, when, he hugged her tightly to him, kissing her lips and hair, and saying to her, "God forgive me, Birdie, I never meant to wrong you and I am going to make amends." The next day when Victor went up to his room he was struck with the peculiar expression of his face--a subdued, peaceful expression which told that he was ready at last to make the great sacrifice--to fold the darkness more thickly around himself and give to Arthur the glorious daylight he once hoped would shine for him and Richard would make this sacrifice in his own way. Edith should read Nina's letter aloud to him, with Arthur sitting near, and then, when it was finished, he would ask if it were true, und why she had not told him before.

Dinner was over, and in the library, where Richard had asked Edith to be his wife, he sat waiting for her now, and for Arthur who had been invited to Collingwood that afternoon. The day was much like that other day when Victor alone sat with him, save that the south wind stealing through the casement was warmer, more fragrant than the breath of May had been. The robin was not now singing in the maple tree, but it would come home ere long, and Richard knew full well the chirping sounds which would welcome its approach. Once he had likened himself to the mated robin, but now, alas, he knew he was but the wounded bird, who finds its nest all desolate, its hopes all fled--I'm a tough old owl," he said, smiling bitterly as he remembered when first he used that term. Edith was right; she could not mate with the owl, he thought, just as Arthur stepped across the threshold, and Edith came flipping down the stairs.

"Sit on a stool at my feet, as you used to do," Richard said to her; "and you, Arthur, sit by me upon this sofa."

They obeyed him, and after a moment he began, "I have sent for you my children, not to inflict pain, but to remove it. Heaven forbid that through me you should suffer longer, or that any act of mine should embitter your young lives. Do not interrupt me," he continued, as Edith was about to speak. "I must hasten on, or my courage all will fail me. Arthur, give me your hands, the hands that saved my life. I will touch them as carefully, as tenderly as I am about to deal with you."

Arthur complied with his request, and pressing the right one, Richard continued,

"I joined this once with another, a tiny, little hand, now laid away beneath the Southern flowers; and you said after me, 'I, Arthur, take thee, Nina, for my wife.' You remember it, don't you?"

Arthur could not speak, and, save the violent start which Edith gave, there came no answer to Richard's question as he went on:

"It is only a few weeks since I learned who was that boy husband of eighteen and that girlish bride of fifteen and a half, but I know it now. I know it all, and this explains much that has been strange in me of late. Edith," and he felt for her bowed head, "Edith, I have here Nina's letter, written by stealth, and brought by Victor to me, and you must read it to us--then tell me, if you can, why I have so long been deceived?"

Edith had glanced at the beginning, and with a choking voice she said,

"No, no, oh, Richard, no. Don't require it of me. Anything but that. I never knew she wrote it. I never meant--oh, Richard, Richard!"

She laid her head now on his knee and sobbed aloud, while he continued:

"You must read it to me, 'Tis the only punishment I shall inflict upon you."

"Read it, Edith," Arthur said, withdrawing one of his hands from Richard's, and resting it upon her head thus to re-assure her,

Richard guessed his intention and laid his own on Arthur's. Edith felt the gentle, forgiving pressure, even through the wounded, bandaged hand, and this it was which gave her strength to read that message, which brought Nina before them all, a seemingly living, breathing presence. And when it was finished there was heard in that library more than one "great cry, like the breaking up of the ice on the Northern ponds."

Richard was the calmest of the three. The contents of the letter were not new to him, and did not touch so tender a chord as that which thrilled and quivered in

Arthur's heart as he listened to the words of his sweet child-wife, the golden haired Nina. Though dead she was all powerful yet, and Nina, from her grave, swayed a mightier sceptre than Nina living could have done.

"Edith," Richard said, when her agitation had in a measure subsided, "you have read the letter, now tell me, is it true? Crazy people do not always see or hear aright. Did Nina? Has Arthur loved you all the time?"

"Spare Edith," Arthur cried; "And question me. I did love Edith Hastings, even when I had no right so to do."

"And would you ask her to be your wife if there were no Richard in the way, and she was free as when you first knew and loved her?"

Arthur knew the blind man was not trifling with him, and he answered promptly,

"I would, but she will bear me witness that never since Nina died, have I sought, by word or deed, to influence her decision."

"I believe you," Richard said; "and now, let us compare our love for her, one with the other. Let us see which is the stronger of the two. Do you love Edith so much that you would give her to another, if you knew she loved that other best? If she were promised to you by a vow she dared not break, would you give her to me, supposing I was preferred before you?"

Arthur was very white, as he answered,

"That would not be one-half so hard as the yielding her to one whom she did not love, and, Richard, I have done this. I have given her to you, even when I knew that a word from me would have kept her from you."

"That is hardly an answer to my question," Richard rejoined, "but it shows how honorable you have been. I question whether I could have done as much. Your sense of right and wrong was stronger than your love."

"But," said Arthur, quickly interrupting him, "you must not think that I loved Edith less, because I did not speak. Silence only fed the flame, and she cannot be so inexpressibly dear to you as she is to me. Oh, Richard, Richard, you do not know how much I love her."

"Don't I?" and Richard smiled mournfully; then turning to Edith, he continued, And you, my darling, I would hear from you now. Is it Richard or Arthur you prefer?"

"Oh, Richard," Edith cried, "I meant to keep my vow, and never let you know. I was going to be a true, a faithful wife, even if it killed me--I certainly was--but, forgive me, Richard, I did love Arthur first, Arthur best, Arthur most of all," and again the "great cry" smote on Richard's ear, touching a chord like that which is touched in a mother's bosom when she hears her suffering infant's wail.

"Edith," he said, "if I insist upon it, will you still be my wife?"

"Yes, Richard, and it will not be so dreadful now that you know I do love Arthur best, for I do, I do, I can't help it, and I have tried so hard. He is young like me, and then I loved him first, I loved him best."

And in this last the whole was embodied. Edith loved Arthur best. Richard knew she did, and turning to Arthur, he continued,

"And what will you do if I insist? Will memories of the love you bore your lost Nina sustain and comfort you?"

Richard spoke half-tauntingly, but Arthur conquered the emotion of anger he felt arising within him at this allusion to the past, and answered mildly,

"As I hope for Heaven, I did love my poor Nina at the last, with a love which, had it been sooner born, would have made me a happier man; and Nina knew it too, I told her so before she died, and I would fain have kept her with me, but I could not, and now, if I lose Edith, too, it will not be so hard, because I did love Nina, and sweet memories of her will keep my soul from fainting, when I am far away from her little grave, far away from you, and far away from Edith."

Arthur arose to leave the room, but Richard held him back, saying to him,

"You have answered well. Now listen to me. Edith Hastings cannot be dearer to you than she is to me, but think you I will compel her to be mine? Should I be happy, knowing that always in her dreams another arm than mine encircled her dear form, that other lips than mine were pressed to hers, which moaned in sleep not Richard's, but Arthur's name? And this would surely be. The wife I mockingly called mine would be yours in spirit; whether on land or sea, and I ask for no such bride. Were I sure I could win her love, even though it might not be in years, not all the powers of earth should wrest her from me. But I cannot. Such is her temperament that she would give me only hatred, and I do not deserve this from her."

"Oh, I wouldn't, I wouldn't," Edith sobbed, and Richard continued,

"Hush, my child, I know how it would be, even if I did forget it for a time. You must not be the blind man's wife, though the giving you up is like tearing me asunder. And now, Edith, let me hold you once more as I never shall hold you again. It will make me strong to do what I must do."

Edith could not move, but Arthur lifted her up, and placing her in Richard's lap, laid one of his own hands pityingly on the head of the blind man, whose tears dropped on Edith's neck, as he breathed over her his farewell.

"Light of my eyes, joy of my heart, you know not what it costs me to give you up, but God in Heaven knows. He will remember all my pain, removing it in His own good time, and I shall yet be happy. It is true, a black, dreary waste stretches on into the future, but beyond it, even in this world, the bright daylight is shining, and Richard will reach it at last,--will learn to think of you without a pang, to love you as his sister. Arthur, I give to you my darling. I release her from her vow, and may the kind Father bless you both, giving you every possible good. Let no sorrow for me mingle with your joy. I shall have grief and heaviness for a time, but I am strong to bear it. Morning will break at last. Let the wedding night be kept the same as is appointed, there need be no change, save in the bridegroom, and of that the world will all approve. And, Edith, if during the coming week I am not much with you, if I stay altogether in my room, do not try to see me. I once thought you would be my wife. I know you cannot now, and you must not come to me at present. But on your bridal night, I shall go with you to the church. It would look strangely if I did not. I shall return with you to the house, shall force myself to hear them call you by another name than mine, and then, the next morning Arthur must take you away--for a time, I mean. I know you will wish to thank me, but I'd rather you would not. God will reward me in some way for the sacrifice I make this day. Now, Edith, kiss me once, kiss me twice, with your arms around my neck. Lay your soft cheek against mine. Yes--so--so--" and over the dark face there broke a shadowy smile, as Edith did his bidding, kissing him many, many times, and blessing him for the great happiness bestowed upon her.

"There, that will do. Now, Arthur, lead me to my room, and sit with me until this horrid giddiness is gone, and my heart beats more naturally."

He put Edith from his lap--passed his hand slowly over her face as if thus he would remember it, and then, leaning heavily on Arthur's arm, tottered from the room--the noble Richard who had made this mighty sacrifice.

CHAPTER XXXVII.
THE BRIDAL.

The week went by as all weeks will, whether laden with happiness or pain, and the rosy light of the 15th morning broke over the New England hills and over Collingwood, where the servants, headed by Grace Atherton, were all astir, and busy with their preparations for the festive scene of the coming night. Edith had made strenuous efforts to have the party given up, sending message after message to Richard, who, without any good reason for it, was determined upon this one point, and always answered "No."

He had adhered to his resolution of staying in his room, and Edith had not seen him since the eventful day when he had made the great sacrifice. Arthur, however, was admitted daily to his presence, always coming from those interviews with a sad look upon his face, as if his happiness were not unmixed with pain. And still Richard tried to be cheerful, talking but little of Edith, and appearing so calm when he did mention her, that a casual observer would have said he did not care.

In the village nothing was talked about save the change of bridegrooms and the approaching wedding, and when the morning came, others than the inmates of Collingwood were busy and excited.

It was a glorious day, for leafy June had donned her gala robes for the occasion, and every heart, save one, beat with joy, as the sun rose higher and higher in the heavens, nearer and nearer the appointed hour. Richard could not be glad, and that bridal day was the saddest he had ever known. Not even Arthur was permitted to be with him, and none save Victor saw the white, still anguish creeping over his face as hour after hour went by, and from the sounds without he knew that they had come whose business it was to array his Edith in her bridal robes of costly satin and fleecy lace. Then two more hours dragged heavily on, and going to his window he felt that the sun was setting. It was time his own toilet was commenced, and like a little child he submitted himself to Victor, groaning occasionally as he heard the merry laugh of the bridesmaids on the stairs, and remembered a time when he, too, felt as light, as joyous as they, aye, and almost as young. He was strangely altered now, and looked far older than his years, when, with his wedding garments on, he sat in his arm-chair waiting for the bride. He had sent Victor for her, knowing it would be better to meet her once before the trying moment at the altar. Edith obeyed the summons, and in all her wondrous beauty, which this night shone forth resplendently, she came and stood before him, saying softly,

"Richard, I am here."

There was no need to tell him that. He knew she was there, and drawing her to his side, he said,

"I am glad that I am blind for once, for should I behold you as you are, I could not give you up. Kneel down here, darling, and let me feel how beautiful you are."

She knelt before him, and her tears fell fast as she felt his hand moving slowly over her dress, pressing her round arms, pausing for a moment upon her white neck, tarrying still longer upon her glowing cheeks, and finally resting in mute blessing upon her braids of hair, where the orange blossoms were.

"I must have a lock of my Birdie's hair, he said. "Let Arthur cut it off to-night. It will be dearer to me than if 'tis later severed, Leave it on the table, where Victor can find it, for, Edith, when you return from your bridal tour, I shall be gone, and I have sent for you because I would talk with you again ere we part--it may be for years, and it may be forever."

"No, Richard, no," Edith sobbed. "You must not go away, I want you here with us."

"It is best that I go for a while," he replied, "I am almost as much at home in Europe as I am here, and Victor is anxious to see Paris again. I have talked with Arthur about it, asking him to live here while I am gone at least and take charge of my affairs. He had thought to rebuild Grassy Spring, but finally consented to defer it for a time and do as I desired. The negroes will be pleased with this arrangement, and as Grace must wish to be rid of them, they will come up here at once. I shall be happier knowing that you are here; and when I feel that I can, I will come back again, but do not let thoughts of the wanderer mar your bliss. I have been thinking it over, Edith, and I see more and more that it was right for me to release you. I do not censure you for aught except that you did not tell me in the beginning. For this I did blame you somewhat, but have forgiven you now."

"Oh. Richard, Richard," Edith burst out impetuously, "I never loved you one half so much as since you gave me to Arthur, and I have wanted to come and tell you so, but you would not let me."

He knew what kind of love she meant, and his heart beat just the same as she continued,

"I wanted to tell you how sorry I am that I was ever cross to you, and I have been many times since that night I promised to be yours. I don't know what made me. I do not feel so now."

"I know what made you," Richard replied. "You did not love the blind old man well enough to be his wife, and the feeling that you must be, soured your disposition. Forgive me, darling, but I don't believe I should have been happy with you after a time--not as happy as Arthur, and it is this which helps me to bear it."

This was not very complimentary to Edith, but it comforted her just as Richard meant it should, and made the future look brighter. Richard was dearer to her now than he had over been, and the tender, loving caress she gave him, when at last Arthur's voice was heard without asking for admission was not feigned, for she felt that he was the noblest, the best of men, and she told him so, kissing again and again his face, and sighing to think how white and wan it had grown within the last few weeks.

"Come, darling, we are waiting for you," Arthur said, as he advanced into the room, and Richard put from his lap the beautiful young girl around whose uncovered shoulders Arthur wrapped the white merino cloak which was to shield her from the night air; then bending over Richard, he said, "Heaven will bless you, even as I do, for the peerless gift I have received from you, and believe me, there is much of pain mingled with my joy--pain at leaving you so desolate. I cannot tell you all I feel, but if a lifetime of devotion can in the smallest degree repay you what I owe, it shall be freely given. Now bless me once more, me and my-- bride."

Richard had arisen as Arthur was speaking, and at the word bride he put out his hand as if to keep from falling, then steadying that on Arthur's head and laying the other on Edith's he whispered,

"To him who saved my life when he believed I was his rival I give my singing bird, who for eleven years has been the blind man's sunshine--give her freely, cheerfully, harboring no malice against him who takes her. My Arthur and my precious Edith, I bless and love you both."

The nerveless hands pressed heavily for a moment upon the two bowed heads, and then Arthur led his bride away to where the carriage waited.

The ceremony was appointed for half-past eight, but long before that hour St. Luke's was filled to overflowing, some coming even as early as six to secure seats most favorable to sight. And there they waited, until the roll of wheels was heard and the clergyman appeared in the chancel. Then seven hundred tired heads turned simultaneously toward the door through which the party came, the rich robes of the bride trailing upon the carpet and sweeping from side to side as she moved up the middle aisle. But not upon her did a single eye in all that vast assemblage linger, nor yet upon the bridegroom, nor yet upon the bridesmaid, filing in one behind the other, but upon the stooping figure which moved so slowly, blind Richard groping his way to the altar, caring nothing for the staring crowd, nothing for the sudden buzz as he came in, hearing nothing but Victor's whispered words, "'twill soon be over."

Yes, it would soon be over. It was commencing now, the marriage ceremony, and Richard listened in a kind of maze, until the clergyman asked,

"Who giveth this woman to be married to this man?"

As Arthur had supposed this part would, of course, be omitted, no arrangements had been made for it, and an awkward pause ensued, while all eyes involuntarily turned upon the dark man now standing up so tall, so erect, among that group of lighter, airier forms. Like some frozen statue Richard stood, and the minister, thinking he did not hear, repeated his demand. Slowly Richard moved forward, and Grace, who was next to Edith, stepped aside as he came near. Reverently he laid his hand on Edith's head, and said aloud,

"I DO!"

Then the hand, sliding from her head rested on her shoulder, where it lay all through that ceremony, and the weeping speculators sitting near, heard distinctly the words whispered by the white lips which dripped with the perspiration of this last dreadful agony.

"I, Richard, take thee, Birdie, to be my wedded wife, to have and to hold, from this day forward, for better for worse, for richer for poorer, in sickness and in health, to love and to cherish, till death us do part, according to God's holy ordinance; and thereto I plight thee my troth."

He said it every word, and when it was Edith's turn, he bent a little forward, while his hand grasped her bare shoulder so firmly as to leave a mark when she put Arthur's name where his should have been, and the quivering lips moaned faintly,

"Don't Birdie, don't."

It was a strange bridal, more sad than joyous, for though in the hearts of bride and groom there was perfect love for each other, there were too many bitter memories crowding upon them both to make it a moment of unmixed bliss--memories of Nina, who seemed to stand by Arthur, blessing him in tones unheard, and a sadder, a living memory of the poor blind man whose low wail, when all was done, smote painfully on Edith's ear.

In a pew near to the altar Victor sat weeping like a child, and when the last Amen was uttered, he sprang to his master's side and said,

"Come with me. You cannot wish to go home with the bride."

Instantly the crowd divided right and left as Victor passed through their midst, leading out into the open air the faint, sick man, who, when they were alone, leaned his head meekly on his faithful valet's arm, saying to him,

"You are all there is left to care for me now. Be good to me, won't you?"

Victor answered with a clasp of his hand and hurried on, reaching Collingwood before the bridal guests, who ere long came swarming in like so many buzzing bees, congratulating the newly-wedded pair, and looking curiously round for Richard. But Richard was not there. He had borne all he could, and on his bed in his bolted room he lay, scarcely giving a token of life save when the sounds from the parlors reached his ear, when he would whisper,

"'Tis done. It is done."

One by one the hours went by, and then up the gravelled walk the carriages rolled a second time to take the guests away. Hands were shaken and good nights said. There was cloaking in the ladies' room and impatient waiting in the gentlemen's; there was hurrying down the stairs, through the hall, and out upon the piazza. There was banging to of carriage doors, cracking of drivers' whips, and racing down the road. There was a hasty gathering up of silver, a closing of the shutters, a putting out of lamps, until at last silence reigned over Collingwood, from whose windows only two lights were gleaming. Arthur was alone with his bride, and Richard alone with his God.

CHAPTER XXXVIII.
SIX YEARS LATER.

The New York and Springfield train eastward bound stood waiting in the depot at New Haven. There had been a slight accident which occasioned a detention of several minutes, and taking advantage of this delay many of the passengers alighted to stretch their weary limbs or inhale a breath of purer air than could be obtained within the crowded car. Several seats were thus left unoccupied, one of which a tall, dark, foreign-looking man, with eyes concealed by a green shade, was about appropriating to himself, when a wee little hand was laid on his and a sweet baby voice called out,

"That's my mamma's chair, big man, mamma gone after cake for Nina!"

The stranger started, and his face flushed with some strong emotion, while his hand rested caressingly upon the flowing curls of the beautiful three-years-old girl, as he asked,

"Who Is mamma, darling? What is her name, I mean?"

"I can tell that a heap better'n Kina," chimed in a boy of five, who was sitting just across the aisle, and joining the little girl, he continued, 'My mother is Edith, so Aunt Grace calls her, but father says Miggie most all the time.

The stranger sank into the seat, dizzy and faint with the mighty shock, for he knew now that Edith's children were standing them before him--that frank, fearless boy, and that sweet little girl, who, not caring to be outdone by her brother, said, in a half exultant way, as if it were something of which she were very proud,

"I've got an Uncle 'Ichard, I have, and he's tomin' home bime by."

"And going to bring me lots of things," interrupted the boy again, "Marie said so."

At this point a tall, slender Frenchman, who had entered behind the man with the green shade, glided from the car, glancing backward just in time to see that his master had coaxed both children into his lap, the girl coming shyly, while the boy sprang forward with that wide-awake fearlessness which characterized all his movements. He was a noble-looking little fellow, and the stranger hugged him fondly as he kissed the full red lips so like to other lips kissed long years ago.

"What makes you wear this funny thing?" asked the child, peering up under the shade.

"Because my eyes are weak," was the reply, "People around your home call me blind."

"Uncle 'Ichard is blind," lisped the little girl, while the boy rejoined, "but the bestest man that ever lived. Why, he's betterer than father, I guess, for I asked ma wan't he, and pa told me yes."

"Hush-sh, child," returned the stranger, fearing lest they might attract too much attention.

Then removing the shade, his eyes rested long and wistfully upon the little boy and girl as he said,

"I am your Uncle Richard."

"True as you live and breathe are you Uncle Dick," the boy almost screamed, winding his chubby arms around the stranger's neck, while Nina standing upon her feet chirped out her joy as she patted the bearded cheek, and called him "Uncle 'Ick."

Surely if there had been any lingering pain in the heart of Richard Harrington it was soothed away by the four soft baby hands which passed so caressingly over his face and hair, while honeyed lips touched his, and sweet bird-like voices told how much they had been taught to love the one whom they always called Uncle. These children had been the hardest part of all to forgive, particularly the first born, for Richard, when he heard of him had felt all the old sorrow coming back again; a feeling as if Edith had no right with little ones which did not call him father. But time had healed that wound too, until from the sunny slopes of France, where his home had so long been, his heart had often leaped across the sea in quest of those same children now prattling in his ear and calling him Uncle Dick. There was another, a dearer name by which they might have called him, but he knew now that 'twas not for him to be thus addressed. And still he felt something like a father's love stealing into his heart as he wound his arms around the little forms, giving back kiss for kiss, and asking which was like their mother.

"Ain't none of us much," Dick replied, "We're like father and Aunt Nina, hanging on the wall in the library. Mother's got big black eyes, with winkers a rod long, and her hair shines like my velvet coat, and comes most to her feet."

Richard smiled, und was about to speak again, when Dick forestalled him by asking--not if he had him something but where it was.

"It's in your trunk, I guess," he said, as his busy fingers investigated every pocket and found nothing savoring of playthings, except a knife, both blades of which were opened in a trice, and tried upon the window sill!

Richard, who, never having known much of children, had not thought of presents, was sorely perplexed, when luckily Victor returned, bringing a paper of molasses candy, which he slyly thrust into his master's hand, whispering to him,

"They always like that."

Victor had calculated aright, for nothing could have pleased the St. Claires more; and when, as she entered at the door, Edith caught sight of her offspring, she hardly knew them, so besmeared were their little faces with molasses, Nina having wiped her hands first upon her hair and then rubbed them upon Richard's knee, while Victor looked on a little doubtful us to what the mother might say.

"There's mam-ma," Nina cried, trying to shake back her curls, which nevertheless stuck lightly to her forehead. "There's mam- ma," and in an instant Little Dick, as he was called, found himself rather unceremoniously set down upon his feet, as Richard adjusted his shade, and resumed the air of helplessness so natural to the blind.

Edith had been to New York with Marie and the children, leaving the former there for a few weeks, and was now on her way home, whither she hoped ere long to welcome Richard, whom she had never seen since the night of her marriage, when Victor led him half fainting from the altar. He would not join them at the breakfast next morning, but sent them his good-bye, and when they returned from their long, happy bridal tour they found a letter for them saying Richard was in Paris.

Regularly after that they heard from him, and though he never referred to the past, Edith knew how much it cost him to write to one whom he had loved so much. Latterly, however, his letters had been far more cheerful in their tone, and it struck Edith that his hand-writing too, was more even than formerly, but she suspected nothing and rather anticipated the time when she should be eyes for him again, just as she used to be. He had said in his last letter that he was coming home ere long, but she had no idea that he was so near, and she wondered what tall, greyish haired gentleman it was who had taken possession of her seat.

"Mother," little Dick was about to scream, when Victor placed his hand upon his mouth, at the same time turning his back to Edith, who, a little surprised at the proceeding, and a little indignant it may be, said rather haughtily, and with a hasty glance at Richard,

"My seat, sir, if you please."

The boy by this time had broken away from Victor, and yelled out, "Uncle Dick, ma, Uncle Dick;" but it did not need this now to tell Edith who it was. A second glance had told her, and with face almost as white as the linen collar about her neck, she reeled forward, and would have fallen but for Victor, who caught her by the shoulder and sat her down beside his master.

Richard was far less excited than herself, inasmuch as he was prepared for the meeting and as she sank down with the folds of her grey traveling dress lying in his lap, he offered her his hand, and with the same old sunny smile she remembered so well, said to her,

"Do you not know me?"

"Yes," she gasped, "but it takes my breath away. I was not expecting you so soon. I am so glad."

He knew she was by the way her snowy fingers twined themselves around his own and by the fervent pressure of her lips upon his hand.

"Mam-ma's tyin," said Nina, and then Edith's tears fell fast, dropping upon the broad hand she still held, which very, very gradually, but still intentionally drew hers directly beneath the green shade, and there Richard kept it, his thumb hiding the broad band of gold which told she was a wife.

It was a very small, white, pretty hand, and so perhaps he imagined, for he held it a long, long time, while he talked quite naturally of Arthur, of Grace, of the people of Shannondale, and lastly of her children.

"They crept into my heart before I knew it," he said, releasing Edith's hand and lifting Nina to his knee. "They are neither of them much like you, my namesake says."

This reminded Edith of the mysterious shade which puzzled her so much, and, without replying directly to him, she asked why it was worn. Victor shot a quick, nervous glance at his master, who without the slightest tremor in his voice, told her that he had of late been troubled with weak eyes, and as the dust and sunlight made them worse, he had been advised to wear it while traveling as a protection.

"I shall remove it by and by, when I am rested," he said.

And Edith hoped he would, for he did not seem natural to her with that ugly thing disfiguring him as it did.

When Hartford was reached Richard found an opportunity of whispering something to Victor, who replied,

"Tired find dusty. Better wait, if you want a good impression."

So, with a spirit of self-denial of which we can scarcely conceive Richard did wait, and the shade was drawn closely down as little Nina, grown more bold climbed up beside him, and poised upon one foot, her fat arm resting on his neck, played "peek-a-boo" beneath the shade, screaming at every "peek," "I seen your eyes, I did."

A misstep backward, a tumble and a bumped head brought this sport to an end, just as Shannondale was reached, and in her attempts to soothe the little girl, Edith failed to see that the shade was lifted for a single moment, while, standing upon the platform, Richard's eyes wandered eagerly, greedily over the broad meadow lands and fields of waving grain, over the wooded hills, rich in summer glory, and lastly toward Collingwood, with its roofs and slender tower basking in the July sun.

"Thank God thank God," he whispered, just as Victor caught his arm, bidding him alight as the train was about to move forward.

"There's papa, there--right across the track," and Dick tugged at his father's coat skirts, trying to make him comprehend, but Arthur had just then neither eyes nor ears for any thing but his sobbing little daughter, whose forehead he kissed tenderly, thereby curing the pain and healing the wounded heart, of his favorite child, his second golden-haired Nina. Dick, however, persevered, until his father understood what he meant, and Nina was in danger of being hurt again, so hastily was she dropped when Arthur learned that Richard had come. There was already a crowd around him, but they made way for Arthur, who was not ashamed to show before them all, how much he loved the noble man, or how glad he was to have him back.

"Richard has grown old," the spectators said to each other, as they watched him till he entered the carriage.

And so he had. His hair was quite grey now, and the tall figure was somewhat inclined to stoop, while about the mouth were deep- cut lines which even the heavy mustache could not quite conceal. But he would grow young again, and even so soon he felt his earlier manhood coming back as he rode along that pleasant afternoon, past the fields where the newly-mown hay, fresh from a recent shower, sent forth its fragrance upon the summer air, while the song of the mowers mingled with the click of the whetting scythe, made sweet, homelike sounds which he loved to hear. Why did he lean so constantly from the carriage, and why when Victor exclaimed, "The old ruin is there yet," referring to Grassy Spring did he, too, look across the valley?

Arthur asked himself this question many times, and at last, when they reached Collingwood and Edith had alighted, he bent forward and whispered in Richard's ear, not an interrogation, but a positive affirmation, which brought back the response,

"Don't tell her--not yet, I mean." Arthur turned very white and could scarcely stand as he stepped to the ground, for that answer, had taken his strength away, and Victor led him instead of his master into the house, where the latter was greeted joyfully by the astonished servants.

He seemed very weary and after receiving them all, asked to go to his room where he could rest.

"You will find it wholly unchanged," Arthur said. "Nothing new but gas."

"I trust I shall not set the house on fire this time," was Richard's playful rejoinder, as he followed Victor up the stairs to the old familiar chamber, where his valet left him alone to breathe out his fervent thanksgivings for the many blessings bestowed on one, who, when last he left that room, had said in his sorrow, there were no sunspots left.

The first coming home he so much dreaded was over now, and had been accompanied with far less pain than he feared. He knew they were glad to have him back--Arthur and his dear sister, as he always called her now. Never since the bridal night had the name Edith passed his lips and if perchance he heard it from others, he shuddered involuntarily. Still the sound of her voice had not hurt him as he thought it would; nothing had been half so hard as he had anticipated, and falling upon his knees, he poured out his soul in prayer, nor heard the steps upon the threshold as Arthur came in, his heart too full to tarry outside longer. Kneeling by Richard, he, too, thanked the Good Father, not so much for his friend's safe return as for the boon, precious as life itself which had been given to that friend.

When at last their prayers were ended, both involuntarily advanced to the window, where, with his handsome, manly face turned fully to the light, Arthur stood immovable, nor flinched a hair, as Edith would ere long when passing the same ordeal. He did not ask what Richard thought of him, neither did Richard tell, only the remark,

"I do not wonder that she loved you best."

They then talked together of a plan concerning Edith, after which Arthur left his brother to the repose he so much needed ere joining them in the parlor below. Never before had pillows seemed so soft or bed so grateful as that on which Richard laid him down to rest, and sleep was just touching his heavy eyelids, when upon the door there came a gentle rap, accompanied with the words,

"P'eae, Uncle 'Ick, let Nina tome. She's all dressed up so nice."

That little girl had crept way down into Richard's heart, just as she did into every body's, and he admitted her at once, suffering her to climb up beside him, where, with her fat, dimpled hands folded together, she sat talking to him in her sweet baby language,

"'Ess go to sleep, Nina tired," she said at last, and folding his arms about her, Richard held her to his bosom as if she had been his own. "'Tain't time to say p'ayers, is it?" she asked, fearing lest she should omit her duty; and when Richard inquired what her prayers were, she answered,

"Now I lay me--and God bess Uncle 'Ick. Mam-ma tell me that."

Richard's eyes filled with tears, which the waxen fingers wiped away, and when somewhat later Victor cautiously looked in, he saw them sleeping there together, Nina's golden head nestled in Richard's neck, and one of her little hands lain upon his cheek.

Meantime, in Edith's room Arthur was virtually superintending the making of his wife's evening toilet, a most unprecedented employment for mankind in general, and him in particular. But for some reason wholly inexplicable to Edith, Arthur was unusually anxious about her personal appearance, suggesting among other things that she should wear a thin pink muslin, which he knew so well became her dark style of beauty; and when she reminded him of its shortcomings with regard to waist and sleeves, he answered playfully,

"That does not matter. 'Twill make you look girlish and young."

So Edith donned the pink dress, and clasping upon her neck and arms the delicate ornaments made from Nina's hair, asked of Arthur, "How she looked."

"Splendidly," he replied, "Handsomer even than on our bridal night."

And Edith was handsomer than on the night when she stood at the altar a bride, for six years of almost perfect happiness had chased away the restless, careworn, sorrowful look which was fast becoming habitual, and now, at twenty-six, Edith St. Claire was pronounced by the world the most strikingly beautiful woman of her age. Poets had sung of her charms, artists had transferred them to canvas; brainless beaux, who would as soon rave about a married woman as a single one, provided it were the fashion so to do, had stamped them upon their hearts; envious females had picked them all to pieces, declaring her too tall, too black, too hoydenish to be even pretty; while little Dick and Nina likened her to the angels, wondering if there were anything in heaven, save Aunt Nina, as beautiful as she. And this was Edith, who when her toilet was completed went down to meet Grace Atherton just arrived and greatly flurried when she heard that Richard had come. Very earnestly the two ladies were talking together when Arthur glanced in for a moment and then hastened up to Richard, whom he found sitting by the window, with Dick and Nina both seated in his lap, the former utterly astounded at the accuracy with which his blind uncle guessed every time how many fingers he held up!

"Father! father!" he screamed, as Arthur came in, "He can see just as good as if he wasn't blind!" and he looked with childish curiosity into the eyes which had discovered in his infantile features more than one trace of the Swedish Petrea, grandmother to the boy.

Arthur smiled and without replying to his son, said to Richard,

"I have come now to take you to Edith. Grace Atherton is there, too--a wonderfully young and handsome woman for forty-two. I am not sure that you can tell them apart.

"I could tell your wife from all the world," was Richard's answer, as putting down the children and resuming the green shade, he went with Arthur to the door of the library, where Grace and Edith, standing with their backs to them were too much engaged to notice that more than Arthur was coming.

Him Edith heard, and turning towards him she was about to speak, when Richard lowered the green shade he had raised for a single moment, and walking up to her took her hand in his. Twining his fingers around her slender wrist he said to her,

"Come with me to the window and sit on a stool at my feet just as you used to do."

Edith was surprised, and stammered out something about Grace's being in the room.

"Never mind Mrs. Atherton," he said, "I will attend to her by and by--my business is now with you," and he led her to the window, where Arthur had carried a stool.

Like lightning the truth flashed upon Grace, and with a nervous glance at the mirror to see how she herself was looking that afternoon, she stood motionless, while Richard dashing the shade to the floor, said to the startled Edith,

"The blind man would know how Petrea's daughter looks."

With a frightened shriek Edith covered up her face, and laying her head in its old resting place, Richard's lap, exclaimed,

"No, no, oh no, Richard. Please do not look at me now. Help me, Arthur. Don't let him," she continued, as she felt the strong hands removing her own by force. But Arthur only replied by lifting up her head himself and holding in his own the struggling hands, while Richard examined a face seen now for the first time since its early babyhood. Oh how scrutinisingly he scanned that face, with its brilliant black eyes, where tears were glittering like diamonds in the sunlight, its rich healthful bloom, its proudly curved lip, its dimpled chin and soft, round cheeks What did he think of it? Did it meet his expectations? Was the face he had known so long in his darkness as Edith's, natural when seen by daylight? Mingled there no shadow of disappointment in the reality? Was Arthur's Edith at all like Richard's singing bird? How Arthur wished he knew. But Richard kept his own counsel, for a time at least. He did not say what he thought of her. He only kissed the lips beginning to quiver with something like a grieved expression that Arthur should hold her so long, kissed them twice, and with his hand wiped her tears away, saying playfully,

"'Tis too bad, Birdie, I know, but I've anticipated this hour so long."

He had not called her Birdie before, and the familiar name compensated for all the pain which Edith had suffered when she saw those strangely black eyes fastened upon her, and knew that they could see. Springing to her feet the moment, she was released, she jumped into his lap in her old impetuous way, and winding her arms around his neck, sobbed out,

"I am so glad, Richard, so glad. You can't begin to guess how glad, and I've prayed for this every night and every day, Arthur and I. Didn't we, Arthur? Dear, dear Richard. I love you so much."

"What he make mam-ma cry for?" asked a childish voice from the comer where little Dick stood, half frightened at what he saw, his tiny fist doubled ready to do battle for mother in case he should make up his mind that her rights were invaded.

This had the effect of rousing Edith, who, faint with excitement, was led by Arthur out into the open air, thus leaving Richard alone with his first love of twenty-five years ago. It did not seem to him possible that so many years had passed over the face which, at seventeen, was marvellously beautiful, and which still was very, very fair and youthful in its look, for Grace was wondrously well preserved and never passed for over thirty, save among the envious ones, who, old themselves, strove hard to make others older still.

"Time has dealt lightly with you, Grace," Richard said, after the first curious glance. "I could almost fancy you were Grace Elmendorff yet," and he lifted gallantly one of her chestnut curls, just as he used to do in years agone, when she was Grace Elmendorff.

This little act recalled so vively the scenes of other days that Grace burst into a flood of tears, and hurried from the room to the parlor adjoining, where, unobserved, she could weep again over the hopes forever fled. Thus left to himself, with the exception of little Dick, Richard had leisure to look about him, descrying ere long the life-sized portrait of Nina hanging on the wall. In an instant he stood before what was to him, not so much a picture painted on rude canvas, as a living reality--the golden-haired angel, who was now as closely identified with his every thought and feeling as even Edith herself had ever been. She had followed him over land and sea, bringing comfort to him in his dark hours of pain, coloring his dreams with rainbow hues of promise, buoying him up and bidding him wait a little--try yet longer, when the only hope worth his living for now seemed to be dying out, and when at last it, the wonderful cure, was done, and those gathered around him said each to the other "He will see," he heard nothing for the buzzing sound which filled his ear, and the low voice whispering to him, "I did it--brought the daylight straight from heaven. God said I might--and I did. Nina takes care of you."

They told him that he had fainted from excess of joy, but Richard believed that Nina had been with him all the same, cherishing that conviction even to this hour, when he stood there face to face with her, unconsciously saying to himself, "Gloriously beautiful Nina. In all my imaginings of you I never saw aught so fair as this. Edith is beautiful, but not--"

"As beautiful as Nina was, am I?" said a voice behind him, and turning round, Richard drew Edith to his side, and encircling her with his arm answered frankly,

"No, my child, you are not as beautiful as Nina."

"Disappointed in me, are you not? Tell me honestly," and Edith peered up half-archly, half-timidly into the eyes whose glance she scarcely yet dared meet.

"I can hardly call it disappointment," Richard answered, smiling down upon her. "You are different-looking from what I supposed, that is all. Still you are much like what I remember your mother to have been, save that her eyes were softer than yours, and her lip not quite so proudly curved."

"In other words, I show by my face that I am a Bernard, and something of a spitfire," suggested Edith, and Richard rejoined,

"I think you do," adding as he held her a little closer to him, "Had I been earlier blessed with sight, I should have known I could not tame you. I should only have spoiled you by indulgence."

Just at this point, little Nina came in, and taking her in her arms, Edith said,

"I wanted to call her Edith, after myself, as I thought it might please you; but Arthur said no, she must be Nina Bernard,"

"Better so," returned Richard, moving away from the picture, "I can never call another by the name I once called you," and this was all the sign he gave that the wound was not quite healed.

But it was healing fast. Home influences were already doing him good, and when at last supper was announced, he looked very happy as he took again his accustomed seat at the table, with Arthur opposite Edith just where she used to be, and Grace, sitting at his right. It was a pleasant family party they made, and the servants marvelled much to hear Richard's hearty laugh mingling with Edith's merry peal.

That night, when the July moon came up over the New England hills, it looked down upon the four--Richard and Arthur, Grace and Edith, sitting upon the broad piazza as they had not sat in years, Grace a little apart from the rest, and Edith between her husband and Richard, holding a hand of each, and listening intently while the latter told them how rumors of a celebrated Parisian oculist had reached him in his wanderings; how he had sought the rooms of that oculist, leaving them a more hopeful man than when he entered; how the hope then enkindled grew stronger month after month, until the thick folds of darkness gave way to a creamy kind of haze, which hovered for weeks over his horizon of sights growing gradually whiter and thinner, until faint outlines were discovered, and to his unutterable joy he counted the window panes, knowing then that sight was surely coming back. He did not tell them how through all that terrible suspense Nina seemed always with him; he would not like to confess how superstitious he had become, fully believing that Nina was his guardian angel, that she hovered near him, and that the touch of her soft, little hands had helped to heal the wound gaping so cruelly when he last bade adieu to his native land. Richard was not a spiritualist. He utterly repudiated their wild theories, and built up one of his own, equally wild and strange, but productive of no evil, inasmuch as no one was admitted into his secret, or suffered to know of his one acknowledged sphere where Nina reigned supreme. This was something he kept to himself, referring but once to Nina during his narrative, and that when he said to Edith,

"You remember, darling, Nina told me in her letter that she'd keep asking God to give me back my sight."

Edith cared but little by whose agency this great cure had been accomplished, and laying her head on Richard's knee, just as a girl she used to do, she wept out her joy for sight restored to her noble benefactor, reproaching him for having kept the good news from them so carefully, even shutting his eyes when he wrote to them so that his writing should be natural, and the surprise when he did return, the greater.

Meanwhile Grace's servant came up to accompany her home, and she bade the happy group good night, her heart beating faster than its wont as Richard said to her at parting, "I was going to offer my services, but see I am forestalled. My usual luck, you know," and his black eyes rested a moment, on her face and then wandered to where Edith sat. Did he mean anything by this? Had the waves of time, which had beaten and battered his heart so long, brought it back at last to its first starting point, Grace Elmendorff? Time only can tell. He believed his youthful passion had died out years ago, that matrimony was for him an utter impossibility.

He had been comparatively happy across the sea, and he was happier still now that he was at home, wishing he had come before, and wondering why it was that the sight of Edith did not pain him, as he feared it would. He liked to look at her, to hear her musical voice, to watch her graceful movements as she flitted about the house, and as the days and weeks went on he grew young again in her society, until he was much like the Richard to whom she once said, "I will be your wife," save that his raven hair was tinged with grey, making him, as some thought, finer-looking than ever. To Arthur and Edith he was like a dearly beloved brother; while to Dick and Nina he was all the world. He was very proud of little Dick, but Nina was his pet, as she was every body's who knew her, and she ere long learned to love him better, if possible, than she did her father, calling him frequently "her oldest papa," and wondering in her childish way why he kissed so tenderly as often as she lisped out that dear name.

And now but little more remains to tell. It is four months since Richard came home, and the hazy Indian summer sun shines o'er the New England hills, bathing Collingwood in its soft, warm rays, and falling upon the tall bare trees and the withered grass below, carpeted with leaves of many a bright hue. On the velvety sward, which last summer showed so rich a green, the children are racing up and down, Dick's cheeks glowing like the scarlet foliage he treads beneath his feet, and Nina's fair hair tossing in the autumn wind, which seems to blow less rudely on the little girl than on her stronger older brother. On one of the iron seats scattered over the lawn sits Richard; watching them as they play, not moodily, not mournfully, for grief and sorrow have no lodgment in the once blind Richard's heart, and he verily believes that he is as happy without Edith as he could possibly have been with her. She is almost everything to him now that a wife could be consulting his wishes before her own, or Arthur's, and making all else subservient to them. No royal sovereign ever lorded it over his subjects more completely than could Richard over Collingwood, if he chose, for master and servants alike yield him unbounded deference; but Richard is far too gentle to abuse the power vested in his hands and so he rules by perfect love, which knows no shadow of distrust. The gift of sight has compensated for all his olden pain, and often to himself he says, "I would hardly be blind again for the sake of Edith's first affections."

He calls her Edith now, just as he used to do, and Edith knows that only a scar is left, as a memento of the fearful sacrifice. The morning has broken at last, the darkness passed away, and while basking in the full, rich daylight, both Richard and Arthur, and Edith wonder if they are the same to whom the world was once so dreary. Only over Grace Atherton is any darkness brooding. She cannot forget the peerless boon she throw away when she deliberately said to Richard Harrington, "I will not walk in your shadow," and the love she once bore him is alive in all its force, but so effectually concealed that few suspect its existence.

Richard goes often to Brier Hill, staying sometimes hours, and Victor, with his opinion of the "gay widow" somewhat changed, has more than once hinted at Collingwood how he thinks these visits will end. But the servants scoffed, at the idea, while Arthur and Edith look curiously on, half hoping Victor is right, and so that matter remains in uncertainty.

Across the fields, Grassy Spring still lies a mass of shapeless ruins. Frequently has Arthur talked of rebuilding it as a home for his children, but as Richard has always opposed it and Edith is indifferent, he will probably remain at Collingwood.

Away to the south, the autumn winds blow softly around Sunnybank, where Edith's negroes are living as happy under the new administration as the old, speaking often of their beautiful mistress who, when the winter snows fall on the Bay State hills, will wend her way to the southward, and Christmas fires will again be kindled upon the hearthstones left desolate so many years. Nor is she, whose little grave lies just across the field forgotten. Enshrined is her memory within the hearts of all who knew and loved her, while away to the northward where the cypress and willow mark the resting-place of Shannondale's dead, a costly marble rears its graceful column, pointing far upward to the sky, the home of her whose name that marble bears. "NINA." That is all. No laudations deeply cut tell what she was or where she died. "NINA." Nothing more. And yet this single word has a power to touch the deepest, tenderest feeling of two hearts at least, Arthur's and Edith's--speaking to them of the little golden-haired girl who crossed so innocently their pathway, striving hard to efface all prints of her footsteps, caring to the last for her "Arthur boy" and the "Miggie" she loved so well, and calling to them as it were, even after the rolling river was safely forded, and she was landed beside the still waters in the bright, green fields of Eden.

And now to the sweet little girl and the noble man who, through the mazy labyrinths of Darkness and of Daylight, have grown so strongly into our love, whose faces were familiar as our own, whose names were household words, over whose sorrows our tears have fallen like rain, and in whose joys we have rejoiced, we bid a final adieu. Farewell to thee, beautiful NINA. "Earth hath none fairer lost. Heaven none purer gained." Farewell to thee forever, and blessings, rich and rare, distil like evening dew upon the dear head of the brave-hearted, generous hero RICHARD HARRINGTON.

www.bookjungle.com *email: sales@bookjungle.com fax: 630-214-0564 mail: Book Jungle PO Box 2226 Champaign, IL 61825*

The Codes Of Hammurabi And Moses
W. W. Davies

QTY

The discovery of the Hammurabi Code is one of the greatest achievements of archaeology, and is of paramount interest, not only to the student of the Bible, but also to all those interested in ancient history...

Religion   **ISBN:** *1-59462-338-4*   **Pages:**132
MSRP $12.95

The Theory of Moral Sentiments
Adam Smith

QTY

This work from 1749. contains original theories of conscience amd moral judgment and it is the foundation for systemof morals.

Philosophy   **ISBN:** *1-59462-777-0*   **Pages:**536
MSRP $19.95

Jessica's First Prayer
Hesba Stretton

QTY

In a screened and secluded corner of one of the many railway-bridges which span the streets of London there could be seen a few years ago, from five o'clock every morning until half past eight, a tidily set-out coffee-stall, consisting of a trestle and board, upon which stood two large tin cans, with a small fire of charcoal burning under each so as to keep the coffee boiling during the early hours of the morning when the work-people were thronging into the city on their way to their daily toil...

Pages:84

Childrens   **ISBN:** *1-59462-373-2*   *MSRP $9.95*

My Life and Work
Henry Ford

QTY

Henry Ford revolutionized the world with his implementation of mass production for the Model T automobile. Gain valuable business insight into his life and work with his own auto-biography... "We have only started on our development of our country we have not as yet, with all our talk of wonderful progress, done more than scratch the surface. The progress has been wonderful enough but..."

Pages:300

Biographies/   **ISBN:** *1-59462-198-5*   *MSRP $21.95*

www.bookjungle.com email: sales@bookjungle.com fax: 630-214-0564 mail: Book Jungle PO Box 2226 Champaign, IL 61825

The Art of Cross-Examination
Francis Wellman

QTY

I presume it is the experience of every author, after his first book is published upon an important subject, to be almost overwhelmed with a wealth of ideas and illustrations which could readily have been included in his book, and which to his own mind, at least, seem to make a second edition inevitable. Such certainly was the case with me; and when the first edition had reached its sixth impression in five months, I rejoiced to learn that it seemed to my publishers that the book had met with a sufficiently favorable reception to justify a second and considerably enlarged edition. ..

Reference   ISBN: *1-59462-647-2*   **Pages:412**
MSRP $19.95

On the Duty of Civil Disobedience
Henry David Thoreau

QTY

Thoreau wrote his famous essay, On the Duty of Civil Disobedience, as a protest against an unjust but popular war and the immoral but popular institution of slave-owning. He did more than write—he declined to pay his taxes, and was hauled off to gaol in consequence. Who can say how much this refusal of his hastened the end of the war and of slavery ?

Law   ISBN: *1-59462-747-9*   **Pages:48**
MSRP $7.45

Dream Psychology Psychoanalysis for Beginners
Sigmund Freud

QTY

Sigmund Freud, born Sigismund Schlomo Freud (May 6, 1856 - September 23, 1939), was a Jewish-Austrian neurologist and psychiatrist who co-founded the psychoanalytic school of psychology. Freud is best known for his theories of the unconscious mind, especially involving the mechanism of repression; his redefinition of sexual desire as mobile and directed towards a wide variety of objects; and his therapeutic techniques, especially his understanding of transference in the therapeutic relationship and the presumed value of dreams as sources of insight into unconscious desires.

Psychology   ISBN: *1-59462-905-6*   **Pages:196**
MSRP $15.45

The Miracle of Right Thought
Orison Swett Marden

QTY

Believe with all of your heart that you will do what you were made to do. When the mind has once formed the habit of holding cheerful, happy, prosperous pictures, it will not be easy to form the opposite habit. It does not matter how improbable or how far away this realization may see, or how dark the prospects may be, if we visualize them as best we can, as vividly as possible, hold tenaciously to them and vigorously struggle to attain them, they will gradually become actualized, realized in the life. But a desire, a longing without endeavor, a yearning abandoned or held indifferently will vanish without realization.

Self Help   ISBN: *1-59462-644-8*   **Pages:360**
MSRP $25.45

www.bookjungle.com email: sales@bookjungle.com fax: 630-214-0564 mail: Book Jungle PO Box 2226 Champaign, IL 61825

QTY

- [ ] **The Rosicrucian Cosmo-Conception Mystic Christianity** by *Max Heindel* — ISBN: *1-59462-188-8* **$38.95**
  The Rosicrucian Cosmo-conception is not dogmatic, neither does it appeal to any other authority than the reason of the student. It is: not controversial, but is: sent forth in the, hope that it may help to clear..
  New Age/Religion Pages 646

- [ ] **Abandonment To Divine Providence** by *Jean-Pierre de Caussade* — ISBN: *1-59462-228-0* **$25.95**
  "The Rev. Jean Pierre de Caussade was one of the most remarkable spiritual writers of the Society of Jesus in France in the 18th Century. His death took place at Toulouse in 1751. His works have gone through many editions and have been republished...
  Inspirational/Religion Pages 400

- [ ] **Mental Chemistry** by *Charles Haanel* — ISBN: *1-59462-192-6* **$23.95**
  Mental Chemistry allows the change of material conditions by combining and appropriately utilizing the power of the mind. Much like applied chemistry creates something new and unique out of careful combinations of chemicals the mastery of mental chemistry...
  New Age Pages 354

- [ ] **The Letters of Robert Browning and Elizabeth Barret Barrett 1845-1846 vol II** by *Robert Browning* and *Elizabeth Barrett* — ISBN: *1-59462-193-4* **$35.95**
  Biographies Pages 596

- [ ] **Gleanings In Genesis (volume I)** by *Arthur W. Pink* — ISBN: *1-59462-130-6* **$27.45**
  Appropriately has Genesis been termed "the seed plot of the Bible" for in it we have, in germ form, almost all of the great doctrines which are afterwards fully developed in the books of Scripture which follow...
  Religion/Inspirational Pages 420

- [ ] **The Master Key** by *L. W. de Laurence* — ISBN: *1-59462-001-6* **$30.95**
  In no branch of human knowledge has there been a more lively increase of the spirit of research during the past few years than in the study of Psychology, Concentration and Mental Discipline. The requests for authentic lessons in Thought Control, Mental Discipline and...
  New Age/Business Pages 422

- [ ] **The Lesser Key Of Solomon Goetia** by *L. W. de Laurence* — ISBN: *1-59462-092-X* **$9.95**
  This translation of the first book of the "Lernegton" which is now for the first time made accessible to students of Talismanic Magic was done, after careful collation and edition, from numerous Ancient Manuscripts in Hebrew, Latin, and French...
  New Age/Occult Pages 92

- [ ] **Rubaiyat Of Omar Khayyam** by *Edward Fitzgerald* — ISBN: *1-59462-332-5* **$13.95**
  Edward Fitzgerald, whom the world has already learned, in spite of his own efforts to remain within the shadow of anonymity, to look upon as one of the rarest poets of the century, was born at Bredfield, in Suffolk, on the 31st of March, 1809. He was the third son of John Purcell...
  Music Pages 172

- [ ] **Ancient Law** by *Henry Maine* — ISBN: *1-59462-128-4* **$29.95**
  The chief object of the following pages is to indicate some of the earliest ideas of mankind, as they are reflected in Ancient Law, and to point out the relation of those ideas to modern thought.
  Religion/History Pages 452

- [ ] **Far-Away Stories** by *William J. Locke* — ISBN: *1-59462-129-2* **$19.45**
  "Good wine needs no bush, but a collection of mixed vintages does. And this book is just such a collection. Some of the stories I do not want to remain buried for ever in the museum files of dead magazine-numbers an author's not unpardonable vanity..."
  Fiction Pages 272

- [ ] **Life of David Crockett** by *David Crockett* — ISBN: *1-59462-250-7* **$27.45**
  "Colonel David Crockett was one of the most remarkable men of the times in which he lived. Born in humble life, but gifted with a strong will, an indomitable courage, and unremitting perseverance...
  Biographies/New Age Pages 424

- [ ] **Lip-Reading** by *Edward Nitchie* — ISBN: *1-59462-206-X* **$25.95**
  Edward B. Nitchie, founder of the New York School for the Hard of Hearing, now the Nitchie School of Lip-Reading, Inc, wrote "LIP-READING Principles and Practice". The development and perfecting of this meritorious work on lip-reading was an undertaking...
  How-to Pages 400

- [ ] **A Handbook of Suggestive Therapeutics, Applied Hypnotism, Psychic Science** by *Henry Munro* — ISBN: *1-59462-214-0* **$24.95**
  Health/New Age/Health/Self-help Pages 376

- [ ] **A Doll's House: and Two Other Plays** by *Henrik Ibsen* — ISBN: *1-59462-112-1* **$19.95**
  Henrik Ibsen created this classic when in revolutionary 1848 Rome. Introducing some striking concepts in playwriting for the realist genre, this play has been studied the world over.
  Fiction/Classics/Plays 308

- [ ] **The Light of Asia** by *sir Edwin Arnold* — ISBN: *1-59462-204-3* **$13.95**
  In this poetic masterpiece, Edwin Arnold describes the life and teachings of Buddha. The man who was to become known as Buddha to the world was born as Prince Gautama of India but he rejected the worldly riches and abandoned the reigns of power when...
  Religion/History/Biographies Pages 170

- [ ] **The Complete Works of Guy de Maupassant** by *Guy de Maupassant* — ISBN: *1-59462-157-8* **$16.95**
  "For days and days, nights and nights, I had dreamed of that first kiss which was to consecrate our engagement, and I knew not on what spot I should put my lips..."
  Fiction/Classics Pages 240

- [ ] **The Art of Cross-Examination** by *Francis L. Wellman* — ISBN: *1-59462-309-0* **$26.95**
  Written by a renowned trial lawyer, Wellman imparts his experience and uses case studies to explain how to use psychology to extract desired information through questioning.
  How-to/Science/Reference Pages 408

- [ ] **Answered or Unanswered?** by *Louisa Vaughan* — ISBN: *1-59462-248-5* **$10.95**
  Miracles of Faith in China
  Religion Pages 112

- [ ] **The Edinburgh Lectures on Mental Science (1909)** by *Thomas* — ISBN: *1-59462-008-3* **$11.95**
  This book contains the substance of a course of lectures recently given by the writer in the Queen Street Hall, Edinburgh. Its purpose is to indicate the Natural Principles governing the relation between Mental Action and Material Conditions...
  New Age/Psychology Pages 148

- [ ] **Ayesha** by *H. Rider Haggard* — ISBN: *1-59462-301-5* **$24.95**
  Verily and indeed it is the unexpected that happens! Probably if there was one person upon the earth from whom the Editor of this, and of a certain previous history, did not expect to hear again...
  Classics Pages 380

- [ ] **Ayala's Angel** by *Anthony Trollope* — ISBN: *1-59462-352-X* **$29.95**
  The two girls were both pretty, but Lucy who was twenty-one who supposed to be simple and comparatively unattractive, whereas Ayala was credited, as her Bombwhat romantic name might show, with poetic charm and a taste for romance. Ayala when her father died was nineteen...
  Fiction Pages 484

- [ ] **The American Commonwealth** by *James Bryce* — ISBN: *1-59462-286-8* **$34.45**
  An interpretation of American democratic political theory. It examines political mechanics and society from the perspective of Scotsman James Bryce.
  Politics Pages 572

- [ ] **Stories of the Pilgrims** by *Margaret P. Pumphrey* — ISBN: *1-59462-116-0* **$17.95**
  This book explores pilgrims religious oppression in England as well as their escape to Holland and eventual crossing to America on the Mayflower, and their early days in New England...
  History Pages 268

www.bookjungle.com *email: sales@bookjungle.com fax: 630-214-0564 mail: Book Jungle PO Box 2226 Champaign, IL 61825*

			QTY
The Fasting Cure *by Sinclair Upton*	ISBN: *1-59462-222-1*	**$13.95**	☐
In the Cosmopolitan Magazine for May, 1910, and in the Contemporary Review (London) for April, 1910, I published an article dealing with my experiences in fasting. I have written a great many magazine articles, but never one which attracted so much attention...	*New Age/Self Help/Health Pages 164*		
Hebrew Astrology *by Sepharial*	ISBN: *1-59462-308-2*	**$13.45**	☐
In these days of advanced thinking it is a matter of common observation that we have left many of the old landmarks behind and that we are now pressing forward to greater heights and to a wider horizon than that which represented the mind-content of our progenitors...	*Astrology Pages 144*		
Thought Vibration or The Law of Attraction in the Thought World	ISBN: *1-59462-127-6*	**$12.95**	☐
by William Walker Atkinson	*Psychology/Religion Pages 144*		
Optimism *by Helen Keller*	ISBN: *1-59462-108-X*	**$15.95**	☐
Helen Keller was blind, deaf, and mute since 19 months old, yet famously learned how to overcome these handicaps, communicate with the world, and spread her lectures promoting optimism. An inspiring read for everyone...	*Biographies/Inspirational Pages 84*		
Sara Crewe *by Frances Burnett*	ISBN: *1-59462-360-0*	**$9.45**	☐
In the first place, Miss Minchin lived in London. Her home was a large, dull, tall one, in a large, dull square, where all the houses were alike, and all the sparrows were alike, and where all the door-knockers made the same heavy sound...	*Childrens/Classic Pages 88*		
The Autobiography of Benjamin Franklin *by Benjamin Franklin*	ISBN: *1-59462-135-7*	**$24.95**	☐
The Autobiography of Benjamin Franklin has probably been more extensively read than any other American historical work, and no other book of its kind has had such ups and downs of fortune. Franklin lived for many years in England, where he was agent...	*Biographies/History Pages 332*		

Name	
Email	
Telephone	
Address	
City, State ZIP	

☐ Credit Card ☐ Check / Money Order

Credit Card Number	
Expiration Date	
Signature	

Please Mail to: Book Jungle
PO Box 2226
Champaign, IL 61825
or Fax to: 630-214-0564

ORDERING INFORMATION

web: *www.bookjungle.com*
email: *sales@bookjungle.com*
fax: *630-214-0564*
mail: *Book Jungle PO Box 2226 Champaign, IL 61825*
or PayPal *to sales@bookjungle.com*

Please contact us for bulk discounts

DIRECT-ORDER TERMS

20% Discount if You Order Two or More Books
Free Domestic Shipping!
Accepted: Master Card, Visa, Discover, American Express

www.ingramcontent.com/pod-product-compliance
Lightning Source LLC
Chambersburg PA
CBHW082109230426
43671CB00015B/2641